Development Economics:
Theory, Practice, and Prospects

Recent Economic Thought Series

Warren J. Samuels, Editor
Michigan State University
East Lansing, Michigan, U.S.A.

This series is devoted to works that present divergent views on the development, prospects, and tensions within some important research areas of international economic thought. Among the fields covered are macromonetary policy, public finance, labor and political economy. The emphasis of the series is on providing a critical, constructive view of each of these fields, as well as a forum through which leading scholars of international reputation may voice their perspectives on important related issues. Each volume in the series will be self-contained; together these volumes will provide dramatic evidence of the variety of economic thought within the scholarly community.

Development Economics:
Theory, Practice, and Prospects

edited by
Thomas R. DeGregori
Department of Economics
University of Houston

Kluwer Academic Publishers
Boston/Dordrecht/London

Distributors for North America:
Kluwer Academic Publishers,
101 Philip Drive,
Assinippi Park,
Norwell, MA 02061, U.S.A.

Distributors for the UK and Ireland:
Kluwer Academic Publishers,
Falcon House, Queen Square,
Lancaster LA1 1RN, UNITED KINGDOM

Distributors for for all other countries:
Kluwer Academic Publishers Group,
Distribution Centre,
Post Office Box 322,
3300 AH Dordrecht, THE NETHERLANDS

Library of Congress Cataloging-in-Publication Data

Development economics : theory, practice, and prospects / edited by
    Thomas R. DeGregori.
        p.   c.m. — (Recent economic thought series)
    Includes index.
        Contents: Four decades of development and development economics /
    Thomas R. DeGregori — Theory and practice in world agriculture /
    N.C. Brady — Population resources and limits to growth / Gunter
    Steinmann — Strategies of development / Kenneth P. Jameson, James
    H. Weaver & Charles K. Wilber — The debate over montetarism / Alan
    Rufus Waters — Donors, development, and debt / Peter Cashel-Cordo
    and Steven G. Craig — Importation and local generation of
    technology by the Third World /Dilmus D. Jones.
        ISBN 0-89838-275-0
        1. Developing countries—Economic conditions.   2. Developing
    countries—Economic policy.   3. Economic development.
    I. DeGregori, Thomas R.   II. Series: Recent economic thought.
    HC59.7.D447 1988
    338.9—dc19   88-8851
                                                                    CIP

CONTENTS

CONTRIBUTING AUTHORS

Nyle C. Brady
Senior Assistant Administrator for Science and
Technology
Agency for International Development

Peter Cashel-Cordo
Department of Economics
University of Houston
Houston, TX 77004

Steven G. Craig
Department of Economics
University of Houston
Houston, TX 77004

Thomas R. DeGregori
Department of Economics
University of Houston
Houston, TX 77004

Peter Delp
ANE/TR/ENR, Rm. 4440
Agency for International Development
Washington, DC 70523

Wendell Gordon
4141 So. Braeswood Blvd., #358
Houston, TX 77025

Dilmus D. James
Department of Economics and Finance
College of Business Administration
The University of Texas at El Paso
El Paso, TX 79968-0543

Kenneth P. Jameson
Department of Economics
University of Notre Dame
Notre Dame, IN 46556

Dr. B. Persaud
Director and Head
Economic Affairs Division
Commonwealth Secretariat
Marlborough House
Pall Mall
London SW1Y 5HX
England

Professor Dr. Gunter Steinmann
Universitat - G H Paderborn
F B Wirtschaftswissenschat
Warburger Strasse 100
D-4790 Paderborn
Federal Republic of Germany

Randal J. Thompson
USAID/Rubat, P.O. Box 120
APO/NY
New York City, NY   09284

Alan Rufus Waters
Department of Finance and Industry
School of Business
California State University - Fresno
Fresno, CA   93740-0007

James H. Weaver
Department of Economics
American University
3800 Massachusetts Ave., N.W.
Washington, DC   20016

Charles K. Wilbur
Department of Economics
University of Notre Dame
Notre Dame, IN   46556

Nyle Brady is Professor Emeritus at Cornell Univrsity where he held several posts, was the Director-General of the International Rice Research Institute (Philippines) and has been Senior Assistant Administrator for Science and Technology, United States Agency for International Development from 1981 through the present (Summer 1988).

Peter Cashel-Cordo is Assistant Professor of Economics, Canisius College, Buffalo, New York. He was formerly with the University of Houston.

Steven G. Craig is Associate Professor of Economics, University of Houston, Houston, Texas.

Thomas R. DeGregori is a Professor of Economics at the University of Houston, Houston, Texas, and author of <u>A Theory of Technology</u>.

Peter Delp is a Foreign Service Officer with the United States Agency for International Development with experience in project evaluation and in science and technology.

Wendell Gordon is Professor Emeritus at the University of Texas at Austin and currently resides in Houston, Texas.

Dilmus D. James is Professor of Economics and Finance with the College of Business Administration, the University of Texas at El Paso, El Paso, Texas.

Kenneth P. Jameson is Professor of Economics and Fellow, Helen Kellog Institute of International Studies, University of Notre Dame, South Bend, Indiana.

Bishnu Persaud is Director and Head, Economic Affairs Division, Commonwealth Secretariat, London, England.

Gunter Steinmann is Professor of Economics, University of Paderborn, Paderborn, Federal Republic of Germany.

Randal Thompson has a background in Philosophy and Systems Analysis and is a Foreign Service Officer with the United States Agency for International Development as a Project Design Officer.

Alan Rufus Waters is Professor of Finance and Industry, School of Business, California State University, Fresno, Fresno, California.

James H. Weaver is Professor of Economics at the American University in Washington, D.C., and Senior Economist in theAgency for International Development's Development Studies Program.

Charles K. Wilber is a Professor of Economics and Fellow, Helen Kellogg Institute of International Studies, University of Notre Dame, South Bend, Indiana.

Development Economics:
Theory, Practice, and Prospects

1 THE DEVELOPMENT CHALLENGE: THEORY, PRACTICE, AND PROSPECTS
Thomas R. DeGregori

INTRODUCTION

Ours is the time of the development revolution. Since World War II there has been a transformation of the lifeways of the inhabitants of the planet that is unprecedented in extent, in depth, and in rapidity. It is truly spectacular and can only be described in superlatives. The indicators for this global transformation are many. In the essays in this collection are references to the more strictly economic indicators such as growth in per capita income and world trade. By any previous standards, the rates of change are considerable, whether aggregated on a global basis or broken down between the developed and the developing countries. If broken down further into regional groupings, particularly for the period before 1980, except for Africa and a few subregions, aggregate economic change has been substantial and, generally, per capita improvement has been widespread.

Other indicators point to changes that have been as impressive and as unprecedented. As one of our authors notes, growth in per capita food production has been a relatively continuous condition of the last four decades. Food production has grown rapidly and has

1

clearly outpaced population growth. One of the
most spectacular of all the transformations has
been in the area of public health, both in
developed and developing countries. Ironically,
this public health revolution has also extended
to some areas where economic indicators of
change are far less favorable. Much the same
is true for education and literacy. In public
health the increases of life expectancy and
declines in infant and child mortality dwarf
any previous changes. All these have
contributed to a growth in population, the rate
and absolute number of which have caught the
public's attention. Whatever problems
population growth may or may not cause, rarely
is it mentioned that it is the consequence of a
series of favorable and extraordinary changes
in the global economy and way of life.

The development revolution is essentially
an unsung and unheralded revolution. In recent
years there has been some media attention to
various miracle economies of Asia, particularly
to the extent that they compete in the U.S.
market. Mainly, the focus in this media
coverage is on a few economies led by Japan,
which has long been developed, and not upon the
broad-based change that has taken place
throughout Asia and other areas of the third
world. In fact, until recently and even to
some extent to the present, a disproportionate
amount of the popular pronouncements on global
trends have been catastrophic. Even in an era
of surpluses in virtually every raw commodity,
food, fiber, or mineral, probably a substantial
majority of the educated, "informed" public in
developed countries believes that the world
food situation is worsening and that major
minerals are being exhausted. In the 1960s and
early 1970s a series of sensational
predictions, some very specific as to time and

extent, were made forecasting a variety of
doomsday outcomes -- from mass starvation and
death to exhaustion of resources. The regular
and continuous falsification of these doomsday
forecasts by events has not lessened their hold
upon the media and upon a segment of the
population. One could reel off a list of
purveyors of gloom and doom who remain
"recognized spokesmen" on problems of the
global economy. In no other areas of the human
endeavor has such persistent error been so
continually glorified. The noise of the
doomsday predictions that have not happened has
drowned out news of the changes that have
occurred. The development revolution has been
a quiet one but no less important. It may be
the most important revolution in human history
up until now.
       The fact that the authors of these essays
and comments are not doomsdayers does not mean
that they do not recognize the existence of
real problems. The progress that is being
discussed flows from both a recognition of the
problems and an offer of active policies to
address them. Clearly, too, there are problems
that development generates. There are problems
of population growth; there are problems of
political instability; there are problems of
environmental degradation. The list is
seemingly endless. Though they are not all
covered in this book, nevertheless they are
recognized. Of course, one also has to
consider the alternative. Would a world
without this unprecedented development have had
fewer or greater problems? To most readers,
the question answers itself. Whatever the
problems of development, they pale in
comparison to the problems of underdevelopment.
Economic development is a problem-solving
process. Solving problems creates new

problems.   That   is   not   incompatible   with
defendable criteria of progress.   It is clear
that   not   solving   problems   is   not   a   way   of
avoiding them; it just makes them worse.

    Some   consistent   themes   emerge   in   these
essays.   That the authors recognize problems
means   there   is   a   sustainability   question   so
often   raised   by   those   against   modern
technology.   For the antitechnology theorists,
sustainability   is   incompatible   with   modern
technological   practice.   Rather,   the   issue
raised,   from   the   agriculture   essay   to   the
technology essay, is: can we keep up the pace
of technological change sufficient to meet the
continued   increases   in   population   and
expectations?   Anyone conversant with what is
going on in science and technology should have
little   doubt   that   the   potential   is   there.
However,   the   direction   and   application   of
science and technology to address the problems
of development will not happen automatically.
The   continuing   political   commitment   to   the
development   process   is   as   vital   as   is   the
science and technology to be applied.   There is
more legitimate skepticism about political will
than   about   technological   potential.   The
continuing potential for using technology for
development   is   a   consistent   theme   of   these
essays.   It is not a call for complacency.
Quite   the   contrary,   the   possibilities   for
success are a motivating force for action and
make inaction immoral.

    The very good news of development is, in a
way, also part of the bad news as well.   If the
unprecedented changes of the last generation
have failed to reduce substantially the number
in poverty, then what kinds and rates of change
will do so?   As we have noted, development has
been widespread.   Growth in per capita income
can mask great and growing inequalities, but it

is difficult for other indicators such as life
expectancy, infant mortality, and per capita
food supply to have grown at the rate they did
without there being many beneficiaries. Still,
despite the controversies over the measures of
absolute poverty, there is evidence that,
though the percentage in poverty may have
declined, population growth has meant that
their numbers remain large. The problems of
poverty in the 1980s and into the 1990s are
compounded by a slowing of global economic
growth rates. Problems of indebtedness also
mean that many countries that once experienced
rapid economic growth are now experiencing
economic stagnation or, even worse, decline.
For many countries in Africa, any stagnation or
decline as a result of debt would make
conditions worse that were already bad in a
region where most of the critical indicators
have been moving for the last decade and a half
in a direction counter to the more favorable
global transformation. The continuing economic
"problems" of the 1980s are frequently
described in terms of excess capacity in a
basic manufacturing process, from steel to
semi-conductors, minerals, in natural and
artificial fibers, in textiles, in oil, and in
numerous internationally traded foodstuffs.
Clearly it is not technology or resource
constraints that have slowed the global
economy. It is institutional indebtedness.
Indebtedness is only one of the international
institutional problems that must be addressed
if we are to accelerate economic growth and
continue with the development process.
        In sum, we can say that there are four
main themes in the essays and comments.

Agree,
Adjustment
Policies and
its negative
effects.

1.   Economic development has brought
      about a rapid and substantial
      change throughout the developing
      world. It has been done in a
      period of time that is brief
      compared to the time for the
      transformation of the developed
      countries.

2.   Technological and scientific
      change are a necessary element
      for understanding the
      fundamental nature and causal
      forces in this transformation.

3.   Despite the dramatic
      improvements in the conditions
      of life in most parts of the
      world, extreme poverty persists.

4.   In the decade of the 1980s, the
      gap is widening between what we
      can achieve and what we are
      actually accomplishing.

These four themes lead to the conclusion that
development policies are important. To some in
the economics profession, development is
suspect as part of the discipline; and to some,
development lacks credibility. Whatever the
case may be, it is certainly an exciting
endeavor. It has been a participant in a
remarkable global transformation. Clearly,
too, the prospects for continuation are
dependent on the theory and practice of
development.
      Both in archeology and in history, there
has been a tendency to label epochs in terms of
the materials or the means by which they made
their tools. There were various stone ages,

then the bronze and iron ages. In many, the
most critical transformations that were
occurring were the way in which people went
about the task of feeding themselves.
Obtaining sufficient food has been a continuing
occupation and preoccupation of most of
humankind. In recent decades, the production
of this food has become the primary
responsibility of an ever-decreasing proportion
of the population while, at the same time, the
per capita availability has been increasing.
Throughout, population has been growing; and
the already high rate of population growth was
itself increasing until about the mid-1970s,
which means that we had to run even faster just
to stand still. Somehow we have run fast
enough to move forward and to move forward at a
rapid rate. Nyle Brady, the author of "Theory
and Practice in World Agriculture," has been an
active participant in this contemporary
agricultural revolution. Brady shows that
throughout its history agriculture has been a
discovery process of "trial and error" and of
"observation, selection, and simple trials."
It has been a cumulative experience, but
learning was largely local. In the last
century, the learning process has become
global, and the inquiry underlying it has
become scientific. The result was that "from
1900 to 1950, worldwide food production
increased only about 1.5 percent annually."
Brady's qualifying term "only" is in reference
to food production growth since then; at the
time it, too, was a global change without known
historical precedent. However, "from the mid-
1950's to 1970-74, global food production
increased at an average annual rate slightly
over 3 per cent." The rate of increase did
slow to 2.2 percent a year from 1970-1974 to
1979-1983. The decline in the growth rate of

food production was accompanied by a roughly
comparable decline in the rate of population
growth.   Consequently, except for Africa, food
supply almost everywhere is keeping ahead of
population, and, globally, surpluses are
growing and are at record highs.   Thus, as
Brady shows, the doomsdayers' forecasts have
not come to pass.

The most fascinating aspect of the essay
on agriculture is the practice that brought the
current conditions into being.   First in order
of priority in Brady's essay is commitment to
agriculture.   What makes the agriculture
revolution of recent decades even more
remarkable is that it occurreed despite the
fact that so many governments gave agriculture
such a low priority compared to
industrialization, that food production was so
often slighted in favor of production for
export, and that urban policy biases manifested
themselves in the form of low prices and taxes
in agriculture.   Where there was commitment,
there were results.

National agriculture policies reflecting
commitment have been vital and are becoming
even more important.   So, too, have been the
cooperative international research
organizations and consultative networks.
Private foundations and donors and development
lenders have played a critical role in the
creation of the research institutions that were
responsible for the Green Revolution.   In fact,
it was the initiative and funding of private
foundations that launched and sustained the
research that produced the "miracle seeds."
Brady served as director of the International
Rice Research Institute in the Philippines.
The contribution of the agricultural research
centers in meeting world food needs is one of
the more significant instances of the critical

Agri

importance   of   technology   and   technology
transfer in the development process.
        One   of   the   continuing   measures   of
commitment   to   agriculture   is   a   government's
willingness   to   assist   in   providing   critical
inputs.   Drawing   on   the   work   of   John   Mellor,
Brady   shows   the   importance   of   agriculture   in
providing   rural   employment   and,   by   so   doing,
spreading   income.   Seeds,   water,   and   chemicals
are   needed   for   agriculture   to   be   successful.
To   the   small   farmer,   this   not   only   means
extension but also credit.   As many have noted,
the   Green   Revolution   was   scale   neutral.
Unfortunately,   therefore,   there   was   often   an
institutional   bias   against   the   small   farmer
which limited the benefits of the new seeds and
other improved inputs.
        Sustainability   is   the   key   to   future
prospects   in   world   agriculture.   Contrary   to
many   critics   of   modern   agriculture,
sustainability   is   not   derived   from   denying
technology   but   from   continuing   it.   Not   only
must   we   develop   new   pesticides   to   counter
emerging resistance to existing pesticides, but
we   must   also   develop   and   diffuse   new   means   of
crop   production   that   allow   for   the   maintenance
of   soil   fertility.   Science   and   technology   in
agriculture,   as   in   all   human   endeavors,   are
ongoing,   problem-solving,   and   problem-creating
processes.   Our   very   successes   require
continuation   of   the   developmental   efforts   that
brought   them.   Equally   important,   as   Brady
shows,   are   policies   that   reflect   government
commitment   and   provide   the   incentives   for
farmers   to   utilize   new   developments   as   they   are
available.   For   it   is   clear   that   biotechnology
among   other   technologies   offers   possibilities
for   continuing   the   agricultural   revolution   and
the benefits that are provided.

Without the agricultural revolution described by Nyle Brady, the population growth chronicled by Gunter Steinmann would not have been possible. There is also the counterargument that without the population growth, the agricultural revolution would not have been possible. To many, this latter assessment seems preposterous and absurd, but it has a reputable pedigree. In some respects, it sounds like a sophisticated restatement of the old adage of necessity being the mother of invention. A major and widely accepted thesis in anthropology is the argument that overpopulation was the driving force in the transition from hunting and gathering to agriculture (Cohen, 1977). Many in anthropology and economics adhere to the more general thesis of Ester Boserup that population pressures tend to lead to more intensive forms of agriculture (Boserup, 1965). The theory of "induced innovation" is more widely accepted among agricultural economists, though its creators question how long such innovations can accommodate sustained high rates of population growth (Hyami and Ruttan, 1987, for a recent version of their often published thesis). Necessity may not be the mother of invention, but, to some, it is the mother of innovation. To the extent that resources, be they agricultural or mineral, are a function of technology, then the question of population and food supply, or population and resources in general, is one of the relationship between population growth and technological change. This issue, moreover, is still unresolved although it is now being studied (National Research Council, 1986; Espenshade and Stolnitz, 1987). Steinmann explores the historical inquiry on population growth and resources, going back to Malthus and continuing

to the more recent limits-of-growth theorists.
The assumption of constant technology is
strongly implied by most who have been fearful
of resource exhaustion. What Steinmann does is
not only to enter the theoretical dispute but
to support his particular perspective with
careful empirical data. The technological
argument for this optimistic perspective on
population and resources has widespread support
in the economic profession, including the
editor of this book (DeGregori, 1987).

Steinmann further argues that population
growth can lead to greater efficiency in
resource use by encouraging more well-defined
property rights. These two arguments appeal to
two distinct traditions in economics. They are
not necessarily complementary, but there are
clearly constituencies for each perspective and
for evidence that the resource base has been
expanding in modern times and not declining.

Price is widely accepted in economics as a
measure of scarcity, though there are those who
strongly dissent from this position. Whether
one accepts price as a measure or not, data
presented by Steinmann are compelling and
consistent with a large body of measurements
that find the real price of commodities, food,
fiber, and minerals to have been falling
steadily for decades. Even from dissenting
traditions, it is hard to imagine a scenario in
which there would be a rapid resource depletion
caused by exponential growth in utilization
that would be accompanied by a long-term,
sustained decline in real price. It is ironic
that one of the dissenting traditions,
institutional economics, which most strongly
questions the validity of price as a measure of
scarcity, pioneered the idea of technology
creating resources. The limits-to-growth
theorists were not only predicting rapid

resource exhaustion, a peaking and even a catastrophic decline in food production, but also real price increases and a concommitant decline in the standard of living.

From the perspective of the mainstream of economics and economic development, Steinmann's argument of better property rights definition and real price declines is partially counteracted by the argument that more rapid growth of population leads to a dilution of capital. Steinmann is balanced in presentation of various contending perspectives on the relationship between population growth and resources. For the purposes of policy consideration, we should separate two closely related but different stands of the thesis. First, much of the catastrophist thinking has been directed to population growth and resource utilization that has been occurring and that one can project to occur. In terms of these real events and the resource implications of them as measured by Steinmann, it is clear that with technology we have been creating resources faster than we have been using them. The optimistic view would seem to prevail, though certainly the pessimists would continue to disagree. There still is the unanswered question as to whether a slower growth in population might have brought a faster or slower improvement in resource-creating technology or even whether the process of increases in scientific and technological knowledge is independent of population change except in extreme circumstances. Steinmann argues that in free societies, faster population growth in the long run facilitates faster economic growth. Whatever his conclusion, he does explore all of the major contending perspectives on the subject.

The significance of Steinmann's contribution can best be understood with some historical perspective. Imagine being an economist of any persuasion in 1950, or, for that matter, imagine being any reasonably well-educated person in that year. What if you were told that over the next roughly 35 years world population would double from 2.5 billion to 5 billion? Who among us would not have predicted mass starvation? The catastrophist forecasts of the late 1960s and early 1970s would have been made earlier had the trends been known, and they would have been widely shared. Imagine also that the high rates of real per capita gross national product (GNP) referred to in other essays in this book had also been forecast. Note that these rates of real GNP per capita are a compounding of the impact of population growth, making aggregate growth in trade and production even greater. Who among us would not have believed in likely resource scarcity? As Steinmann indicates, it was success in public health, food supply, or whatever other factors lowered death rates that have been the sole cause of the increase in population growth rates. One could reverse the argument and say that it is technological change that causes population growth. Many countries that experienced rapid economic success also experienced a similar rapid decline in death rates and a consequent growth in population. There are generally the same countries that now have low fertility rates and low and often declining population growth rates. One does not have to have a Panglossian best-of-all-possible-worlds perspective to suggest that population growth has been an almost inevitable outcome of nearly four decades of successful economic transformation.

If there is good news in Steinmann's article, there is also some implicit bad news. For the last decade or so, there has been a decline in the global rates of population growth. Many developed countries are concerned about negative growth. Many parts of the developing world are close to stabilizing their population. The most rapid rates of population growth are in places like Africa where economic success has been minimal. In some instances, the economies have been contracting while population growth rates have been increasing. One can even accept the argument of Steinmann and many others that in Africa it is not a resource problem but a policy problem, be it economic or political. There are still some demonstrable regional population problems, and unless we can find another pathway than that which has been followed over the previous decades for world population change, then there are real possibilities that the situation in Africa and other regions will get worse before it has a chance to improve. In any case, from Brady and from Steinmann we understand that we are not currently facing the global food and resource problems that were so vividly forecast for our times.

If the good news of population growth, resource creation, and food supply also has a down side, so, too, does the good news of rapid economic development, as shown in the article, "Strategies of Development," by Jameson, Weaver, and Wilber. The authors quote Paul Streeten's famous dictum that "every solution creates its own problem." The three refer to a series of unprecedented economic changes and a number of other "significant improvements in literacy, life expectancy, infant mortality, access to education, health services, and potable water." However, problems like "unequal income distribution" and "rural poverty" continue. On the positive side, one can say that never have so many people lived in such conditions of economic sufficiency, food security, literacy, and expectations of an extended lifespan. The percentage of the world's population in absolute poverty has fallen. However, given the increase in population, many argue that the absolute number in poverty has remained constant. It is such a condition that leads the authors to refer to "mixed results" and a suggestion "that the development process would be a long one."

There is an implicit and important message in the "Strategies of Development" essay. Thirty years of development from 1950-1980 have brought transformations that can only be described in superlatives such as <u>unprecedented</u>. Yet the results are still mixed, and poverty continues. The question, then, is whether the slowing of growth in the 1980s will undo some of the benefits of previous development. And certainly the character of the policies that are being followed in the slower growth regimen, such as attempts at restricting consumption and employment in order to meet international debt obligations, are not designed to address any of the outstanding problems of development except inflation and indebtedness. The authors speak of dependency theory. There is an overriding dependency; it is the global dependency on continued high rates of economic growth. Thirty years ago, growth was viewed as desirable. After growth has been widely experienced, lack of economic growth becomes intolerable and unacceptable.

There have been almost as many strategies of development as there have been developing countries. Since there have been great

variations in the outcomes of policy from
spectacular success to dismal failure, the
issue of development strategy is of
considerable significance and not merely an
academic exercise. Few would argue that
economic strategy has been the only factor
determining these varied outcomes.
Nevertheless, it is widely recognized as a
critical variable. Jameson, Weaver, and Wilber
do an admirable job in grouping these diverse
strategies into a workable number of analyzable
and recognizable categories.

The authors use the metaphor of a three-
ring circus with a couple of additional
sideshows. In the center ring today of the
development discourse are policies for freeing
up markets, restraining monetary growth,
privatizing public sector enterprise, and other
restructuring activities designed to enhance
efficiency. Restructuring has become a theme
of both capitalist and socialist states. In
both cases, it generally means reducing the
role of government and allowing for a greater
private initiative. Thirty years ago, the
center ring of economic development concern was
interventionist; now it is antiinterventionist.
Restructuring, then, meant intervening to
overcome market bias, inherited colonial
practice, or any traditional structure,
international or domestic, that favored those
who had power. Restructuring today almost
always means removing the hand of the
government. The one consolation that
interventionists can draw today is the argument
that the restructuring reforms of the 1950s and
1960s created the conditions that now allow for
freeing up market forces that were in earlier
decades restrained by nongovernmental forces.

The old adage that failure is an orphan
but success has many fathers is no more true

than in development strategies. As the authors show, the recognized super success stories of development are four Asian economies: Singapore, Hong Kong, Korea, and Taiwan, known as "the Gang of Four." Socialist, Marxist, and dependency theorists do not claim them, but everyone else does. They have been most often cited as examples of free market or more open export-oriented economies. Many have countered that these economies, particularly Korea and Singapore, have had the heavy but efficient and effective hand of government directing their economic success.

Most of the attention within the discipline and without has been on the mainstream strategy debates, particularly those with ideological overtones. We are all familiar with capitalism versus socialism, intervention versus nonintervention, or export-oriented versus import substitution. Jameson, Weaver, and Wilber show that the development debate is much richer than these few dichotomies. More important, they argue that some of the nonmainstream approaches have strongly influenced policy in the past, and some are poised to do so in the future. However reformist the communist countries may be, they are still likely to have considerable central direction and therefore are managing the economic fortunes of about a quarter of the world's population. There are other approaches that the authors illustrate with grassroots programs that may not command the attention of governments as a comprehensive strategy but nevertheless influence development through their implementation in projects. Few governments practice development policies that are derived strictly from a political economy perspective. Yet in both domestic and international policy debates, few can

completely escape the issues raised by
political economists of historical
circumstances and current conditions of unequal
power. The authors are particularly strong on
the need to understand the peculiarities of a
country's cultural and historical past before
trying to frame a development strategy for it.
Such a case-by-case approach might not be
strongly supported by economists but would find
considerable support from development
practitioners with backgrounds in other social
sciences.

        If the Jameson, Weaver, and Wilber essay
demonstrates that there remains a rich
diversity of development strategies, it also
shows by implication and omission, at least,
that some have dropped from contention. When
the authors discuss grassroots development, it
is seen as a strategy operating at the micro-
level within the context of varied macro-
strategies. In the 1970s, similar programs
were proferred as part of a go-it-alone program
under the general heading of self-reliance. It
was a strategy that followed from dependency
theory and the presumed need to break the
economic bonds of dependency. It is a strategy
that has produced no successes and some
confessed failures. There may be many
successful local projects, but basically, most
of us are in some way tied to the global
economy. No development strategy can ignore
the conditions of the world economy and the
economies of countries that are competitors or
trading partners. The extraordinary
developments of the last 30 years or so have
bound our fate together in this world as it has
never done before.

        "The Debate Over Monetarism" by Alan Rufus
Waters stands in sharp contrast to the previous
essay. It is a vigorous essay and to some may

sound strident. If this book had an essay by
an equally strong proponent of Marxism,
dependency, or possibly even of a political
economy approach, then the judgments and even
the language could well have been as harsh; for
the debate over monetarism or Marxism, or
whatever, is more than an academic exercise.
It is even more than growth in GNP per capita,
though that is at the heart of the issue. With
wide variations in growth rates and the
compounding impact of exponential growth, the
end results have meaning not only in enormous
differences in GNP but also, in developing
countries, in human lives saved or lost.

      The debate over monetarism in development
has thus far been one of proponents' or
opponents' selecting countries and comparing
growth rates. Proponents of monetarism, as we
have noted, have used the Gang of Four to make
their case. Sometimes the same country is used
by proponents and opponents alike, each
selecting a different time period within the
span of its presumed monetarist policies.
Countries frequently cited in the debate, such
as the Gang of Four, have never claimed to be
monetarist. The debate may be heated, though
it is in some respects sterile. There are
enough different countries with sufficient
diversity of presumed policy and outcome that
any advocate can select a sample to prove or
disprove a point.

      Waters performs the necessary functions
for this book by studying the history of the
monetarist idea, defining the term carefully,
and then giving us a flavor of the debate, even
if it is from a highly partisan perspective.
Waters goes beyond the current debate and seeks
fundamentally to recast the issue. Monetarism
is much more than a verbal declaration; it is a
basic policy about restrained, sustained, and

predictable growth in the money. Waters would
not have us judge whether a policy was
monetarist by proclamation but by outcome. In
his empirical study of a number of countries,
Waters really did not find any who fit the
monetarist paradigm. Indonesia appears to have
had stable growth until one notices that the
relatively flat line defines variations in
money supply growth between close to 0 to close
to 100 percent. Most of the countries share
periods of rapid decline in the rate of money
supply growth which probably reflect the
application of monetarist medicine to a
particular problem such as inflation and not a
consistent use of monetarist policy.

     For an essay written by a staunch
monetarist, we are left with some fascinating
implications which are probably not satisfying
to monetarists. By a rigorous definition of
monetarism, it would appear that it is
difficult to find any developing country that
qualifies. From the perspective of the debate,
this means that monetarism does not have any
failures to explain. But neither do they have
successes, and there have been many more of the
latter. Further, there is the even more
substantive question as to whether a monetarist
policy is even possible for small developing
countries. Stated differently, do these
countries have sufficient control over the
growth of their domestic money supply so as to
be able to consistently implement a monetarist
policy? This is really questionable given all
of the international forces of trade, loans,
investment, capital flight, etc. that can so
significantly impact upon policy outcomes.

     In seeking to reframe the debate between
monetarists and their critics, Waters has also
created the need to rethink issues among
monetarists as they relate to developing

countries' policies.   Clearly, Waters is no
less of a monetarist now that he has run his
data than he was before.   The real issue for
monetarists is whether their analyses require a
different set of policies in order to create
the conditions of stability and predictability
in the money supply and economy for capitalist
work in a manner consistent with their
theories.

On no issue are questions concerning
monetarism more relevant than in "Donors,
Development, and Debt."   Thus far we have been
talking of long-term policies or strategies of
development.   Whatever the policy attempted,
however long- or short-term the policy ends up
being, the major determining factor tends to be
primarily domestic political forces.   But for a
large number of countries, short-term
monetarist type policies are imposed upon them
as a condition for some needed external
support.   The International Monetary Fund (IMF)
has long established formal "conditionality" as
a basis for help in refinancing debt or other
forms of foreign exchange assistance.
Conditionality has generally involved
monetarist type policies of restrained monetary
growth, as well as restraint on the growth of
money wages, and removal of restraints on
prices.   Clearly, it is a policy of getting
your prices right.   In recent years, the World
Bank has increasingly played an IMF type of
role, sometimes being more vigorous in
implementation than the IMF itself.   And donors
are calling for a policy dialogue with
recipients that generally involves a
prescription consistent with monetarist theory,
e.g., freeing markets and restraining the
growth of money supply and government
expenditures.   In some instances the terms of
conditionality are contractually established

with a representative of IMF on the scene to enforce it. The benefits of conditionality are often debated. This is particularly true for currency devaluation as part of conditionality. Instances can be called upon both of successes as well as failures.

Currency devaluation is a very public and knowable response. But in measuring the success or failure of conditionality, a more comprehensive measure of domestic effort is needed. In addition, for aid agencies there is always concern that their assistance will substitute for local effort rather than enhance it. To limit the possibility that their aid is merely a substitute for what would have been carried out anyway, donors often require some form of domestic contribution. This may minimize donor assistance being spent on the purely frivolous, but it still avoids the fundamental commitment or effort. Cashel-Cordo and Craig address this critical issue.

The overall policy changes involved in conditionality are broadly similar for donors and lenders across a wide spectrum, but the specific effort required varies according to the purposes of the donor or lender and the problems that they are addressing. Lenders who are assisting in dealing with inflation, indebtedness, or balance of payments difficulties design conditionality to reduce public and private spending. Donors and lenders involved in projects are seeking efforts that increase development expenditures and sometimes taxes, though they may at the same time be seeking to reduce other forms of nonessential spending. The outcomes, if successful, are considerably different. Conditionality that reduces overall spending reduces economic growth and may even lead to an economic downturn. Such an outcome is widely recognized and seen by its proponents as essential in generating the sustainable export surpluses necessary to service debt. If a donor or lender project is truly developmental, then the local effort should also be one that contributes to economic growth. The former effort often facilitates the outflow of resources, while the latter effort is a condition for receiving and presumably effectively using an inward flow of resources.

As with the Waters essay, Cashel-Cordo and Craig are not merely trying to define the current state of thinking on debt and development. In most instances there is widespread agreement as to what the loans or aid and the accompanying conditions are supposed to achieve. But there is, unfortunately, previous little evidence as to whether the imposed policies achieve these results. The use of loans and aid as leverage is not for the purpose of policy change but for the outcomes that these policy changes are supposed to achieve. The policy dialogue is always framed in terms of the corrective necessary to achieve the universally desired goal of enhanced rates of economic growth.

Donors and lenders and recipients alike wish to know whether strings on assistance and conditionality work. It relates directly to the larger, frequently asked question as to whether aid has actually been beneficial. A major empirical find of Cashel-Cordo and Craig will come as no surprise to those active in development. Since it provides solid evidence for what has been widely perceived, it is no less important. Namely, that aid donors and lenders have difficulty getting local governments to come forward with the tax effort necessary to meet expenditure requirements. Where they do tax, it is often of the wrong

kind, such as those who lean heavily on
agriculture. Conversely, Cashel-Cordo and
Craig show that IMF conditionality has been
successful in reducing central government
expenditures. To those who support IMF policy,
they will be seen as validating policy. But to
many others, it will confirm their worst fears.
To these dissenters from IMF, policy
prescriptions are a major factor in the slowing
of economic growth in the decade of the 1980s.
In places such as Latin America, the 1980s are
being called the lost decade.

If growth has slowed in the 1980s, the
technological and scientific means of expanding
production have not slowed. What this means is
that there has been a widening gap between what
we can achieve and what we are achieving. This
is evident from the ever-growing production of
commodities, food fibers, and minerals, and
their frequent surplus status this decade. It
is evident in so many industries that are
viewed as having excess capacity. Quite
possibly in the 1950s, 1960s, and into the
1970s, there was greater capability than was
used; but, given the extraordinary overall
performance of those decades, it is hard to
fault this achievement. The tragedy of our
time may be the growing disparity between
rapidly advancing technological capability and
the institutional ability to utilize it.
Without question, indebtedness and policy
responses to it are a major element in this
growing gap. Clearly, we need to understand
and do better. Lives depend on it.

Although the power of our technology to
facilitate development may be growing, as
Dilmus James argues in "Importation and Local
Generation of Technology by the Third World,"
the means of access to it by developing
countries may be becoming more costly and more

difficult.   James   is   writing   within   the
framework   of   Institutional   Economics,   a
perspective   that   is   shared   by   the   editor   of
this   book.   To   James,   this   unprecedented   and
unpredicted   period   of   growth   since   1950   is   also
not   understandable   from   the   theoretical
framework   of   mainstream   economics.   James   is
clearly   at   odds   with   the   mainstream,   monetarist
arguments   of   Alan   Rufus   Waters.   It   is
interesting   that   one   of   the   fundamental
differences   goes   beyond   economics   to   the   realm
of   political   and   philosophical   discourse   on   the
nature   of   freedom.   Waters   found   freedom   in
conditions   of   economically   noninterventionist
governments   and   free   markets.   James   is
unabashedly   interventionist   and   counters   that
"it   is   ironic   in   the   extreme   that   a   brand   of
economics   which   takes   pride   in   maximizing
freedom   of   individual   choice   could   not   be
introduced   or   sustained   in   these   countries
without   an   oppressive,   totalitarian   political
system."   He   is   referring   specifically   to   the
Southern   Cone   countries   of   Latin   America.
     The   "instrumental   approaches   for   acquiring
technological   prowess"   that   follow   from
institutional   economics   are   illustrated   with   an
analysis   of   Korean   development.   The   Korean
success   story   has   yet   another   parent.   It   is
not   that   Korea   intervened   but   that   Korea
intervened   intelligently.   She   "made   very   wise
and   extensive   use   of   market   forces"   and   "went
to   some   pains   to   get   prices   right."   For   Korean
policy   makers   made   "technological   matters   very
close   to   the   heart   of   industrialization
strategies."   To   James,   "Korea's   experience
cannot   be   understood   fully   in   neoclassical
terms."   This   statement   sums   up   his   analysis   of
not   only   Korean   development   but   the   entire
realm   of   economic   development   since   World   War
II.   Technology   transfer   and   change   have   been

at the very heart of this extraordinary
transformation. Not only was it not predicted
by mainstream neoclassical economics; but, to
James, it was also unpredictable in those terms
because it is also inexplicable. The
institutional theory of technology provides the
framework for understanding this process.

In many respects, James' essay is readable
but also highly technical, surveying the
literature and practice of technology transfer.
Some of the forces that he diagnoses as
restraining technology transfer are
international economic structures and the power
relations that they imply. Inequitable
distribution of wealth and power, both
international and domestic, is not only a
social and ethical issue; but, to James, it
also adversely affects the selection and
utilization of technology. The complex range
of issues involved in the choice of technology
are comprehensively covered in this essay.

The implications of James' analysis are
interesting. The extraordinary growth that
occurred was recognized by him and other
authors as being caused by technological change
and transfer. If such results could be
achieved when the process of technology
transfer was so laden with errors in selection
and inequities of power, imagine the possible
results if the process of technology transfer
were handled better. And doing the job better
is really what James' essay is about. One can
look at every nuance of the analysis and
practice of technology transfer as he does, one
can offer the theoretical framework of
institutional economic theory, but the purpose
of this exercise is to offer an understanding
that leads to programs for more effective
action in the realm of technology transfer. If
institutional economics has much to say to the

development process, it is equally true that the experience of development and technology transfer, done well or done poorly, has had much to add to the richness of institutional economics and economic theory in general. James has himself been a pioneer in the concept of technological blending. It avoids the sterile either/or argument of the 1970s. The appropriate technology movement was then noted for its advocacy of exclusive reliance on a particular type of technology. Most practitioners of appropriate technology today are far more pragmatic in the choice of technology. James, in his call for technological pluralism, is in fact bringing forward the best in institutional economic theory. The instrumental process that he describes is one in which one judges a theory or action in terms of the consequence that flows from it. Technologies are not to be judged in terms of aprioristic criteria but in terms of their consequences for the human endeavor.

If one takes a pluralistic instrumental conception of technology, there are further implications. Too often the transfer of a technology was viewed as an end in itself rather than as an end in view. It is not technology as a thing that needs to be transferred but technology as ideas and processes. The criteria for the instrumental assessment of a given technology is not merely the short-term benefit but also the ongoing stream of technologies and benefits that can be expected from the continuation of the process. Things in themselves do not produce this stream of emerging technologies, but humans understanding the ideas embodied in a technology can use these ideas to create new technologies. Technology as ideas may be the seminal contribution of institutional economics, going back to Veblen at the turn of the century. The dynamism of technology, understood by institutionalists from Veblen to James, is derived from the rapidly cumulating power of ideas. The embodiment of ideas in things is a necessary part of the process, but this embodiment is often confused with the totality of the process itself.

The approach to technology of James and the institutionalists is holistic. Unfortunately, the term holistic has become a cliche. It is one of those ideas that everyone favors, but few really know what it means. As used in this context by James, the term has a long and useful history. A holistic approach requires that one understand technologies as they operate in the context of institutions and culture. James spells these out in sufficient detail to make the concept useful. Institutional economics has always looked at the power relations involved in the use of technology and the belief systems that lead people to accept or reject a technology on other than instrumental grounds. To an institutionalist trained in this tradition in the 1940s, 1950s, and 1960s, the reasonable expectation would be the power of technology as described in this essay and its frequent rejection by end users, particularly groups like peasant agriculturalists. What should have come as a pleasant surprise to institutionalists is the rather rapid and continued adoption of technologies by precisely the groups that were expected to resist it. For third world countries, as James has noted, the complaint has been about the power relations that have denied them access to desired technologies, and not their failure to seek access to it. A minority of institutionalists, rather than being surprised, have joined the pessimists and denied the transformations that have taken place. Fortunately, Dilmus James is not one of them.

Institutional economics, as noted by James, is evolutionary and valuational. So, in many ways, is development. It is valuational because it is about changing the lives of people. Economists distinguish between economic growth which is quantitative and development which involves structural changes, many of which are valuational. The experience of development over the last decades is evolutionary in many respects. The sustaining of change through time would be sufficient to warrant that designation. That it was unpredicted means that it was also a discovery and emergent process. These are further characteristics of evolution in its larger sense. It is emergent in the sense that it has generated properties that did not previously exist. The practical actions involved in the development process have also been a path of discovery, as we have learned from each step along the way. The real excitement is in the magnitude of the changes in the lives of the 5 billion people on the globe. Equally exciting is what we have learned about how it was done, how we can do it better, and what is the theoretical implication of what we have learned. As with all intellectual endeavors, the issues are far from settled, and there remains considerable controversy. The essays and comments in this book reflect both what we have learned and where we disagree. These disagreements are anything but unimportant. The success of past decades has established the criteria to measure the present and the future. The irony is that as we have learned more about the success of the process, we seem less and

less able to turn this to the account of
continuing it. We know the potential. We also
know that we are far below it. Our economic
theories and policies do make a difference.
Few books have the privilege of debating issues
that affect the lives of so many people. The
challenge of development economics is to keep
the debate open and the intelligent issues
clearly laid out. Electorates and policy
makers must choose; development economists must
provide the framework to assist choice. Our
generation has the opportunity to exceed the
achievements of the past but only if we
understand them. The choices of our time are
both opportunities and challenges. We must
accept the challenge or accept a failure that
can only be measured in the enormous
opportunities foregone.

The authors of five of the six essays are
academics, though most have considerable
development experience. Conversely, three of
the four comments are written by development
practitioners. All have solid academic
credentials. Agencies involved in the
development process have made considerable use
of highly trained economists, both as members
of their organization and as consultants from
firms or academic institutions. Basic economic
concepts such as cost benefit analysis are part
of the lending or project's process. Yet it
doesn't take much contact with those in the
field to detect a large measure of skepticism
concerning orthodox economic constructs.
Economics as a discipline has sufficient
respect for its technical achievements that
this distrust is often muted in public. Though
development practitioners may find that
economic theories do not hold true in their
area of endeavor or that such theories are not
particularly helpful in guiding their actions,

if they are not professionally trained
economists, their criticism is often
circumspect.
     Economics is not the only source of
dissatisfaction by development practitioners.
Various alternative theories of development
have not withstood their scrutiny and testing
against actual practice. If some economists
have been rigid in their neoclassical
orthodoxy, it is equally true that an abundance
of theories of economics and technology were
offered in the 1960s and 1970s as cures for our
development ills. Their proponents too often
were limited in their knowledge of the economic
development theories from which they were
dissenting. Practitioners have also been
skeptical of these alternative views. It is
not that the practitioners do not need or want
theory; they want theory that works. As Peter
Delp in his comment on "Strategies of
Development" notes, there is a continuing
"fascination" with appropriate technology or
with development theories that incorporate its
basic tenets, such as empowering people on
village level development. Undoubtedly, Delp
and others find the "lofty goals" of these
theories to be appealing; however, he, along
with most of his fellow development
practitioners, is not "convinced" that these
theories and the movements built around them
will be other than components or complements to
the larger development process. They may
capture a lot of the rhetoric, but the
development action will still be largely in
terms of the major existing strategy. Delp
similarly doubts that any of the strategies
that gained prominence in the late 1970s will
move to the "forefront . . . in many parts of
the world." Religious beliefs, such as the
interpretation of Islam currently holding sway

in Iran, involve the totality of human
activity, including economics. Politically
these concepts may be highly significant and to
many, threatening. They have a capability for
disruption but not for development. As such,
then, they are unlikely to be emulated by many
in the long run except those who are willing to
forego development for the sake of other
values.

From 1950 to 1980, development was
widespread; 1980 is seen as a turning point,
though the roots of this transition are seen by
both Delp and the authors of the "Strategies of
Development" essay as having roots in the 1973-
1974 run up of oil prices. Jameson, Weaver,
and Wilber see this transition as calling into
question the long-term viability of the
policies that brought both the extraordinary
growth and our current inability to sustain it.
Thus, they see a number of development
strategies reemerging from the current crisis
as influential policy prescriptions. To Delp,
the critical issue may not be the multiplicity
of different development policies that will be
followed, but rather, amidst this diversity,
"how to maintain the structure of a globally
integrated economy despite such groupings."

Delp, the development practitioner, sees
certain trends and technologies emerging that
would almost make formal economic development
strategies a sideshow issue. He illustrates
with food policies and information
technologies. From an aggregate global
perspective, postwar food production has been a
roaring success. In fact, from a producer's
point of view, it has been too much of a
success. Within the context of this success,
as Delp shows, is the contrast between the
failure of those who sought food self-
sufficiency and the more widespread success of

those who sought food security through both the
production of food and the earning of foreign
exchange in order to buy food. Even here,
where food policy has been a "success,"
malnutrition may still exist because many lack
the income to gain access to food that is
readily (and often cheaply) available. Food
policies are as political as they are economic.
Food policies are not only political, but in
order to understand all the complex
interconnections, one must understand politics,
economics, trade, agriculture, and nutrition.
Delp would undoubtedly concur that his brief
analysis of food policy is, in many respects, a
metaphor for the complex integrated analysis
necessary for the comprehension of most all
development problems, be they in health, in
housing, or in education. Development analysis
must be "holistic."

It is ironic that, as the development
revolution has been slowing, the information
revolution has been gathering momentum. As
Delp demonstrates, this information revolution
holds the promise of revitalizing the
development process. It is compatible with a
variety of different development strategies.
New information technologies can be
centralizing or decentralizing. They can be
effective tools for interventionists in the
planning process, or they can be used by
capitalists to make markets work more
effectively. Even so, though formal power may
be centralized, development and the
microelectronics described by Delp are likely
to have a decentralizing, democratic impact.
In the Soviet Union, for instance, there is a
recognized need to expand rapidly the use of
microcomputers in the workplace and, at the
same time, a fear that they will be a force
challenging centralized, political control. As

the implications of the information revolution
are better understood, it could well be that it
will   transform   the   context   in   which   we
understand and debate development strategies.

    One   of   the   most   vociferous   debates   in
development circles and in the media continues
to be on food policy and food security. Bishnu
Persaud's comment on "Theory and Practice in
World Agriculture" reflects the complexities of
the   issues   involved.   Persaud   accepts   the
"overall thrust of the paper" but raises some
questions about interpretation.   There is no
question that technological change has brought
a rapid growth in food supply and has led to
growing stocks of surplus commodities in many
areas.   But   the   global   picture,   however
important   it   may   be,   can   sometimes   obscure
regional   differences   and   difficulties.
Unfortunately,   it   has   too   often   been   the
doomsdayers who have sought to frame the issues
in global terms such as "world hunger" and,
therefore, have shifted the discourse away from
emphasis   on   very   real   regional   differences.
Refutation of catastrophic visions of global
famine does not deny the fact that there is an
array of severe food problems around the globe.
On this point, Brady and Persaud would agree.

    Though most of the world's population has
been able to increase and regularize its food
production or access to food, Persaud shows
that 21 countries in Africa and approximately
30   countries   overall   have   experienced   a
decrease in per capita food production in the
two   decades   prior   to   1985.   For   these
countries,   their   food   situation   is   getting
worse.   World food surpluses keep food prices
low, making imports affordable to food-deficit
countries and providing the stocks for food aid
and   famine   relief.   However worthwhile these
achievements   may   be,   and   their   significance

should not be underestimated, it is clear that
they are at best a mixed blessing. Cheap food
is a boon to the consumer but at the same time
serves as a disincentive for third world
farmers to increase production. Persaud raises
serious questions about the protectionist
policies such as those of the European Economic
Community (EEC) that brought some of these
surpluses into being, the policies of dumping
them on world markets and the way in which
"they distort prices and discourage production
in those developing countries with a
comparative advantage in their production."
Everyone favors famine relief, but the benefits
of food aid are fiercely debated; and there are
those who argue that in the long run it does
more harm than good by discouraging food
production.

Protectionist agricultural policies by
developed countries raise ancillary issues
about protectionism overall and its economic
impact upon developing countries. It is not
too great an oversimplification to say that
colonialism was a system that sought to make
the colonies producers of raw commodities and
to reserve most processing and manufacturing to
colonial countries. Many of these policies
have continued in the postcolonial era with
tariff structures that begin with little or no
tariffs on tropical raw commodities, and they
increase in severity with each stage in
processing. As Persaud states, "agro-
processing is often protected also, even in
cases where the agricultural raw materials are
only produced in developing countries." He
adds that "this discouragement of agro-
processing in developing countries is a further
discouragement to food production in these
countries."

     Persaud   notes   what,   in   this   author's
judgment, is one of the neglected factors in
increasing food production in parts of Asia,
land reform.   "In the Republic of China and
Taiwan, and in South Asia, land redistribution
has been important in contributing not only to
output,   but   also   to   welfare,   since   it   has
helped to absorb family labour and to bring
about a better distribution of output."   To the
countries   he   mentioned,   we   might   add   the
Republic   of   Korea   and,   before   that,   Japan.
These   reforms   were   early   in   the   development
process and generally effective.   And with the
exception of the People's Republic of China,
they were generally carried out by governments
that would be considered conservative.
     Some of us congenital optimists can get
carried away by the extraordinary increase in
such indicators of human well being as growth
in world food supply and the existence of world
food surpluses.   It is always important to add
the   qualification   that   food   surpluses   are
relative to the demand for food.   The demand
for food is dependent upon income and is not
synonomous with the need for food.   In many
areas where income is growing, we often find
the demand for food to be growing more rapidly
than population or food supply, as people are
demanding more food and better quality food.
In the case of "better quality" food it means
an   even   greater   increase   in   primary   food
production such as coarse grains to provide
animal feed in order to produce the meat, eggs,
milk, cheese, etc., that people wish to consume
in larger quantities.   At the time, the demand
for food includes large numbers of people who
would like to increase their consumption and
improve their nutrition but lack the income to
do so.   From Persaud, we learn that "India and
other populous countries in Asia still have a

long way to go to enable their people to
satisfy minimum food needs. During 1982-84 the
caloric value of average daily food supplies
was below the minimum accepted as being
compatible with a healthy life in forty-five
developing countries -- twenty-eight in Africa,
nine in Asia, six in the Americas and two in
Oceania."

Finally, as to food policy, Persaud makes
an important point. Economists are among the
most vociferous critics of failed agricultural
policies in developing countries, particularly
those in Africa: the countries that made the
wrong policy choices in the 1950s and 1960s,
and later are responsible for the failures that
followed. However, as Persaud states, " . . .
some eminent development thinkers at that time
saw a shortcut to development in concentration
on industrialization." In fact, among some
economists, models of using "surplus" labor
from agriculture to build industry and
infrastructure were close to being the
prevailing dogma of the time.

In his comments on "Population, Resources
and Limits to Growth," Bishnu Persaud stresses
the importance of the distinction between
short-term and long-term effects of population
growth. Much of the pessimistic writing on
population focuses on long-term projections of
population growth and the consequent and
seemingly horrendously large populations that
result from varied assumptions. Both Steinmann
and Persaud are not unduly concerned about the
long run. But Persaud expresses some doubts
about poorer countries, particularly those in
sub-Saharan Africa, being able to manage their
current high rates of population growth. Their
income and savings are inadequate to meet the
health and education levels necessary for their
expanding populations. The long run population

optimism of both Steinmann and Persaud is
predicated on the thesis that more people mean
more intelligence, creativity, and resource
creation, and therefore the wealth to sustain
them. Neither, I presume, would subscribe to
the view often attributed to Marx and Marxists,
that raw labor power creates its own future.
Invention and creativity as we know it today
requires a modicum of health and education. An
increase in population that remains mired in
poverty, ill health, and lack of education is
unlikely in Persaud's assessment to transform
the conditions sufficient to bring greater
wealth for a larger population.
     Persaud differs on another vital point.
He recognizes that "poor economic management
has been a significant cause of economic
distress in sub-Saharan Africa." He sees "much
effort at policy reform."   But, he argues,
policy reform is not enough to address the
magnitude of Africa's economic and population
problems. In the past decade, there have been
a series of severe setbacks to the African
economies, including drought, desertification,
and soil erosion, that make it difficult for
these governments to utilize existing resources
let alone create new ones. When African
countries are not facing famine, they find
themselves confronting low prices for their raw
commodity products. Clearly, from Persaud's
perspective, in order to address successfully
Africa's population and resource needs,
continuing policy reforms have to be matched
with considerable coordinated regional and
international efforts and resources. The
current political prospects for a substantive
increase in international aid are dim. If the
effort were made, the potential of science and
technology, particularly in areas such as
biotechnology, could create the possibility for

"a very hopeful future." Even with current technology, Africa could greatly increase its food production instead of experiencing the declining per capita food production which is the condition of most countries in sub-Saharan Africa.

Persaud closes his comment on an idealistic and optimistic note. The hundreds of millions of people living today in poverty and without the benefit of education, adequate nutrition, or good health constitute the greatest underutilized resource in human history. Unfortunately, "current thinking" does not "lend much support to global cooperation" to develop this resource not only for the benefit of those involved but also in recognition that this "brain power of the new born of the third world" are resources that could yield high returns to investment in them." Under these circumstances, the unleashing of the "dormant and stultified brain power" could mean a higher standard of living and improved quality of life for everyone.

This development revolution that we have been describing has been making the economies of the world more closely related and interdependent. World trade has grown even more rapidly than production. Our strategies of development, to be workable and sustainable, have to take into consideration all global economic realities. A development strategy that stimulates the economy to fuller utilization of resources can eventually lead to balance-of-payments difficulties, followed by domestic inflationary pressures. Getting one's prices right loses all meaning when inflation is out of control. Prior success in development may be undone and productive capacity underutilized by policies that restrict consumption in order to generate

export surpluses to service foreign debt. In
the 1980s, success of development strategies is
tied to monetary policies and the possibility
of successful debt management.

In   the   1980s,   on   questions   of   money
management,   monetarist   policies   prevail.   Or,
at   least,   there   is   a   verbal   commitment   to
monetarist   policies,   even   though,   as   Waters
notes,   the   actual   reality   of   policy   may   be   at
considerable   variance   from   the   statement   of   it.
Monetarism   is   noninterventionist.   But,   as
other   authors   in   this   book   observe,   it   requires
various   forms   of   intervention   to   achieve
nonintervention.   Granted,   "structural
adjustment"   may   be   a   process   to   get   government
out   of   a   number   of   endeavors,   but   still   some
minimum   of   government   involvement   is   a   source
of   difficulty.   Wendell   Gordon   explores   the
"policy   implementation"   problems   implicit   in
the   monetarist   analysis   of   Alan   Rufus   Waters.

The   3   to   4   percent   growth   in   money   supply
is   a   governmental   function.   Monetarists
concede   the   necessity   for   this   action   but   wish,
even   here,   to   keep   the   discretion   of   the
monetary   authorities   to   a   minimum.   Beyond
that,   as   Gordon   observes,   if   the   policy   is
going   to   work,   it   requires   private   sector
cooperation.   Private   commercial   banks,   other
lenders,   and   sellers   can   increase   purchasing
power   by   lending   money   or   extending   credit.
Further,   he   maintains   that   the   inflationary
impact   of   lending   will   be   in   part   a   function   of
the   productivity   of   the   use   to   which   the   loans
are   put.   If   the   loans   are   made   for
consumption,   its   inflationary   result   will   be
far   greater   than   the   loans   that   are   used   to
expand   production.   A   rigorously
noninterventionist   policy   allows   for   no
mechanism,   market   or   otherwise,   to
differentiate   and   regulate   these   differential

types of economic behavior. Consequently,
Gordon concludes, controlling the money supply
is at best only part of the solution to
inflation.

Gordon readily concedes that much of what
we call money, particularly paper money,
originated as a result of private sector
initiatives. He maintains that the intrusion
of government into the process was not because
government was necessarily an essential
instrument to create a money supply, but
because the existing methods led to abuses. At
the risk of some oversimplification, one can
define a fundamental difference between Gordon
and Waters and, more important, between
interventionists and noninterventionists in
terms of the conception of the nature of
government. To Gordon, governments intervened
in monetary matters because there were abuses
and because the public or some part of it
sought help from the government. To Waters,
those in government seek to expand their
authority by intruding deeper into the lives of
its citizens, and its response to the "public"
is more a response to special interest seeking
favors at the expense of the public.

Beyond perspectives on government, Gordon
is arguing for political, social, and economic
processes as being an ongoing, problem-solving,
learning endeavor in continuous need of
intelligent adjustment and correction. Trade
gives rise to a need for a medium of exchange;
the private sector creates money instruments.
Abuses arise; government becomes involved.
Government involvement itself creates other
problems; means have to be found to solve them.
Philosophically, this view is remarkably
similar to that of the noninterventionist
monetarist except that the continuous
correcting, problem-solving process works

within markets, and the role of government is
to establish rules under which markets operate.
The differences between the perspectives may in
some sense be small; in terms of real world
application, the chasm between them is
seemingly unbridgeable.

However one views the role of government,
Gordon maintains that the simple fact is that
the public in developing and developed
countries alike will not accept an "unfettered
private creation of the medium of exchange."
In Waters' essay, Gordon finds that there is a
recognition of a dependency on some kind of
legally constituted monetary authority, even if
that authority may be that of a larger, more
developed economy with a history of stable
money policy. The debate over the relevance of
monetarism for third world countries will
continue.

The difficulty of defining and getting the
type of "responsible behavior" that Gordon
thinks is necessary for intelligent monetary
and development policy is compounded by the
problems of the indebtedness of the
economically less developed nations. Two
propositions on indebtedness are widely
accepted. First, finding some means for an
ongoing resolution of the indebtedness problem
is vital for all countries, creditors, debtors,
or those whose international accounts are
essentially in balance. Second, most of the
debtor nations cannot meet their obligations
without external assistance. A third
proposition is gaining wide acceptance, namely,
that growth has to be the pathway out of the
indebtedness trap. This leads to the central
point of the Cashel-Cordo and Craig essay;
namely, what are the mechanisms available to
lenders and donors so that their external
support will facilitate growth and effective

debt management.   Gordon clearly agrees with
the goal of facilitating growth; however, he
questions whether the conditions imposed by
lenders and donors actually contribute to
growth or to recession.   In this regard, his
views are widely shared by development
economists and by recipient countries.   Gordon
makes a further important point that is
frequently overlooked.   In a world where
conditionality and structural adjustment are
attempts to minimize intervention, there are a
vast number of structural changes that are
ignored.   Redirecting resources into areas such
as health or education, or agricultural
development, particularly for the poor, may be
vital for inaugurating the growth that may be a
precondition of sustained effective debt
management.   Gordon's point is that
conditionality, either as required by the IMF
or as measured by Cashel-Cordo and Craig, does
not address issues which in his judgment may be
the most critical.

Of all the fields of economics, macro,
micro, industrial organization, regional, etc.,
development is the only one whose name implies
an activity as well as a system of thought.
Implicit, then, is a judgment that development
theories should be tested by the usefulness in
development practice.   This is the criteria
that Randal Thompson applies to the
institutional theories of technology transfer
set forth by Dilmus James.   Thompson is a
project design officer and is therefore
professionally involved in translating theory
into practical reality.   To a "large extent," a
project design officer is a "technology
broker."   To the development practitioner in
the field, there is an additional dimension,
the necessity for "accountability," a condition

that is not always imposed upon the academic
theoretician.
     The "multi-disciplinary, flexible method"
of doing development is a very human endeavor
of successes and failures.   To Thompson, the
virtue of the approach to technology transfer
set forth by James is that we learn from our
mistakes in a way that enhances both theory and
practice.   "Tool using behavior" carries with
it "a presumed cultural context, a whole array
of ideas, an institutional framework, and a
complex of skills to reinforce, use, and
maintain it."   The institutional approach to
technology transfer seems almost axiomatic to
someone involved in project design who has to
understand a technology in terms of the people
who will use it and the culture in which it
operates.
     The continuing task of economists
concerned with technology transfer is one of
"fleshing out of operational guidelines" for
use in the actual transfer process.   Though the
task may be "extremely difficult," the
interaction between academic theoreticians such
as Dilmus James and development practitioners
such as Randal Thompson is an important
ingredient in specifying the criteria to be
used in the selection of technology.
     It is interesting that in these essays and
comments, it is Thompson, a development
practitioner, who seeks to go beyond technology
as hardware to a "broader concept of technology
as ideas."   One could argue that the entirety
of the development process is primarily one of
ideas and the way people think.   We have noted
the importance of research and the role it has
played in the development of world agriculture
and in our ability to feed ourselves.   On
population, demographers are increasingly
recognizing the importance of the spread of

ideas.   In family planning, few ideas are more important than the simple recognition that people can choose their destiny and the number of children they wish to have.   We have also argued that technology creates resources. Resources are not things but properties of things that come into being because people have ideas and abilities to use them for human purposes.   The debate about strategies is a debate about ideas, as is that over monetarism or how to manage the debt problem. And, as the vast differences in growth rates throughout the world show, ideas do make a difference. One of the most important ideas is the idea of the intelligent use of technology for development.

The most powerful idea in the world today is that people no longer need to be poor or hungry. The task of economic development is to harness the power of that idea and to make it a reality.   The evidence of the past 40 years is one in which vast numbers of people have arisen from the depths of some of the most degrading poverty to the threshold of industrialization and some of the trappings of affluence. Many have been left behind, leaving much that still must be done.   Development economics is concerned with both the past achievements and the future possibilities. The following essays and comments involve a dialogue between theorists and practitioners about what we have done and how we can do it better in the future. There are over five billion people on this earth. The task of development economics is to play a vital role in defining the means by which they can have a better, longer life.

REFERENCES

Boserup, Ester. The Conditions of Agricultural Growth: The Economics of Agrarian Change Under Population Pressure. Chicago: Aldine, 1965.

Cohen, Mark Nathan. The Food Crisis in Prehistory: Overpopulation and the Origins of Agriculture. New Haven, CT: Yale University Press, 1977.

DeGregori, Thomas R. "Resources Are Not: They Become - An Institutional Theory." Journal of Economic Issues XXI (3): September 1987, pp. 1241-1263.

Espenshade, Thomas J., and Stolnitz, George J. (eds.). Technological Prospects and Population Trends. Boulder, CO: Westview Press, AAAS Selected Symposium No. 103, 1987.

National Research Council. Population Growth and Economic Development: Policy Questions. Washington, D.C.: National Academy Press, 1986.

2 THEORY AND PRACTICE IN WORLD AGRICULTURE

N. C. Brady

> Grant us a common faith that man
> shall know bread and peace . . . .
>
> from a prayer by
> Stephen Vincent Benet

INTRODUCTION

Human history provides the foundation for modern agricultural theory. It started with the first agricultural revolution some 10,000 years ago when a few of our early ancestors realized that hunting and gathering was not the most efficient way to put food "on the table." From the numerous plants and animals around them, they selected a very limited number of crop varieties to cultivate and a few animals to domesticate. In doing so, they were better able to meet their food requirements. Their choices predetermined much of the human diet, even to the present day. By trial and error, the first elements of the science of agriculture were born.

Through observation, selection, and simple trials, those early farmers accumulated a growing body of agricultural knowledge that was enhanced from generation to generation. Until a few hundred years ago, however, this learning process was provincial, pertaining only to locally raised crops and animals. Only when scientists were able to complement the farmers' knowledge of <u>what</u> to do with explanations of <u>why</u> it should be done was progress really made.

For example, for centuries farmers had known the beneficial effects of materials such as barnyard manure, ashes, and lime, but it was not until the nineteenth century that Von Leibig proved that the mineral elements in these additives were responsible for much of the crop stimulation. The gaining and sharing of this knowledge of what to do and why, first among scientists and then among farmers, broke down the insularity, and international agriculture came into being.

THE DOOMSAYERS OF THE 1960s

"The battle to feed all of humanity is over. In the 1970's . . . the world will undergo famines -- hundreds of millions of people are going to starve to death . . . ." So wrote Dr. Paul Ehrlich in 1968. And it seemed to be true.

Twenty-five years ago, the world's agricultural product was not perceived as being adequate to fully support human life of the future. Concern about the earth's limits to growth which began in the eighteenth and nineteenth centuries acquired new urgency. Experts anxiously observed that human population was growing at an ever-increasing rate while agricultural production was comparatively stagnant.

Their fears were well founded. The impact of famines, epidemics, and wars or massacres-- the three major factors that caused excess mortality throughout human history -- was greatly reduced by the middle of the twentieth century. Medical advances dramatically increased human longevity, significantly reduced infant mortality, and somewhat increased the birth rate (Sauvy, 1961).

The impact of these demographic changes was evident. World population which had doubled only about every 1,000 years from 7000 BC to 1650 AD, to reach 500 million, doubled again in 200 years to 1 billion in 1850, once more in 80 years to 2 billion in 1930, and would double again in 44 years to reach 4 billion in 1974 (A.I.D., 1987). The implications of this accelerating population growth were clear and frightening. Extreme food shortages for growing numbers of people seemed unavoidable.

Continued food deficits were projected to increase the incidence of inescapable poverty and widen the gulf between industrial and developing countries, conditions that would exacerbate existing political problems. Many knowledgeable individuals predicted unavoidable catastrophe for the earth's inhabitants.

In 1966 William and Paul Paddock wrote that the collision between stagnant food production and population increases was inevitable and that widespread famine would become a recurrent condition. In the same year, population expert Roger Revelle called attention to the fact that while developing countries had twice as many people to feed as industrial countries, they occupied only about half of the earth's approximately 3 billion hectares that were already cultivated or potentially arable. This problem promised to become particularly acute in Asia which then contained over half of the world's population

and where most of the potentially arable land
was already being farmed.

     In his 1967 State of the Union Message,
President Lyndon B. Johnson said, "Next to the
pursuit of peace the really greatest challenge
to the human family is the race between food
supply and population increase.   That race is
being lost."   In the same year, the President's
Science   Advisory   Committee   issued   a
comprehensive   report   on   "The   World   Food
Problem," one conclusion of which was that "The
scale, severity, and duration of the world food
problem   are   so   great   that   a   massive,   long-
range, innovative effort unprecedented in human
history will be required to master it."   These
were only a few of the many expressions of deep
concern about humanity's ability to feed its
growing numbers.

AGRICULTURE IN THE THIRD WORLD IN THE 1950s

     In the 1950s, agriculture, our first and
more essential endeavor, was being neglected in
the   developing   world.   Agricultural   systems
were stagnant.   The capacity to create needed
technologies   was   extremely   limited   because
there were few educated and trained scientists
and   technicians.   Many   third   world   leaders
viewed industrialization as the key to economic
success and regarded agriculture as a necessary
but   backward   occupation   not   deserving   of
serious   attention   or   improvements.   These
attitudes were exemplified by the heavy tax
burden borne by the agricultural sector in many
countries to provide resources for industrial
development.

     Technical cooperation with the third world
was a very new endeavor, and the knowledge and
vision of donors was still rather limited.   The

United States and other national and multilateral donors sincerely believed that brisk development could be fostered in emerging countries through efficient transfer of proved industrial-world technologies. They shared the developing-country view that a belated "industrial revolution" could quickly bring about the desired economic transformation and did not consider that dynamic agricultural improvements were essential to that process. The developing countries needed only to borrow and use outside technologies, not try to create their own. For this reason, extension and institutional development activities received heavy emphasis.

Very little donor support was given to exploring the possibilities for creating technologies specifically suited to the developing countries. Support for agricultural research was essentially nil since such research was not deemed to be essential and, in any case, it took too much time. The major agricultural efforts focused on plant and animal disease and pest control, development of irrigation and extension systems, and institutional and resource development (United States Technical Cooperation Congressional Presentation). Failure of this simplistic approach to stimulate agricultural production in the third world added fuel to the doomsday fire of the pessimists.

WORLD AGRICULTURE TODAY

A glance at the world food situation today shows little evidence of the catastrophic events that were predicted 30 years ago. On the contrary, just the opposite is true. The world appears to be awash with food, and

several industrialized nations, including the
United States and European Economic Community
countries, have food surplusses and record
costly food stocks with which to contend.
Several developing nations such as China,
India, and Indonesia have greatly reduced their
need for some food imports, and have even
exported modest quantities of other products.

    In most other developing countries where
unprecedented population pressures during the
last two decades required extraordinary food
increases, food needs have been met. In Asia
and much of Latin America, access to family
planning, general economic development, and per
capita food production have all improved. Most
Asian countries have kept food production
growth rates ahead of rates of population
increase, and the dire predictions of the
doomsayers were thus proven false. Today, food
production increase rates in most developing
countries are staying ahead of population
growth rates -- in some cases just barely
ahead, but ahead.

    From 1900 to 1950, worldwide food
production increased only about 1.5 percent
annually. From the mid-1950s to 1970-1974,
global food production increased at an average
annual rate slightly over 3 percent. Although
the rate fell to an annual average of 2.2
percent in 1970-1974 to 1979-1983, by 1986
worldwide exportable surplusses and stocks of
grain were at all-time high levels (FAO, 1982).

    It would be incorrect to assume that world
agriculture had fully achieved its goals during
the past 25 years. There are at least 500
million souls, a majority of them children, who
still go to bed hungry every night. Many of
them suffer from malnutrition and associated
illnesses.

But the catastrophic famines predicted by the well-meaning experts of the 1960s have been averted.   Furthermore,   credit   for   averting these disasters must be given to the countries in which the disasters were to have occurred. While the United States and other traditional food   suppliers   have   responded   to   fill   in significant gaps, more of the needed food has been   produced   in   the   developing   countries themselves.   The only exception to this general statement is Africa south of the Sahara which will   receive   special   attention   later   in   this chapter.

THEORY PUT INTO PRACTICE

Experiences   of   the   past   25   years   have contributed to the formulation of theories of agricultural   development   in   the   third   world. While the future may bring further refinements, the   remarkable   record   of   the   past   quarter-century provides us with the major elements of agricultural   development   theory   and   tell   us what   elements   must   be   present   to   encourage   if not   assure   success.   Of   these   elements,   I   am suggesting   that   the   following   seven   were largely responsible for what we call the Green Revolution.

Commitment to Agriculture

The   first   element   of   success   was   the recognition   at   all   levels   in   society   that agriculture was not only important but was the cornerstone   of   national   development.   The notion had to be disspelled that only through industrialization   could   these   countries succeed.   No   longer   was   it   thought   to   be

appropriate to overtax agriculture to provide
finances for industrialization. Nor was it
appropriate to ignore the training and
educational needs of farm families.

The commitment of national leaders was
especially essential to the agricultural
development process. Agriculture had to
receive high priority in national development
plans. Resources needed to produce the food
and fiber, and systems to harvest and market
the produce had to be created and implemented.
Social and economic rewards had to be made
available. Everyone had to recognize that
agriculture is where human economic development
begins.

John Mellor, in a simple and
straightforward manner, presents the case for
agriculture as the foundation for
industrialization. He shows the essentiality
of producing as much as possible of the
country's food and fiber needs, but he also
emphasizes the critical role of agriculture in
increasing rural incomes. These increased
incomes mean greater purchasing power for the
majority of the people, which in turn
stimulates both the agricultural and
nonagricultural economies of a country.

Policy Modifications

National commitments to the Green
Revolution were most evident in the area of
public policies. In most countries, the
success of this revolution hinged on the
commitment of national governments to alter
their policies and attitudes which in the past
had discriminated against agriculture. Price
structures were no longer set to provide low-
cost foods to the urban consumers and high-

priced   inputs   (fertilizers,   seeds,   and
chemicals) to the farmer.   Export levees were
not set so high as to depress the purchase
price from the farmer.   Policies were
instituted which made it profitable for farmers
to   adopt   the   yield-producing   technologies.
Furthermore,   policies   did   not   discriminate
against the small, subsistence farmer.   Poor
farmers with small land holdings responded to
profit incentives with the same enthusiasm as
larger scale farmers, thus quelling the myth
that small-scale farmers resist change.

Policies   were   also   established   to
encourage the development of institutions, both
public and private, to serve the farmer.   Farm
cooperatives are an example.   They provided a
means of encouraging farmer participation in
the process of procuring inputs and marketing
outputs.   Likewise, private entrepreneurs were
encouraged to initiate agro-industries which
became   integral   parts   of   the   agricultural
development systems.

Agricultural   production   increases   were
most dramatic in countries where the need to
improve food output was recognized and
addressed by leaders at the highest level and
where   specific   policy   changes   were   made.
Countries such as India and Indonesia, in which
improvements in agricultural productivity were
regarded   as   an   essential   ingredient   in
development process, were eminently successful.
On   the   other   hand,   where   agriculture   was
neglected, as it was in some African countries,
growth in food production has been slow, in
many cases not even keeping up with the rate of
population growth, and their economies have
suffered.

Technology Creation and Transfer

No other element of agricultural development was more important in stimulating the Green Revolution than was the creation of new and improved technologies. When properly orchestrated, these technologies provided new and exciting yield levels which had previously only been dreamed of. The most widely known of these technologies were the high-yielding, short-statured varieties of wheat and rice which became known as the "miracle seeds." When these varieties were properly fertilized and supplied with water, their yields were double or even triple those of the traditional varieties. Furthermore, their growth period was shorter by one to three months than those of native cultivars. And they resisted lodging (falling over) before harvesting.

The creation of these new technologies required teamwork among national and international agricultural research centers. The transformation from traditional to intensified agriculture was accelerated by scientific efforts sponsored by the Rockefeller and Ford Foundations. In 1941, the Mexican government and the Rockefeller Foundation undertook a joint effort to develop superior varieties of wheat and maize. The success of the semidwarf wheat varieties developed under this program led the Rockefeller and Ford Foundations and the Philippine government, in 1960, to cooperatively establish the first major international agricultural research center, the International Rice Research Institute (IRRI), in the Philippines.

In 1962, IRRI began research to develop a highly productive and hardy rice variety, IR-8. This "miracle rice" was a revolution for farmers and scientists alike. It opened up a

new era of technology improvement and
stimulated the work of national rice-
improvement centers. In the meantime, the crop
research programs in Mexico were rebuilt on the
IRRI model, and emerged in 1966 as the Centro
Internacional de Mejoramiento de Maiz y Trigo
(CIMMYT). CIMMYT not only produced a number of
outstanding cultivars but, more importantly, it
quickly fed these cultivars into the crop
improvement programs of national centers.

Additional centers focusing on other
agricultural crops and environments were
formed, and in 1971 the Consultative Group on
International Agricultural Research (CGIAR) was
created to support and coordinate the efforts
of this growing number of international
research facilities.

The CGIAR is an informal network of
countries and other public and private
development donors who are committed to
improving food and economic security in the
developing world. The early work of the CGIAR
centers was confined to a few major grain crops
cultivated under very specific conditions that
prevailed in much of Asia.

As countries strengthened their own
research capacities, national agricultural
researchers, an increasing number of whom were
educated and trained in their own countries,
provided leadership for research which led to
improved technologies. National scientists
quickly used the new cereal cultivars on
farmers' fields and in their own research
programs to develop more specific technological
solutions to their countries' problems.
Technology produced by a strong national
research system, such as in India, is based on
both the broad expertise of the international
centers and the more precisely focused
knowledge and understanding of their own

scientists. While some of these science-based technologies were successfully transferred from industrial nations, most were created in the tropical environments for which they are meant.

Today, the 13 CGIAR research centers work with developing-country national research programs on a variety of agricultural problems, and the emphasis has shifted to the more variable needs of African farmers and the harsher environments in which they cultivate crops. The original rice and wheat breakthroughs and subsequent improvements in other cereal crops were founded on basic plant knowledge and systems which are put under strain in dryland areas.

Availability of Inputs

A fourth element which contributed to the success of the Green Revolution was the timely availability of reasonable prices of inputs such as seeds, fertilizer, irrigation water, and credit. While both private and public sources were used to provide farmers with these inputs, their availability at price levels which encouraged production was made possible by public policies which reflected the commitment of national leaders to agricultural development.

Seeds. As new seed varieties became available from the scientists' test plots, they had to be increased and their genetic purity maintained. Initially, government-operated seed farms were given primary responsibility for this seed increase. In time, farmer cooperatives and private companies were given an opportunity to participate in this process. Today, in most countries at least a share of

the improved seeds come from private
organizations, some of which are also involved
in research to further improve the cultivars.
In any case, the need to develop and maintain
high-quality seed was recognized by national
governments, and some kind of arrangements were
made to provide farmers with these improved
materials.

Irrigation. Improved seeds alone could
not have created the remarkable production
increases of the Green Revolution. Expanded
use of irrigation has been a major factor in
the food production increases of the last 25
years. The irrigated area in developing
regions has increased over 2 percent annually
since 1960 (FAO, 1982). About 160 million
hectares, one-fifth of the cropland harvested
globally, were irrigated in 1982.
Approximately two-fifths of the annual crops in
developing countries are produced on irrigated
land. Other highly productive areas have
relatively favorable rainfall.

But the expanded area of irrigation does
not tell the full story of the influence of
irrigation on crop production. Research has
helped develop improved irrigation systems to
increase the efficiency of the water applied.
Likewise, research has helped alleviate the
problems of poor drainage and salinity, and has
highlighted the importance of individual
farmers and their organizations in improving
water-use efficiency.

Chemicals. Judicious application of
chemical inputs is another essential component
of improved crop yields. The use of chemical
fertilizer has increased about eight-fold in
developing countries since 1960 (FAO, 1982).
Used only in irrigated areas, the fertilizers

have helped the new cereal cultivars more nearly achieve their potential. Chemical pesticides have also contributed to improved and reliable agricultural productivity in areas where pests are a serious problem.

Research has played a critical role in identifying the importance of fertilizers and other agricultural chemicals. While the transfer of technology from industrialized countries was important in showing the essentiality of chemical nutrients, research in the tropics identified means of greatly increasing the efficiency of applied fertilizers. For example, root-zone placement of nitrogenous fertilizers in wetland rice was found essentially to double the efficiency of that nutrient.

Financial Resources. Credit was an essential component of food production systems. In most countries, credit available to low-income farmers initially was highly subsidized by the government, with mixed success. Payback by the small farmers was often woefully deficient. In time, other procedures involving small, rural banks and credit cooperatives evolved, and stringent restrictions were imposed on lenders. Likewise, mechanisms to encourage farmers' savings were initiated. These became more and more effective as rural incomes benefitted from the Green Revolution technologies. In any event, government policies which took into account the needs of small farmers were planned and implemented with at least some degree of success.

The creation and use of improved technologies played a major role in agricultural progress in Asia and Latin America in the past quarter-century. Today, about half of the wheat and rice hectarage in those regions is planted with the improved varieties developed at national and international research institutions. In the United States, semidwarf varieties were grown on nearly 60 percent of the area planted to wheat in 1984. The proportional use of improved cereal varieties is sure to increase in both developing and industrial countries.

Building and Education and Training Base

The relationship between human and institutional strength and increased agricultural productivity has long been recognized. It is exemplified in the U.S. land-grant system of colleges and universities that has placed this country at the zenith of agricultural science. Improving their human resource base was one of the critical achievements of those countries in which the Green Revolution was most successful. The developing countries recognized that through the creation of an in-country agricultural scientific community they could foster linkages between academic education and activities in research and extension. The countries sought a critical mass of educated and trained scientists and technicians to teach others and to carry out research and extension activities that focus on remediating the specific agricultural problems in their country.

Assistance donors were acutely conscious of this critical need, and no country more so than the United States. Our land-grant system is an unmatched and expanding resource of agricultural knowledge and expertise combined with broad, coordinated government support. Accessing this system, we have helped many emerging nations to build and vitalize their own scientific communities and institutions. Today, a number of these countries have technological bases of significant caliber which they continue to develop through participation in the world scientific community. Three examples will be given.

India. India is a case in point. From 1947 to 1967, this newly independent country requested and benefitted from assistance provided by six U.S. land-grant universities. India was helped to establish nine new agricultural universities, was host to over 300 faculty members from the involved U.S. institutions, and sent more than 1,000 agricultural faculty members and graduate students to the United States for further education. The dramatic increases in India's agricultural production over the last several years could not have been achieved without the human and institutional resources thus developed.

The success of India's universities has been enhanced through countrywide coordination of research by the Indian Council for Agricultural Research (ICAR). Among ICAR's most successful efforts are coordinated trials for crop improvement and soil management which the agricultural universities help plan and implement throughout India. The remarkable results of this enhancement are evident in India's food production figures. Between 1969-1971 and 1985, India's annual wheat production more than doubled from less than 21 to over 44 million metric tons, and annual rice production increased from less than 63 to over 91 million metric tons (USDA, 1981; FAO, 1985).

Indonesia. Developments in Indonesia over the last two decades also exemplify how human and institutional resource development can create an agricultural revolution. Indonesia emerged from World War II independent but very poor in human and institutional resources. Until 1967, human resource development, particularly in agriculture, was delayed by social and political unrest.

In the early 1970s, increased agricultural production became a priority, and the U.S. universities of the Midwestern Universities Consortium for International Agriculture (MUCIA) helped Indonesia develop the needed human and institutional resources. Hundreds of Indonesian postgraduate students came to the United States for further study and returned home well qualified to fill academic and government positions.

Today Indonesia's agricultural scientists effectively select, plan, and implement necessary research programs. The dynamic increase in annual rice production from just over 19 million metric tons annually in 1969-1971 to over 38.6 in 1985 clearly testifies to the caliber of Indonesian agricultural research and application (USDA, 1981; FAO, 1985).

Nigeria. While a number of Asian countries have successfully developed human and institutional resources for agricultural research, in Africa Nigeria has made the most progress. However, the road to agricultural success has not been smooth. The shortage of trained professionals was critical when the country achieved independence in 1959, and the subsequent emphasis on very sophisticated agricultural technologies and management practices ignored the needs of the small-scale farmer majority. Civil War in the late 1960s and postwar emphasis on oil production further delayed agricultural development.

A new forward momentum was fostered during the 1960s and 1970s by academic relationships between three newly founded Nigerian universities and three U.S. land-grant universities: Ahmadu Bello University (ABU) with Kansas State University; the University of Ife (Ife) with the University of Wisconsin; and the University of Nigeria/Nsukka (UNN) with Michigan State University. ABU most closely emulates the U.S. land-grant model with its teaching component coupled with locally relevant research and an effective program of extension to reach local farmers. ABU's success is due, at least in part, to the inclusion in the university's operations of long-established national agricultural research centers with important linkages in the agricultural community.

The Nigerian system works and has contributed to remarkable agricultural production increases. Corn production more than doubled, and rice production more than tripled during the 15-year period that ended in 1985 (USDA, 1981; FAO, 1985).

Participant Training. Educational opportunities in U.S. institutions have made it possible for developing country students and professionals to continue their training beyond what is presently available in their own country or region. They return home to apply their new knowledge and expertise. A.I.D.'s participant training program, therefore, is an important element in the development process.

The myriad of American universities, public and private organizations, and businesses that offer academic and practical on-the-job experience to graduate students and mid-career professionals from the developing world make this program possible. The training experiences range from short-term observation of Americans at work in agriculture, industry, administration, health services, and other key fields, to long-term study toward advanced degrees. The individual programs are carefully tailored to the human resource needs of the participant's country, and the time spent in the United States is enriched through a variety of contacts and experiences that help the participant to appreciate better the unique American way of life.

They bring back to their countries not only the increased knowledge for which they came but also a first-hand assessment of our customs and institutions, and an appreciation of the private-sector achievement upon which we base our success. For them, a policy climate that promotes and strengthens private institutions, credit systems, and other private-sector entities takes on new meaning in the context of their countries' development goals.

The Contribution of the Social Sciences. Despite the strength and scope of technical assistance, the biological and physical science breakthroughs would have been much less effective without the simultaneous inclusion of other supportive changes. Through research, social scientists have gained a better understanding of how people relate to and interact with their natural environments, governments, and institutions. For example, the role of private initiative in stimulating savings and the proper use of credit has been clarified. These insights help the development community to meet more precisely the needs and

aspirations of farmers and other aid recipients
in the developing world.

   Postcontract Linkages. The collaborative
work of American educators, researchers, and
technicians with developing ocuntries often
leads to individual and institutional
relationships that continue well beyond formal
project activities. We are now considering the
possible provision of modest support to help
the involved institutions sustain and expand
these valuable contacts.

Sustainable Agriculture

   The countries with successful Green
Revolutions learned a sixth important principle
as they progressed -- agricultural development
must be sustainable. The success of
agricultural practices that required inputs
largely dependent on outside assistance was
short-lived. Likewise, systems built around
the use of chemical pesticides to which the
pests quickly became resistant were soon
modified to emphasize integrated pest control.
   In less favorable agricultural
environments, they learned that protection of
the land from the ravages of soil erosion often
must be accomplished through the use of
alternative farming systems. Traditional modes
of cultivation such as "slash-and-burn" must be
replaced by more sustainable systems such as
"alley-cropping." In this agroforestry system,
annual food crops are alternated with rows of
perennial trees and shrubs. The larger,
usually leguminous plants reduce soil erosion
by providing some ground cover, recycling soil
nutrients from levels well below the roots of
crop plants, and furnishing leaf and stem

materials to reduce moisture loss and increase
soil fertility. Other similar systems involve
mixed cropping of leguminous and nonleguminous
food plants, and continuous small applications
of fertilizer at crucial times in the growing
cycle. The ultimate aims of such alternative
systems are to reduce erosion of precious
topsoil, maintain soil fertility, and increase
land productivity at minimal cost while
conserving scarce or threatened natural
resources.

Enhancing Individual Opportunities and Responsibilities

The seventh element deals with enhancing
the opportunities and responsibilities of
individual small-scale farmers. Thirty years
ago, only the large landholders had at their
disposal the knowledge and needed inputs to
increase agricultural production. Likewise, in
the centrally planned economies large state
farm communes dominated agricultural
production. These systems allowed little
opportunity for individual small-farmer
initiative.
Although this situation can be further
improved, great progress has been made to
increase individual responsibility. Seeds and
farm credit have become available to small
farmers, and adoption records show that farmers
respond. For example, adoption of hybrid maize
by small-scale farmers in Kenya and Zimbabwe
amazed national leaders. Likewise, the
remarkable increase in food production in the
People's Republic of China is due in no small
part to a degree of privatization which gave
the individual farmer a greater degree of both
responsibility and opportunity.

Since the revolution 40 years ago, China has developed a significant cadre of fairly well-trained agricultural workers, and an effective program to test, evaluate, and disseminate improved seeds and management technologies. With these improvements, Chinese agricultural production made significant progress. The research program and the progress it generated were curtailed somewhat during the Cultural Revolution. But recent steps to ensure private initiative of individual farmers have helped them to increase their overall agricultural output by more than 52 percent between 1978 and 1984 (USDA, 1985). The policy changes of this period significantly altered the way Chinese farmers live and work, and provided opportunities for wage earners to move out of agriculture and into other rural occupations such as transportation and construction that were vitalized by the increased agricultural output. A second wave of privatizing reforms now underway will help to bring pricing policies and distribution mechanisms into conformation with the greatly increased production levels.

WHAT THE FUTURE HOLDS

While some forward momentum has been achieved, we cannot consider this enormous job even close to being done. The cumulative resources of our planet could conceivably feed many more than the approximately 10 billion people projected by the year 2050 (World Bank, 1984). Nevertheless, in the twenty-first century, many poor people still may be victims of hunger and malnutrition. The great volume of rich arable land is located in the temperate regions of the industrial world, while the most prolific populations are the rural poor of less developed nations, particularly in the tropics, many of whom do not have the technology or resources to obtain adequate diets. These growing numbers of people need access to more and better food.

Focus on Agricultural Policies

The lessons we learned in Asia must now be adapted for application in these new, often less favorable circumstances. First, governments must make a commitment to agriculture and to policy changes that will bring about nationwide food security. The efforts of farmers must be augmented through access to improved plant and animal technologies. Policies must be adopted that make farming profitable enough to encourage increased productivity in both highly favorable and less favorable agricultural environments. The improved production resulting from those efforts will lead to economic growth and, ultimately, to increased incomes that will give people at all levels of the economic scale better access to more varied diets and other basic necessities.

Developing nations must also be encouraged to foster economic growth through policies that promote private sector endeavors. Development planners must keep in mind that economic growth and the elimination of poverty will produce long-lasting, positive results, and that food self-sufficiency is not the only path to food security.

There are some examples of countries which have already adopted enlightened policies that encourage agriculture and that give private enterprise and individuals incentives to

produce.   Agriculture in Botswana, Kenya, and
Zimbabwe has responded to these policies, and
food production has increased accordingly.
Small landholders in Zimbabwe surprised even
their strongest supporters as they adopted
newly created maize hybrids and associated
production technologies.   Other countries such
as Mali are turning more to the free market
economy in an attempt to bolster their food
production.   Such actions are essential if
Africa's downward trend of per capita food
production is to be reversed.

Agricultural Technologies

     Second, new agricultural technologies must
be developed and adopted.   In areas where the
resource base is strong and sustainable, use of
such   improved   technologies   can   greatly
intensify both plant and animal production.   In
the   more   fragile   areas,   particularly   in
countries   most   in   need   of   economic
improvements,   food   security   rarely   can   be
achieved by rapid increases in production of
food.   In such environments, more modest,
sustainabeg improvements in productivity must
be   achieved   through   introduction   of
technologies that use limited water resources
and fragile soils with great care to prevent
further damage.   Already research efforts to
provide more drought-tolerant crop varieties
are   beginning   to   pay   off.   During   the
widespread   droughts   in   1984-1985,   the
superiority of new sorghum varieties produced
by national scientists and counterparts in the
International Crops Research Institute for the
Semi-Arid Tropics (ICRISAT) was demonstrated.
If   research   institutions   are   supported

adequately, we can expect similar results with this and other crops in the years ahead.

Research to increase water use efficiency must be continued and expanded. The benefits from simple land-forming procedures for soils high in expanding clays which were developed at ICRISAT should be explored further. Likewise, improved agroforestry techniques must be sought to permit crop production while reducing water runoff and erosion.

Technologies must also be designed to control the insects and diseases that are most damaging to plant and animal production. Again, such resistance is beginning to appear in the improved varieties coming from research institutes around the world. Using the same principles that governed the development of insect- and disease-resistant varieties of wheat, rice, and maize, scientists have created new pest-resistant varieties of crops such as beans, cowpeas, and cassava. In addition, at the International Institute for Tropical Agriculture (IITA) in Nigeria, biological control methods have been developed for the control of the cassava mealy bug.

The cost of animal diseases to African agriculture must be fully recognized. Not only are animals a source of milk and meat but, for many subsistence farmers, also the only source of on-farm power. Scientists must diligently apply the best available research techniques to control or eradicate the most prevalent and damaging of these diseases. Methods for controlling East Coast fever of cattle are being developed at the International Laboratory for Research on Animal Diseases (ILRAD) in Kenya. These are examples of what can and must be done if Africans are to be able to feed themselves.

These are broad goals, but ones that can be accomplished if we diligently apply both new and long-proved scientific approaches. We are doing just that.

Using the modern methods of biotechnology, for example, agricultural scientists are beginning to develop plant cultivars that will tolerate the adverse soil and climatic conditions, and resist the insects and diseases so common in much of Africa and in other areas that have major constraints against productive agriculture. These new techniques yield results much more rapidly than traditional plant breeding methods, and greatly reduce the experimental time required. They also allow researchers to choose, isolate, and incorporate the precise stress-resistant characteristics needed for a specific constraint in a particular environment.

Tissue and cell culture techniques are already being used in crop improvement in the tropics. Such methods have made possible viable crosses between traditional rice varieties and wild rice cultivars which were previously incompatible. Already these methods are being used to incorporate stable resistance to insect pests of the rice plant. Likewise, tissue culture techniques have expedited the ready exchange of disease-free potato germ plasm, thereby accelerating the development of improved varieties.

These newer biotechnological methods are being employed in tandem with traditional breeding experiments to augment plant and animal research programs throughout the world. While many of the initial applications of biotechnology will be more useful in the industrialized nations, some are already being used in the low-income countries. Furthermore, as these tools become more precise, their application to plants and animals in the developing countries will improve and will be increased accordingly. Certainly, developing country scientists and technicians must be ready to employ the new scientific research methods and should now sharpen their expertise in this important new field.

Innovative biotechnology must be employed not only in the laboratories of developed countries but in counterpart laboratories of the low-income countries. Third world scientists must receive training in the new techniques and must focus the methods they learn on the food production problems of their own countries. They cannot afford to await only the spillover from science in the United States and other industrialized nations.

Sustainable Systems

The third major issue that must be addressed is conservation of natural resources, most particularly in tropical regions. We already know how much damage can be caused by incautious use of fragile and scarce natural resources as people struggle to grow enough food for survival. The welfare of future, even more numerous generations will depend upon protection of those resources. We must learn how to make development and conservation not only compatible but mutually reinforcing.

Sustainable agriculture must be further explored. New agroforestry techniques supplemented by modest fertilizer inputs will need to be developed. The biological research needed to create new approaches must be complemented by social science studies which focus on the cultural and economic needs of the cultivators. In Africa much greater attention must be given to the needs and role of women in these systems.

The aim is to produce more and better food in a resource-conserving manner. To do this, the small-scale farmer will require superior products and methods that are financially and technologically accessible, and that will not abuse the resources upon which future productivity depends. In addition to biotechnology, scientists and technicians are employing computer and satellite technology, and are emphasizing the development of environmentally sound agricultural management systems that minimize reliance on chemical fertilizers and pesticides for success.

Emerging computer-based tools have the potential to revolutionize our ability to predict crop-production levels in different agroecosystems without on-site experimentation. Interdisciplinary teams of climatologists, plant physiologists and breeders, and soil and water scientists are using environmental crop models to accelerate agrotechnology transfer from one experimental site to others with similar characteristics.

This approach is being used by a group of international cooperators associated with the International Benchmark Sites Network for Agrotechnology Transfer (IBSNAT) which is funded by A.I.D. A basic system of soil classification, called Soil Taxonomy, is the key used by researchers to identify areas of common soil characteristics throughout the world. Collaborating scientists from different countries identify potentially productive crops for specific soil/climate/management combinations. Computer simulation models help them to predict the likely success of various proposed combinations.

When this methodology is fine-tuned, it will be possible, for example, to predict the probable success of a new technology in a wide variety of agroecological systems from the results of a few carefully managed trials. Because of its universal applicability, this fairly new field of research is linking scientists from different disciplines in the industrialized and developing countries.

The development community is employing computerized data processing in many other ways, and these promising applications must be fully explored. Computer mobels simulating different population growth rates, agricultural productivity, forest resource depletion, energy use, weather patterns, and other relevant variables help developing country decision makers to grasp the magnitude of problems that can ensue from the complex world in which we live. The models also demonstrate how thoughtful current strategies can help countries avoid "worse-case" scenarios in the future. Predictive models also bring them face to face with the reality that while today's concerns may seem to preclude consideration of tomorrow's needs, wise current investments of time, money, and personnel can greatly reduce future demands on these resources.

CONCLUSION

Agriculture is as old as the first human attempt at cultivation and as new as this morning's scientific breakthrough. But always, it is the basic force behind economic development.

Despite the dire predictions made from time to time, this little planet can feed us all. Technology-based agricultural systems can produce the needed food, generate income for other human needs, and help to create both on- and off-farm employment.

We must enlarge our vision to encompass all of the human family, so that ever fewer of us lie down hungry at night. We cannot consider ourselves really self-sufficient or safe until our agricutural bounty is available to every man, woman, and child on this earth.

REFERENCES

A.I.D. Human Population Doubling Time, 7000 BC to 2023 AD. Science and Technology Directorate for Population, 1987.

Ehrlich, Paul R. The Population Bomb. Ballantine Books, 1968, p. xi.

FAO Production Yearbook, various years.

FAO at Work, October/November 1986, p. 2.

FAO. Agricultural Inputs in Developing Countries, 1960-79. World Bank, 1982.

Johnson, Lyndon B. President's Science Advisory Committee, Food vs. People. Excerpts from "The World Food Problem," p. 3.

Mellors, John W. "Agriculture on the Road to Industrialization." Development Strategies Reconsidered, edited by John P. Lewis and Valeriana Kallab. Overseas Development Council, published by Transaction Books, 1986, pp. 67-89.

Paddock, William and Paul.   <u>Famine - 1975</u>.
Boston: Little, Brown & Company, Ltd., 1966,
p. 9.

Revelle, Roger. <u>Symposium on the Prospects of
the World Food Supply</u>.   National Academy of
Sciences, 1966, p. 26.

Sauvy, A.   <u>Humanity and Subsistence</u>.   Annales
Nestle, 1961, pp. 29-30.

United   States   Technical   Cooperation
Congressional Presentation 1958, various
country data.

USDA.   <u>World Indices of Agricultural and Food
Production</u>, 1981, various pages.

USDA.   Economic   Research   Service,   <u>China,
Outlook and Situation Report</u>, July 1985, p. 5.

World Bank.   <u>World Development Report 1984</u>, pp.
192-193.

COMMENTARY BY B. PERSAUD

This is a very useful survey of developments in world agriculture in relation to man's capacity to feed himself. In view of this theme and that of the book, the chapter inevitably focuses on developments and prospects for food production in the developing countries.

The author points to the great strides that have been made in increasing food production since the late 1960s when many commentators saw the Malthusian spectre looming once again in the world. Much of the chapter describes the reasons for this success, and it has an optimistic tone. It goes on to deal with some essential requirements if this progress is to be sustained.

I do not have any major quarrel with the overall thrust of the chapter. However, differences with the detailed formulation are significant and lead to some differences of emphasis, both in the overall analysis and in prescriptions.

From the author's background, it is understandable that technological change and U.S. assistance to third world agriculture are given much relative attention. While in the latter case this results in neglecting the contribution of other bilateral donors and the multilateral development institutions, in the former, the great emphasis given to technological change, in relation to both

recent progress and the future, is not
misplaced.

The author does not also allow his origin
and involvement in a major donor agency to
cloud his view of the great contribution made
to progress by the efforts of the developing
countries themselves. From my own experience
in international cooperation, I can say that
this is unusual and is therefore very
commendable. Donors and multilateral agencies
have too great a tendency to take credit for
policy reform in developing countries. They do
not recognize enough that developing countries,
too, can learn from their mistakes.

Again, in relation to the overall
assessment, I believe that the author has
overestimated the progress made and expectedly
therefore underplays future difficulties. It
is true that progress has been substantial in
some of the major developing countries with
huge populations, e.g., countries in South and
East Asia. However, while in terms of the
world's capacity to produce food and in
relation to major third world countries, there
have been substantial achievements, it is still
true to say that the majority of developing
countries continue to face serious food
problems and are very vulnerable to climatic
failures and crop pests and diseases. In the
two decades up to 1985, per capita food
production had fallen in about 30 developing
countries, 21 of which were in Africa.

Global figures on food production
increases can be a misleading guide to the
improvement of capacity to avert famines. The
incidence of famines in Africa in the last
decade and the large impact of the recent
monsoon failure in India tell the tale.
Although work by Professor Amartya Sen (1980)
and others, including the World Bank, have

increased awareness that such factors as income distribution and general economic growth are also important in considering vulnerability to famines, too much emphasis is still given to world food production capacity in assessing progress in achieving food security. The author to some extent falls into this trap. The chapter treats too much in global terms-- progress and prospects -- and does not give enough attention to the important role of overall economic progress in individual developing countries in resolving their food problems.

It is surely too sanguine to say that the "world appears to be awash with food," and, going beyond China, India, and Indonesia, that "in most other developing countries where unprecedented population pressures during the last two decades required extraordinary food increases, food needs have been met." The experience not only of Ethiopia and the Sahel but of other parts of Africa including countries such as Kenya shows this to be unwarrantedly optimistic.

While for some developing countries, e.g., the small newly industrializing or service- oriented countries, economic progress does not depend on progress in food production, and increasing food imports might be affordable, for the vast majority of developing countries expanding food production is either crucial to economic progress or could greatly facilitate it. And in spite of the good progress in food production and in agriculture generally in some developing countries, for most of these countries agriculture has the potential to make a greater contribution to development.

Seemingly one reason for the sanguine attitude is that the author does not distinguish between progress in meeting

effective demand and the much larger demand,
which remains unsatisfied, to meet minimum
nutritional requirements. Thus he seems to
make the usual mistake of regarding the food
problem as only or mainly a sub-Saharan African
problem. India and other populous countries in
Asia still have a long way to go to enable
their people to satisfy minimum food needs.
During 1982-1984 the caloric value of average
daily food supplies was below the minimum
accepted as being compatible with a healthy
life in 45 developing countries -- 28 in
Africa, 9 in Asia, 6 in the Americas, and 2 in
Oceania.

In relation to the failure in the pre-
1970s, too much blame is attached to policy
makers. A significant part of the problem was
the wrong guidance to policy provided by
development theory. Some eminent development
thinkers at that time saw a short-cut to
development in concentration on
industrialization.

In terms of specifics, two significant
issues were almost completely neglected:
protectionism in the major countries and their
impact on food production in developing
countries; and the contribution to progress in
developing countries made by land reform.

The author cites the large food stocks in
the European Economic Community (EEC) and the
United States and evidence of current great
food production capacity. However, especially
in the case of the EEC, these stocks result
from the high levels of protection provided to
farmers; and while their availability
encourages the provision of food aid to needy
countries, these surpluses are also dumped on
world markets where, as in the case of sugar,
they distort prices and discourage production
in those developing countries with a

comparative advantage in their production. Actual and potential food exports from developing countries are thus adversely affected. Besides sugar, other notable examples include wheat, rice, cassava, beef and vegetable oil.

Some commentators have justified the creation of surpluses because of their ready availability as food aid to ease food shortages and malnutrition in developing countries. While such surpluses encourage generosity, their adverse long-term effects on food production and exports through distribution policies which sometimes affect production incentives in developing countries and through dumping point to the need for reduced protection and surpluses, but without a reduction in the level of assistance concerned with removing malnutrition in food deficit countries. Surpluses in affluent countries which discourage production where it is greatly needed arean impediment to solving the world food problem.

Protection extends beyond support for farmers in industrial countries. Agro-processing is often protected also even in cases where the agricultural raw materials are only produced in developing countries, through the levy of greater effective tariffs on imports of finished goods than on imports of the raw materials from whicht hey are produced. This discouragement of agro-processing in developing countries is a further discouragement to food production in these countries. The level of protection and their effectson developing countries are not on the whole insignificant. An authoritative study by Valdes and Zietz shows that for 99 commodities, if the level of protection was reduced by about

one-half, exports from developing countries
could have increased by about 11 percent.

The author does not include reform in the
'seven elements' which he highlighted as being
largely responsible for agricultural progress
in recent times. This is a significant
omission since in many developing countries
with high man:land ratios, giving farmers
access to land through redistribution from the
state sector, from traditional plantation
agriculture or from other large land holdings
has encouraged agriculture of the appropriate
cultivation intensity both in terms of the
crops and methods chosen. In the Republic of
China and Taiwan, and in South Asia, land
redistribution has been important in
contributing not only to output but also to
welfare since it has helped to absorb family
labor and to bring about a better distribution
of output. This is a contribution of state
action which the extreme proponents of free
markets seem to neglect because they do not
recognize enough the importance of state action
in agriculture in removing institutional
impediments to progress.

There are a number of other points on
which some refinements are possible. Progress
is seen as starting too abruptly around 1970 or
just before. Yet as the statistics in the
chapter itself show, global food production
increased by over 3 percent per year from 1950
to 1974, a higher rate than the period
immediately following. In the case of India,
the buildup of progress began in the 1960s.

In discussing institutional improvements,
the chapter mentions cooperatives only in
favorable terms. Yet while there has been some
success in this form of economic organization
in agriculture, there has also been much
failure. In fact, the record of cooperatives

seems to be worse in developing countries than in developed ones because of management difficulties.

The author recognizes the contribution which has been made by policy reforms in developing countries, e.g., agricultural pricing policies. He seems, however, to give the impression that these reforms have gone further than is the case. This imbalance may have been due to the tendency toward generalization noted above. The extent to which reforms have been adopted varies widely, and there is still much scope for policy improvements in many countries in such areas as pricing, land reform, and in the relative distribution of public expenditure between agriculture and other sectors.

One policy reform outside of agriculture which has been contributing to agricultural progress is the correction of overvalued exchange rates. This is not mentioned by the author, yet it is doing much to improve the agricultural terms of trade.

While much attention is given to the contribution that could be made by technological progress and especially by biotechnology, the future is seen too much as depending on prior advances in the industrial countries. Biotechnology could do much to accelerate agricultural transformation in developing countries, and much of the applied work is not beyond the capacity of developing countries in terms of both technical skills and resources. While these require supplementing by economic assistance, much of the work must be done in the developing countries themselves.

A particular problem for the future is the unfavorable trend which is developing in capital flows to developing countries. This is not mentioned in the chapter because it has not been given adequate attention in terms of its past contribution. Yet the World Bank, through both the International Bank for Reconstruction and Development (IBRD) and the International Development Association (IDA), has done much to finance agricultural improvements both in terms of infrastructure as well as irrigation and methods of production. In South Asia, particularly, World Bank financing has made a tangible and obvious contribution to output increase.

This comment has inevitably concentrated on differences in points of view. However, there is much agreement with the chapter both in thrust and details. Some of the points are mere refinements which may have been captured by the author himself had he been able to attempt a more comprehensive treatment. These views, it is hoped, will serve as a supplement to the chapter in helping to provide a wider and more balanced understanding of this important subject.

REFERENCES

Sen, A. K. Poverty and Famine: An Essay in Entitlement. London: Oxford University Press, 1980.

Valdes, A., and Zietz, J. Agricultural Protection in OECD Countries: Its Cost to Less-Developed Countries, IFPRI, 1983.

3 POPULATION, RESOURCES, AND LIMITS TO GROWTH

Gunter Steinmann

INTRODUCTION

On July 11, 1987, the world population reached 5 billion. Although the exact birthday of the 5 billionth person is unknown, the United Nations Fund for Population Activities (UNFPA) adopted this date to increase public awareness of the dynamics of current population growth. UNFPA also reported the newest projection that world population will increase to 6 billion before the turn of the century and will continue to grow to 7 billion in 2010 and to 8 billion in 2022.

Is this good or bad news? Many newsmen, readers, and policy makers are alarmed by the figures. They fear the apparently inevitable explosion of the world population and are concerned about the consequences. They take for granted that the unprecedented increase in the number of people aggravates famine, unemployment, economic backwardness, illiteracy, and other problems of underdevelopment, and precipitates more pollution and faster depletion of natural resources in the world. The widespread concern led to numerous proposals and initiatives for prompt actions to slow down and eventually stop

the growth of world population. Some
pessimists even argued that in some countries
population has already grown beyond capacity
limits and that there is no way to avoid mass
starvation and economic collapse in those
countries.

The purpose of this chapter is to show
that the fears of a world population explosion
as it relates to hunger catastrophies and other
miseries are exaggerated and unjustified. This
first part of the chapter briefly describes the
current demographic trends in the developing
countries and analyzes the causes of the rapid
population growth. The second part deals with
the economic consequences of the demographic
change.

I present first the demographic data, then
enter into the controversy on the historical
uniqueness of the present population growth.
The fertility and mortality of the developing
countries are compared with the fertility and
mortality of the developed countries in the
last century, and the similarities and
dissimilarities between the present and the
previous process of demographic transition are
shown.

After this I turn to the consequences of
population growth, beginning with a discussion
of the limits of this growth. Malthus had
argued that population is checked by the
scarcity of food and resources, and that
population growth is therefore impossible
unless technical improvements increase the
carrying capacity of the territories. Malthus'
argument shows the necessity of studying the
links between population and technology and of
analyzing the immense progress in expanding the
capacity limits on earth. Having accepted the
principal possibility of long-run population
growth, we are still confronted with the

question of whether further population growth is desirable. This question, which is in the very center of the modern population debate, is discussed in the remainder of the chapter. We show that population growth can be an obstacle to economic development in the short run, but that it can also hasten economic progress in the long run. The assessment of the economic consequences of population growth then depends on the time horizon of the society.

THE DEMOGRAPHIC TRENDS

In 1950 there were about 1.8 billion people in the less developed countries[1] (68 percent of the world population). My mid-1986 population had more than doubled and was estimated at about 3.8 billion (76 percent of the world population). In terms of sheer numbers, the increase was 2 billion. That corresponds to an average annual population growth rate of about 2.1 percent.

These rates, however, reflect the global trend only. They conceal the significant differences of the rates of population growth between different parts of the third world and between different time periods after World War II. They do not contain any information about the birth and death rates that led to the population growth.

Figure 3-1 shows the average annual population growth rates in less developed regions for 1950-1985. The population growth accelerated in the 1950s and 1960s, peaked with 2.5 percent in the late sixties, and slowed down again in the seventies and eighties. The current rate is 2 percent, and the rate projected for the nineties is 1.8 percent.

Figure 3-1.   Average Annual Population Growth
               Rates in More Developed and Less
               Developed Regions, 1950-1985

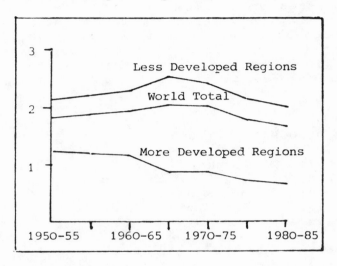

Source: World Resources Institute, <u>World
          Resources 1986</u>, New York, 1986, p. 11.

        Population grew at very different rates in
different parts of the third world (see table
3-1).   The greatest decline in growth rate
occurred in East Asia, and most of that was
accounted for by China, where the growth rate
fell from 2.7 percent in 1965-1973 to 1.5
percent in 1973-1980 and 1.2 percent in 1980-
1985 due to strict enforcement of antinatalist
policies by the Chinese government.   The
decline of China's growth rate was the primary
cause of the deceleration of the population
growth in the less developed countries.   The
growth rate of the less developed countries
<u>excluding China</u> in 1980-1985 is still 2.4

Table 3-1.   Estimates of Demographic Variables for Major Third World Regions

Region	1985 Population (in millions)	Annual Percentage Growth Rate 1950-1955	1980-1985	Crude Birth Rate per 1,000 1950-1955	1980-1985	Crude Death Rate per 1,000 1950-1955	1980-1985	Total Fertility Rate per 1,000 1950-1955	1980-1985	Life Expectancy at Birth 1950-1955	1980-1985
Total Developing Regions	3,763.4	2.10	2.00	45.0	31.0	24.0	11.0	6.1	4.1	41.4	56.9
Sub-Saharan Africa	449.8	2.00	3.03	48.0	47.6	28.0	17.5	6.4	6.6	34.4	47.9
Latin America	406.2	2.72	2.30	42.5	31.8	15.5	8.2	5.9	4.1	51.0	64.1
East Asia and Pacific (except Japan)	1,498.9	2.07	1.40	44.8	21.8	24.1	7.7	5.9	2.8	41.1	64.8
South Asia	1,052.6	1.86	2.16	45.7	35.7	27.0	14.0	6.6	4.8	39.0	51.6
Middle East and North Africa	180.9	2.64	2.98	50.5	42.3	23.0	12.3	7.2	6.1	43.6	57.0

Source: National Research Council (U.S.), Working Group on Population Growth and Economic Development (eds.), Population Growth and Economic Development: Policy, Questions. Washington, D.C., 1986, p. 3.

percent and significantly higher than the 2.0
percent shown in table 3-1 for the less
developed countries including China. China is
the most spectacular, but not the only case of
declining rates of population growth. At the
beginning of the period, Latin America was the
fastest growing region and now has a growth
rate of 2.3 percent compared to 2.7 percent in
1950-1955. India's population growth dropped
from 2.5 percent in 1950-1955 to 2.0 percent in
1980-1985, and the decrease is similar in most
other Asian countries. Africa took a different
demographic development. The growth rate of
African population in the eighties was
considerably higher than it was in the fifties,
with Africa overtaking Europe to become the
world's third most populous region.

The large demographic change in the
developing countries since World War II becomes
evident when we consider the development of the
birth rates and the death rates that led to the
population growth[2] (see figure 3-2). The death
rates fell substantially in all regions during
the whole period. The death rate of all
developing countries was 11 per 1,000 in 1980-
1985 or less than half of the rate of 1950-
1955, with the strongest improvements in East
Asia (decline by more than two-thirds) and the
smallest improvement in sub-Saharan Africa
(decline by about one-third). Decreasing birth
rates started in the mid-sixties. The births
fell dramatically in China but remained nearly
constant in sub-Saharan Africa. In the other
regions, the birth rates were about one-fifth
lower in 1980 than in 1950.

Figure 3-2. Birth Rates, Death Rates, and
Population Growth Rates in
Different Regions, 1950, 1965, and
1980

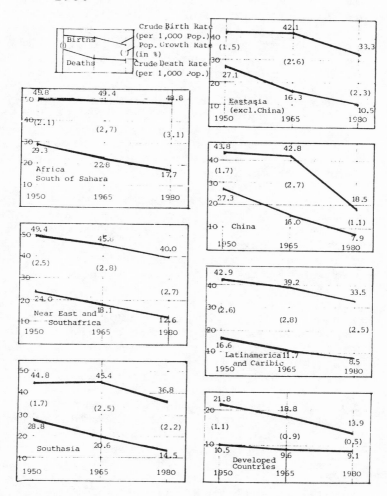

Source: World Bank, <u>World Development Report
1984</u>, Washington, D.C., 1984.

        Death rates and birth rates are affected
by the age structure of population and can
therefore not be used as indicators of
mortality and fertility. However, the changes
of life expectation at birth clearly indicate
the immense improvement of mortality in all
developing countries (see table 3-1).
Fertility is measured by the total fertility
rate (number of births per woman). The
fertility rates slightly increased in sub-
Saharan Africa but decreased in the other
regions. The decrease of the fertility rates
exceeded the decline of the birth rates. This
confirms that the process of declining
fertility is underway in all developing regions
except sub-Saharan Africa.
        The current level of fertility in the
developing countries is still high compared to
the level reached in the developed countries,
and there is no reason to expect that the
fertility decline has come or will come to an
end soon. On the contrary, it is likely that
the downward trend will continue and spread to
sub-Saharan Africa, too. On the other hand,
the process of mortality decline will certainly
slow down. Future improvements of life
expectancy will be more difficult to achieve
when the mortality gap between the developing
and the developed countries is relatively
small. We expect, therefore, that fertility
will decline faster than mortality in the
future. This development will retard
population growth in the next decades but will
not stop it. In 1980 about 40 percent of the
population of the developing countries were
younger than 15. These people already have
reached child-bearing ages in 1987 or will
enter into them within the next years. The
large increase in the numbers of persons in
child-bearing ages will offset the effects of

lower fertility and will guarantee a positive
growth rate of population for many more decades
even if fertility would instantly fall to the
low level that prevails in the industrialized
countries now.

To put the present population growth of
the developing countries into perspective, it
helps to look back at the population growth of
the developed countries in the eighteenth and
nineteenth centuries.   Before the Industrial
Revolution   dramatically   changed   the
demographics of Europe, Europe experienced
large fluctuations of the death rate and the
size of population.   Population density had
slowly increased, but the average annual rate
of population growth was 0.5 percent or less.
The beginning of industrialization also marked
the beginning of the demographic revolution.
The recurrent peaks of the death rates almost
totally disappeared.   The decline of mortality
caused   an   acceleration   of   the   population
growth.   The growth rates reached between 1 and
1.5 percent.   The peak rates were considerably
lower than the growth rates that the developing
countries experienced after World War II.   The
discrepancy between the historical growth rates
of the developed countries and the contemporary
growth rates of the developed countries is due
to   differences   in   fertility,   mortality,   and
migration.

European women showed much lower fertility
in   the   last   century   than   the   women   of   the
developing countries did in the middle of this
century.   The birth rates never exceeded 40 per
1,000 in Northwest Europe.   England had a birth
rate of 34 per 1,000 in 1850 when fertility
began to decrease, and the rates were close to
30 per 1,000 in many other European countries.
Compared   to   these   figures,   the   developing
countries experienced very high rates in the

1950s.   Their birth rates were well above 40
per 1,000 and ranged from 48 per 1,000 in sub-
Saharan   Africa   to   42.5   per   1,000   in   Latin
America.
      How   are   the   different   experiences   of
Europe   and   the   developing   countries   to   be
explained?   The   European   countries   of   the
seventeenth   and   eighteenth   centuries   had
effectively   checked   fertility   through   a
complicated   network   of   rules,   customs,   and
societal pressure that made it difficult for a
couple to marry.   The average age of women at
marriage was late at about 25, and never more
than 45 to 50 percent of the women in child-
bearing ages 15 to 50 were married at any time.
It   was   not   before   last   century   that   the
barriers to marriage were lifted and lost their
importance.   The   developing   countries,   on   the
other hand, had a very different system.   They
had not installed social mechanisms to prevent
a   couple   from   marrying.   Their   system
encouraged them to marry early by making the
marriage an economic necessity both for men and
women.   The   lack   of   social   preventions   to
marriage and the low ages of women at marriage
caused the high fertility that prevailed in the
developing countries until recently.
      A   second   important   difference   between
European   demographic   history   and   the
demographic situation of developing countries
after World War II concerns mortality.   At the
beginning of European industrialization, the
death rates were about 30 per 1,000.   At the
beginning of this century, they had fallen to
20 per 1,000.   Some European countries had even
higher death rates.   The developing countries,
however, started both with lower death rates
and also experienced a sharper fall in them.
The death rates were at about 24 per 1,000 in
1950-1955   and   reached   11   per   1,000   only   30

years later. This tremendous reduction was almost universal and was unprecedented in history. It largely contributed to the phenomenon of "population explosion" and is the main reason why the rates of population growth were twice as high as the peak rates in European demographic history.

A third difference is in the scale of international migration. At the end of the last century mass emigration absorbed about one-fifth of the national growth of European population. The ratio was higher for certain regions (especially for Ireland) in certain periods. However, when the population growth of the developing countries accelerated after World War II, the alternative of mass emigration was no longer open. Although international migration continued to exist and to influence population growth of the immigration countries and of some emigration countries, it did not play a significant role for the developing countries.

The preceding observations point to the uniqueness of the present demographic situation of the developing countries. Their rapid population growth since World War II has mainly been caused by the sharp decrease of the death rates. The negative assessment of the population growth is therefore wrong and misleading. The population growth does not demonstrate growing misery. It rather gives evidence of the strong and unprecedented fall of mortality, which is tantamount to a tremendous improvement of the quality of human life in the developing countries. Although the process of fertility decline has already started, it will be decades before population growth will come to an end. The growth rates will become smaller and will fall well below the peak rates of the past decades.

RESOURCES AND THE EARTH'S CARRYING CAPABILITY

What are the consequences of the population growth in the future? Will the developing countries be able to keep mortality low and to nourish the large and growing numbers of people in the coming decades? Will they continue to improve the quality of life of their population or will they be constrained by increasing scarcity of land and resources and threatened by setbacks and catastrophes?

To many observers the deleterious consequences of population growth have appeared obvious. Doomsayers from Malthus (1798) to Meadows (1972) and the other modern ecologists have argued that the resources of the earth are finite and that more people by definition means fewer natural resources per person. The argument led to the idea of a "race" between population on the one side, and agricultural and industrial production on the other side.

The concept of finitude of resources, however, is not self-evident. And often it is even not clear what people mean by resources. All the factors that render economic goods and services are resources in a wide sense. In what follows, we confine the definition to the "natural resources" that are used to produce economic goods and services. We can distinguish between two types of <u>natural resources</u>: (1) exhaustible resources like fossil fuels and nonfuel minerals and (2) renewable resources like forests, fisheries, and agricultural land. While the latter can be renewed as long as their regenerative capability is not damaged, the exhaustible resources are partially destroyed when they provide economic services so that the world's stock declines.

We have underlined the term <u>natural</u> <u>resources</u> because it depends upon technology whether specific raw materials and energy sources are or are not to be considered resources. A mineral may represent a resource under specific technological conditions but may be substituted by plastics under other technological conditions and cease to be a resource. The concept of finitude of resources is therefore only applicable to a world with constant technology but is vacuous and wrong to a world with technological change. Resources are not "natural" but are related to specific technologies. As a consequence, the stock of resources is indeterminate and undefinable unless we neglect technical progress and assume that the existing technology is the only technology that is available. Only if we make this assumption can we define the resources and, principally, also determine their quantity (although the problems of definition and measurement are big and difficult to solve). This quantity is, of course, finite.

The indeterminateness of the stock of resources does not mean that the stock is infinite. The infiniteness of resources requires the infiniteness of technical choices, and it is disputable whether this is the case. The optimists are confident that new inventions and innovations provide us with so many technical alternatives and new resources that the stock of resources rather increases than decreases, as it always has been in the past. The empirical proof for the growing plentifulness of resources is the long-run fall of the prices of raw materials and energy relative to the prices of consumer goods and labor that is shown in figure 3-3 for three representative materials. (All other raw materials show similar behavior.) The

Figure 3-3a.   The Scarcity of Copper As
                Measured by Its Price Relative to
                Wages

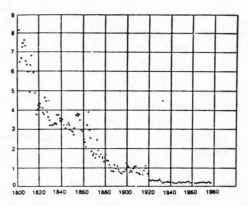

Source: <u>Historical Statistics of the U.S.</u>

Figure 3-3b.   The Scarcity of Copper As
                Measured by Its Price Relative to
                the Consumer Price Index

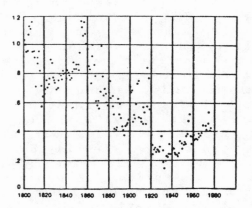

Source: <u>Historical Statistics of the U.S.</u>

Figure 3-3c.   The Price of Oil Relative to
               Wages

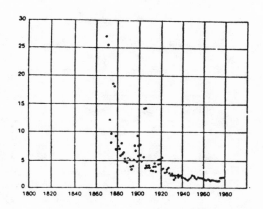

Source: <u>Historical Statistics of the U.S.</u>

Figure 3-3d.   The Price of Oil Relative to the
               Consumer Price Index

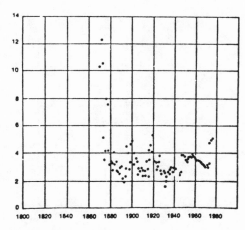

Source: <u>Historical Statistics of the U.S.</u>

Figure 3-3e.   The Price of Wheat Relative to
                Wages in the U.S.

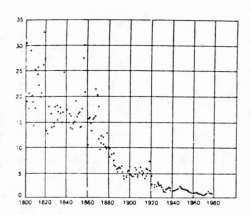

Source: _Historical Statistics of the U.S._

Figure 3-3f.   The Price of Wheat Relative to
                the Consumer Price Index

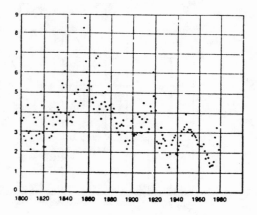

Source: _Historical Statistics of the U.S._

pessimists concede the trend to lower prices of resources in the past but deny that these experiences have any relevance for the future. They point out that there is never logical entailment that past trends will continue their direction, and they argue that the growth of new technical knowledge will not keep up with the growing demand for new technology in the future and that the resource situation, hence, will grow worse rather than better.

An increase of population affects the resources in different ways. First, in the short run, i.e., when technology is unchanged, population size and growth affect the demand for resources. This is the well-known Malthusian argument. Second, population size and density determine the optimal technology that will be adopted and, thereby, the materials that actually form resources. This link between population and the stock of resources is contrary to all Malthusian thinking and has especially been emphasized by Ester Boserup. Third, population is the source of the new ideas and inventions that lead to the endless process of upgrading formerly useless material into potentially valuable resources and to the permanent extension of the stock of resources. This view is stressed by Julian Simon who argues that the human imagination coupled with the human spirit is the ultimate resource.

Assume first a Malthusian world with given technology and, hence, a given and finite stock of resources. Furthermore, neglect for a moment the renewable resources and only consider the exhaustible resources. In this hypothetical Mathusian world a more rapid population growth can certainly advance the date at which the exhaustible resources will be depleted. The number of people, however, who

can enjoy a certain standard of resource
consumption is fixed and independent of the
rate of population growth. The limits of
growth are imminent in this world, and a
decrease of population growth and even of
population size can never break the resource
constraints. It makes the queue thinner but
longer, and this cannot do more than to delay
the process of resource depletion.[3] And it is
even questionable whether this delay will take
place at all. For the great differences in the
consumption of resources between the developed
and the developing countries show that it is
the income level rather than the population
size that is the key determinant of the demand
for exhaustible resources. In 1981, for
instance, the shares of the industrialized
countries and of the developing countries on
world energy consumption were 75 percent and 25
percent, respectively, while the shares on
world population were 25 percent and 75
percent, respectively. In the Malthusian
world, with given technology, diminishing
marginal returns to labor are likely to lower
the per capita income of larger populations
and, hence, to reduce the resource consumption
per capita. The decrease in the level of
consumption counteracts the increase in the
number of consumers. The net effect of
population growth on the aggregate demand of
exhaustible resources is, therefore, uncertain
and depends upon which of the two factors
predominates.

There is a second argument as to why
population growth may decelerate the process of
resource depletion instead of accelerating it.
The needs and incentives to define property
rights on the resources are positively related
to the number of people who seek access to the
resources at the time being. The establishment

of property rights leads to the development of resource markets or alternative social institutions to govern the access to resources. Market prices or nonmarket forms of rationing allocate the resources among alternative uses and over time, and curtail present resource consumption. It is, therefore, possible that the resources will be more effectively conserved in the case of strong population pressure and consumption rationing than in the case of low population density and free access to common-property resources.

Renewable resources are distinct from exhaustible resources because they are not necessarily subject to a tradeoff between present and future consumption. The people alive at a moment of time can use the renewable resources without restraining future generations from potential consumption if they do not damage the regenerative capabilities of the renewable resources. They can, however, also interfere in the process of regeneration and thereby temporarily or permanently deplete the stock of renewable resources. An overexploitation will diminish the stock at least for a while, and the extinction of plants and species can never be undone.

Population size and growth rates can jeopardize the regeneration process. This is another potential link between population and resources. Unlike in the case of exhaustible resources, the size and growth of population at a moment of time can have an impact on the number of people who are able to use a given quantity of renewable resources. If the nature's surplus of renewable resources had already been used up by men, then a further increase in the number of people must either lead to lower consumption per capita or to the excessive use and diminished regeneration of the renewable resources or to both. This is the fundamental argument of Malthus and his disciples and has been repeated by the environmentalists again and again. Notice, however, that the Malthusian proposition abstains from the possibility that people can switch to new technologies and that they can increase the stock of resources by new ideas and inventions. The concept of diminishing returns to labor stems from the assumption of constant technology and cannot be derived without that. It is evident that this condition is not (and probably never has been) fulfilled either in the developed or developing countries, and this mainly explains the failure of many studies to prove the existence of diminishing returns to labor in the developing countries.

Arable land is the most important renewable resource of the developing countries. Many people consider usable land as a typical example of a fixed natural resource and forecast that food production cannot grow with the rate of population because increasing land scarcity will depress the marginal productivity of labor. Malthus firmly believed in the existence of land limits and diminishing returns to labor, and characterized his population principle as a law of nature. Ricardo added the argument that population pressure will cause the conversion of nonfarmland with low soil quality into farmland which also leads to a negative relation between population growth and food production per capita. The assumptions of a nonaugmentable input land and a negative link between population and labor productivity have been made by many other economists and are standard in many textbooks.

The data, however, tell a different story. Food production has grown faster than population in most countries of the world (see table 3-2). (The different experiences of Africa will be discussed below.) Farm output in the developing countries has risen and grown at 3.8 percent in the last decade and 4.1 percent annually in the eighties.[4]

The explanation for this is that land is just as little natural and fixed as any other natural resource. The stock of arable land is constantly being increased by humans. New farmland is being added by the clearing of new land or reclamation of wasteland (see table 3-3). The gain in the developing countries is particularly significant. Contrary to what Ricardo has thought, the productivity per acre of land is being increased (see Table 3-4). It increased because people adopted new agricultural technologies and substituted land by labor and labor-intensive capital investment, when population growth led to higher demand for fod. Growing demand for food also set incentives to convert nonfarmland far distinct from consumers but of high soil quality into farmland. These reactions show that arable land, like any other resource, is being created by human efforts instead of being fixed and given by nature.[5] The idea of stationary technology and hence of finitude of resources and diminishing returns to labor is anything but self-evident. It is a restrictive theoretical hypothesis that is contrary to all empirical experiences of the past and the present.

Table 3-2. Food and Agricultural Production / Index of Food Production, 1964-1966 = 100

	Total		Per Capita	
	1979-81	1983-85	1979-81	1983-85
Africa	140,9	153,5	92,6	88,9
North and Central America	140,9	145,1	111,1	107,8
South America	156,3	167,2	109,9	107,7
Asia	151,5	177,3	108,7	118,5
Europe	133,3	141,3	122,0	126,8
USSR	133,3	144,0	116,3	122,1
Oceania	142,9	155,7	108,7	112,0
World	142,9	157,1	106,4	108,5

Source: World Resources Institute, World Resources 1987, New York, 1987, p. 276.

Table 3-3. Changes in Land Use

| | Percentage Distribution | | | | | | | | Percentage Change 1964-66 to 1982-84 | | | |
| | Cropland | | Permanent Pasture | | Forests and Woodland | | Acreland | | Cropland | Permanent Pasture | Forests and Woodland | Acreland |
	1964-66	1981-83	1964-66	1981-83	1964-66	1981-83	1964-66	1981-83				
Africa	5	6	26	26	25	23	43	44	+ 13.5	- 0.8	- 7.6	+ 3.3
North America	12	13	17	17	33	32	38	39	+ 7.8	- 3.1	- 5.8	+ 1.8
South America	6	8	24	26	57	53	13	13	+ 34.6	+ 9.2	- 6.9	- 2.4
Asia	16	17	25	24	21	21	38	38	+ 4.1	- 3.0	+ 0.9	- 0.3
Europe	28	30	20	18	32	33	20	19	+ 10.5	- 4.3	+ 7.0	+ 3.2
USSR	10	10	17	17	41	41	32	32	+ 1.3	+ 0.1	+ 8.3	- 9.7
Oceania	5	6	55	55	22	18	19	21	+ 23.5	- 1.2	- 15.4	+ 16.5
World	10	11	24	24	33	31	33	33	+ 8.9	- 0.3	- 2.6	+- 0.0

Sources: World Resources Institute, World Resources 1986, New York, 1986, pp. 256f.; and World Resources 1987, New York, 1987, pp. 268f.

Table 3-4. Changes in Crop Yields

	Crop Yields					
	Cereals			Roots and Tubers		
	Kilograms per Hectar	Percentage Changes over		Kilograms per Hectar	Percentage Change over	
	1983-85	1964-66	1974-76	1983-85	1964-66	1974-75
Africa	951	13	- 5	7,478	22	13
North America	3,532	44	22	19,196	23	6
South America	2,015	42	23	11,043	- 1	1
Asia	2,477	77	36	14,021	58	16
Europe	4,102	76	29	20,018	19	9
USSR	1,563	35	7	11,985	13	8
Oceania	1,611	25	13	10,772	13	8
World	2,441	58	25	12,476	21	9

Source: World Resources Institute, World Resources 1987, New York, 1987, pp. 276f.

Furthermore, the carrying capacity of the earth is even <u>under the existing agricultural technologies</u> sufficient to support a population many times larger than the present world population. This is demonstrated by a study of the U.N. Food and Agriculture Organization (FAO) and the International Institute for Applied Systems Analysis (IIASA). The authors of this study evaluated the maximum number of people who can be fed in the developing countries at three alternative levels of farming technology: low, equivalant to subsistence farming; intermediate, with some fertilizers, pesticides and improved seeds, conservation measures, and improved patterns on half the land; high, with full use of all inputs, full conservation measures, and the most productive mix of crops on all land-- equivalent to Western European levels of farming. The authors find that, taken together, the entire land resources of the 117 developing countries studied would have been able to support twice their total 1975 population of 1,956 million using low inputs. With intermediate inputs, they could support almost 7 times, and with high inputs, more than 16 times their 1975 population. By 2000, the potential supporting capacity is 1.6 times the projected population size of 3,589 million, using low inputs, and 4.2 and 9.3 times, using intermediate and high levels, respectively (see table 3-5). Notice that the corresponding ratios for Africa and South America are still higher.

The calculated figures for the ratios between potential capacity and population size support the view that population can continue a long time without reaching limits set by the exhaustion of resources. The results must, however, not be overrated. First, capacity

Table 3-5. Regional Potential/Needs Ratios (Potential population-supporting capacities divided by 1975 or 2000 populations)

YEAR 1975 RATIOS

Input Level	Africa	SW Asia	South America	Central America	SE Asia	Average Average
Low	3.0	0.8	5.9	1.6	1.1	2.0
Intermediate	11.6	1.3	23.9	4.2	3.0	6.9
High	33.9	2.0	57.2	11.5	5.1	16.6

YEAR 2000 RATIOS

	Africa	SW Asia	South America	Central America	SE Asia	Average Average
Low	1.6	0.7	3.5	1.4	1.3	1.6
Intermediate	5.8	0.9	13.3	2.6	2.3	4.2
High	16.5	1.2	31.5	6.0	3.3	9.3

Source: FAO, Land, Food and People, Rome, 1984, p. 16.

ratios cannot simply be taken from agricultural
statistics but have to be estimated under more
or less plausible hypotheses on the potential
output levels of the alternative technologies.
The computed numerical values are, therefore,
more or less disputable and need not coincide
with the uncertain real values. Second, the
ratios show technical capabilities rather than
economic possibilities. In most cases, the
production is limited by economic constraints:
inefficiency of the market-, price-, and
transport-system. It is true that the
technical capabilities constitute the
hypothetical ceilings of food production, but
they do not represent the real limits. Third,
and most important, the maximum potential
capacity is derived under the assumption that
agricultural technology cannot be improved
beyond the level currently adopted in Western
Europe. This is nothing else but the well-
known argument of finitude applied to the case
of technological knowledge. Only the limits
are assumed to be relatively far (technological
standard of Western Europe) and, consequently,
not to be reached before long.

The ingenuity of a large and growing
number of people is, however, not finite. Ever
since human beings appeared on earth they
created new knowledge when they needed it for
surviving. The needs led to the solutions.
There is no reason to fear that the future will
be different from the past. Even the most
optimistic man at the end of the eighteenth
century could probably not have imagined that
the earth would be able to feed 5 billion
people. In 1987, the 5 billion people are not
only alive but are also fed better than the
approximately 800 million people who were alive
two centuries ago. In addition, many countries

have food surpluses and try to stimulate food
demand instead of food supply.
      The doomsayer's warnings of increasing
famine in the world turned out to be wrong in
the past, and there is no reason to expect that
the alarms deserve more credit in the future.
The world's food prospects are better than they
have ever been.   The risk of a <u>worldwide</u> food
shortage is definitively averted.   This does
not mean, however, that famine is or will be
absent everywhere in the world.   Famine is a
regional problem and stems from failures to
balance regional disparities in food supply.
      The region with the greatest food problems
is Africa.   It is the only continent where the
population grew faster than food production.
The FAO index of food production per capita
shows for Africa a decrease from 108 in 1964-
1966 to 96 in 1983-1985 (1979-1981 = 100).   FAO
and many other international organizations are
deeply concerned about Africa's prospects of
feeding its future populations.   The continent
has a massive land area of 2,878 million
hectares (excluding South Africa); but 47
percent of the area is too dry for rain-fed
agriculture, and only 19 percent of soils have
no inherent fertility limitations.   Despite
this, Africa has a very large area of potential
rain-fed cropland -- 789 million hectares, not
including marginal land -- most of this in the
humid tropics.   In 1975, only 168 million
hectares were cultivated (FAO, 1984, p. 21).
These FAO data clearly indicate that land and
other natural resources are available and less
scarce in Africa than in the other continents.
      The existence of large unused land
reserves explains why Africa's potential
carrying capacity exceeds many times the
current population size.   The FAO estimated
that Africa as a whole is capable of supporting

with low inputs the 1975 population 3 times, with intemediate inputs 12 times, and with high inputs 34 times.   Hence, the reasons for Africa's actual food problems cannot be sought in too many people and too little land and natural resources.   It is rather that Africa has very few other resources not to be found in nature ("societal" resources), such as functioning firms and markets, good farm-to-market-transportation, and, last but not least, democracy and political stability. Paradoxically, a greater population density can reduce the likeliness of famine in Africa, as has been the case in Europe in the nineteenth century.   The concentration of population produces some of those societal resources that are urgently needed.   The bunching of food demand is a precondition for the existence of large and well-organized markets.   Higher population density also causes better roads and transportation, and thereby creates and improves the links between the regional markets.   The concentration of population facilitates the formation of social organizations and political institutions.   We may also note that population growth may cause a rigid structure to break up.   This is Boserup's thesis applied to simple, small societies, and Lal (1981) has, for the history of India, made this case effectively.

POPULATION GROWTH: DESIRABLE OR UNDESIRABLE?

Modern growth theory departs from Malthus's stagnation theory by including technical progress in the analysis and, hence, does not share the alarmist view that population bears the risk to grow beyond the earth's food capacity.   Growth theorists

believe in the continuing growth of technical
knowledge that continually widens existing
resource constraints and allows more and more
people to make their living. But this view
does not automatically lead to a positive
assessment of population growth.   On the
contrary, the overwhelming majority of growth
theorists still judges faster population growth
as undesirable because it yields a lower
consumption level than does slower population
growth. This is the outcome of the Solow-Swan
model with exogenous technical progress, and it
results from the need to devote more of the
total output to investment in order to equip
additional new workers when labor force growth
is higher (capital dilution effect).

The disadvantageous capital dilution
effect attributed to faster population growth
is, however, in contradiction to Kuznets'
empirical findings, that the decades with the
fastest growth of per capita income of the
European countries in the last century also
have been the decades with the fastest
population growth. The negative standard
growth-theoretical assessment of population
growth is also open to theoretical criticism
because it is based upon one of three
alternative conditions: (1) either that the
rate of technical progress is <u>independent</u> of
population size or growth, or (2) that the
positive effect of population size or growth on
technical knowledge is <u>too weak</u> to overcome the
adverse effect of capital dilution, or (3) that
the stimulation of technical knowledge <u>needs
more time</u> than the capital dilution effect so
that the latter prevails in the meantime.

The first condition is certainly
unrealistic. Population and technical
knowledge are linked in many ways: more people
implies more ideas and thereby better technical

knowledge.   This   argument   was   expressed   by
Petty:[6]

> As   for   the   Arts   of   Delight   and
> Ornament, they are best promoted by
> the   greatest   number   of   emulators.
> And it is more likely that one
> ingenious curious man may rather be
> found   among   4   million   than   400
> persons   .   .   .   .   And   for   the
> propagation and improvement of useful
> learning,   the   same   may   be   said
> concerning   it   as   above-said
> concerning . . . the Arts of Delight
> and Ornament (Simon, 1986, p. 16).

Simon Kuznets took the same view:[7]

> The   greatest   factor   in   growth   of
> output per capita is, of course, the
> increasing   stock   of   tested,   useful
> knowledge.   The   producers   of   this
> stock are the scientists, inventors,
> engineers, managers, and explorers of
> various description -- all members of
> that population whose growth we are
> considering. Assume now that, judged
> by native capacities (and they do
> differ),   0.05   per   cent   of   a   given
> population are geniuses, another 2.0
> per cent are possessors of gifts that
> may   be   described   as   talent,   and
> another 10.0 per cent have distinctly
> higher   than   average   capacity   for
> fruitful   search   for   facts,
> principles,   and   inventions: (The
> grades   of   native   ability   and
> percentages are, of course, purely
> illustrative, and would probably be
> changed by an expert in this field.).

Since we have assumed the education, training, and other capital investment necessary to assure that the additions to the population will be at least as well equipped as the population already existing, the proportion of mute Miltons and unfulfilled Newtons will be no higher than previously. Population growth, under the assumptions stated, would, therefore, produce an absolutely larger number of geniuses, talented men, and generally gifted contributors to new knowledge-- whose native ability would be permitted to mature to effective levels when they join the labor force.

Phelps (1966) implicitly made a similar point. He proposed a technical progress function in which the rate of technical progress is determined by the amount of resources and labor that a society devotes to research. This links the growth rate of technical knowledge to the size of population if the number of research workers (for the amount of resources for research) can be considered to increase with the labor force. That result has been made explicit by Simon and Steinmann (1980, 1981).

Population growth also causes technical change by making the substitution of labor and capital for land and the replacement of scarce resources by newly created and relatively plentiful resources both possible and necessary. This is the 'population push' hypothesis developed by Ester Boserup (1965, 1981). She emphasizes that men have known several technological alternatives ever since

the beginning of history and, hence, have been
able to make technological choices. Societies
always adopted the best technology that gave
them the largest output and switched to a
different technology when increasing shortages
of labor, capital, land, and other resources
made the existing technology inferior to the
new one. The "population push" hypothesis
explains the new adoption of previously known
technical knowledge rather than the invention
of new knowledge.

     Another link between technology and
population can be derived from the learning-by-
doing hypothesis. This hypothesis states that
the production costs fall with experience. It
was originally found and discussed in empirical
studies, before Arrow combined it with a macro-
model to study the economic implications of the
phenomenon. Simon and Steinmann, working with
a model like Arrow's, show that the learning-
by-doing hypothesis can positively relate
population growth and, even more importantly,
population size with the rate of technical
progress. For a country that has twice the
size of population and output of another
country (notice that this means that both
countries have the same output per capita!)
makes the production experiences faster and,
hence, gets the fruits of learning-by-doing in
half the time of the smaller country. This
result does not require identical levels of
output per capita as a necessary condition. It
is rather sufficient to the country with the
larger population to have the larger aggregate
output to possess the advantage of greater
experience and, therefore, the lead in
productivity over the country with the smaller
population.

     While more recently the stimulating effect
of population growth on technical progress has

been widely discussed and accepted, it is still
controversial whether the positive effect of
population growth on productivity is strong
enough to neutralize or even to exceed the
negative effect of capital dilution. The issue
is central for assessing the income effects of
population growth. Most development theorists
and policy makers have been educated in the
Malthusian tradition and judge population
growth as unfavorable. They are convinced that
the stimulating effect of population growth on
technology is uncertain and small in comparison
to the dilution effect from providing more
people with capital and natural resources.
They refer, in addition, to the time lag
between the growth of population and the
increase of labor force and technical
knowledge. A newborn baby, who instantly needs
goods and services, will not produce goods and
services until he or she has grown up.
        While the last argument is certainly true,
there is no evidence for the view that the
capital dilution effect succeeds the
stimulating effect on technical knowledge so
that population growth has a negative impact on
the growth of output per capita even in the
long run, when it promotes the creation of new
technical knowledge. Cross-sectional
regressions with the World Bank data of the
growth rates of gross national product (GNP)
per capita and population for the developing
countries in various decades after World War II
do not show any significant, positive or
negative, correlation between the two growth
rates for the developing countries. It is only
if we also include the developed countries in
the regressions that we get the asserted
negative correlation coefficients. This
result, however, is vacuous and cannot be
interpreted as testimony to an inverse

relationship between the growth of population and the growth of income per capita because the economic and demographic conditions in the two groups of countries are totally different and incomparable.

Theoretical growth models with technical progress functions like Boserup's, Phelps', or Arrow's lead to the result that population growth and population size may well have positive effects upon the rate of economic growth through their positive efects on the rate of technical progress (see Steinmann and Simon, 1980; Simon and Steinmann, 1981, 1984, 1985, 1987; and Simon, 1986). The models produce the positive effects with reasonable assumptions about the parameter values of the production function and the technical progress function. Negative effects, however, are also possible and prevail from other less reasonable assumptions about the parameter values. We cannot enter here into the details of these models and, therefore, must skip discussing the properties required for a positive solution. Perhaps the most important conclusion is that growth models with endogenous technical progress call into question the easy generalization drawn from growth theory with technical progress exogenous that population growth is negatively related to the growth of output per head. They rather indicate that it seems more likely that faster population growth implies a faster equilibrium rate of growth of the standard of living. And this result is comfortably embodied in growth theoretical models without upsetting the basic structure of that theory.

Differences in the economic and social climate for the development of new knowledge may explain why population growth has stimulated technical progress and economic

development in certain circumstances and has
failed to do so in others. If all factors are
fixed and there is no capacity to create new
resources, additional people clearly cause
economic disruption and resource scarcity. In
such a system, additional people imply less
output to go around. Hence, it is necessary to
distinguish the effects of population growth in
free market economies from the effects in
economies where there either is central
planning or the market does not operate
effectively because of other social rigidities.

In circumstances where, due to adverse
institutional and cultural conditions, there
will be relatively little new creation of
resources in response to the "pressure" and
opportunity of population increase, the effect
of more people may be quite negative for a long
time because total output will not rise much
and output per person will fall; Africa's
currently unfree countries make a good example,
as did China at some times in her past, and
(according to Lal, 1981) as did India for
millenia until early in this century. But the
United States, Europe from 1600 onward
(especially the Netherlands), Taiwan, and some
other countries allow(ed) and even promote(d)
freer and more rapid response. Hence the
negative capital dilution effect of additional
people in such places is short-lived, while the
long-run effect is positive.

The time horizon that people have in mind
when they make the assessment of population
growth plays the key role whether population
growth is judged good or bad. This is due to
the fact that the positive and negative
externalities of an additional person for those
already alive prevail at different periods in
the present and the future. A child consumes
the time of his parents and requires individual

and social services that otherwise could have been used elsewhere. When he or she has grown up and has entered the labor force, the additional worker leads to the dilution of capital and, therefore, the reduction of output per worker.

On the discovery side, the impact of the additional person also needs time. The response obviously is lagged, and posterity thereby gains more than do contemporaries from the arising of new problems. There are several reasons for the lag between the "need" revealed, for instance, by the jump in price and the onset and end of the responses. It takes time for ideas to be produced. It also takes time for ideas to be evaluated by the demanders and for the better ideas to shoulder aside the poorer ideas (which certainly is not done perfectly). Then it takes time for adoption of new ideas throughout the industry. Last, but perhaps most important, new ideas breed other new ideas, some of which have nothing at all to do with the original problem; and this process of self-perpetuating idea generation may go on almost infinitely.

The conclusion is that the length of the time period taken into account is pivotal for the assessment of the costs and benefits of population growth.[8] When people's welfare in the near future is the criterion, then it is likely that the negative effects resulting from transfer payments and capital dilution predominate the overall judgments about the social welfare of population growth. When, however, the long run future is allowed to weigh heavily in the judgment, then faster population growth can almost always be expected to lead to better results than slower population growth. The only exception is when the political and social system prevents men

from developing ingenuity and, hence, delays or
stops the continuing process of resource
creation.

CONCLUSION

The standard argument that population
growth leads to increasing scarcity of capital
and natural resources must be qualified. It is
neither theoretically justified nor empirically
founded. Population growth must not be an
obstacle to long run economic development,
though it may pose economic problems in the
short run.

The real limits of long run economic
development are the adverse institutional and
cultural conditions that prevail in many
developing countries. It is true that
additional people cause problems in the short
run, but they also boost human efforts to
create and adopt new knowledge that helps to
solve the problems. The result of these
efforts has often been that people eventually
were better off when they had to overcome
problems than if the problems had never arisen.
It is only in circumstances where human efforts
and technical progress are being counteracted
by the political and social system that
additional people must lead to a decrease of
the long run standard of living. This is the
case when the political and social
organizations conserve the traditional
economic, technical, and institutional
structure and prevent the necessary changes.

It is not the natural resources that limit
long run development. The ultimate resource is
people or -- more exactly -- the human
imagination coupled to the human spirit. And
this, in turn, requires a political and social

system that is open and encourages rather than discourages human endeavors to solve the problems.

NOTES

1.   More developed regions, following the U.N. classification, comprise all of Europe and North America, plus Australia, Japan, New Zealand, and the USSR. All other regions and countries are classified as less developed.

2.   The influence of international migration on the growth rate of population of the developing regions is small and can be neglected.

3.   "Unless one is more concerned with the welfare of people born in the distant future than those born in the immediate future, there is little reason to be concerned about the rate at which population growth is depleting the stock of exhaustible resources" (Committee on Population, 1986, pp. 15f).

4.   Data from New Scientist, 19 (1987), quoted by DeGregori, 1987, p. 70.

5.   The phenomenon that the area of arable land is being expanded and the productivity of land is being improved simultaneously is also traceable in the history of European agriculture (see Boserup and Ester, 1987).

6.   Petty, William, Another Essay in Political Arithmetic (1692/1899), p. 474, quoted by Simon (1986, p. 16).

7. Kuznets, Simon, <u>Population Change and Aggregate Output</u> (1960), p. 328, quoted by Simon (1986, pp. 16f).

8. It is also important whether only the interests of those already alive are considered or whether the interests of future generations are included, too; notice that population growth is beneficial in any case from the view of those who will be born only when population grows fast!

REFERENCES

Boserup, Ester. <u>Population and Technology</u>. Oxford: Basil Blackwell, 1981.

Boserup, Ester. <u>The Conditions of Agricultural Growth</u>. London: Allen and Unwin, 1965.

Boserup, Ester. Population and Technology in Preindustrial Europe, 1987 (mimeo).

Chesnais, Jean-Claude. <u>La Revanche du Ties Monde</u>. Paris: Robert Laffont, 1987.

Cipolla, Carlo M. <u>The Economic History of World Population</u>. 7th edition, Harmondsworth: Penguin Books, 1978.

Committee on Population. <u>Population Growth and Economic Development: Policy Questions</u>. Washington, D.C.: National Academy Press, 1986.

DeGregori, Thomas R. <u>A Theory of Technology</u>. Ames, Iowa: The Iowa State University Press, 1985.

DeGregori, Thomas R. Population, Technology, Cognition and Resource Creation: Humanizing the Environment for Habitation and Higher Achievement, Some Modest Musings by a Non-Demographer. Paper Prepared for the First European Population Conference in Finland, 1987 (mimeo).

FAO. Food and Agriculture Organization of the United Nations, Land, Food and People. Rome, 1984.

Lal, Deepak. Cultural Stability and Economic Stagnation, India 1500 BC - 1980 AD, manuscript, University College London, unpublished, 1981.

Phelps, Edmund S. "Models of Technical Progress and the Golden Rule of Research," Review of Economic Studies, 33: 1966, 133-145.

Pingali, Prabhu, Bigot, Yves, and Binswanger, Hans P. Agricultural, Mechanization and the Evolution of Farming Systems in Sub-Saharan Africa. Baltimore and London: The Johns Hopkins University Press, 1987.

Simon, Julian L. The Economics of Population Growth. Princeton, N.J., Princeton University Press, 1977.

Simon, Julian L. The Ultimate Resource. Princeton, N.J.: Princeton University Press, 1981.

Simon, Julian L. Theory of Population and Economic Growth. Oxford: Basil Blackwell, 1986.

Simon, Julian L., and Steinmann, Gunter. "Population Growth and Phelp's Technical Progress Model: Interpretation and Generalization," Research in Population Economics, 1981, pp. 239-254.

Simon, Julian L., and Steinmann, Gunter. "On the Optimum Theoretical Rate of Population Growth," Jahrbucher fur Nationalokonomie und Statistik, 200/5: 1985, 508-531.

Simon, Julian L., and Steinmann, Gunter. Population Growth, Natural Resources, and the Long Run Standard of Living, 1987 (mimeo).

Steinmann, Gunter, and Simon, Julian L. "Phelp's Technical Progress Model Generalized," Economic Letters, 5: 1980, 177-182.

World Bank. World Development Report 1984. Washington, D.C., 1984.

World Resources Institute. World Resources 1986. New York, 1986.

World Resources Institute. World Resources 1987. New York, 1987.

COMMENTARY BY B. PERSAUD

Steinmann's chapter deals with the major issue of whether the world is becoming overpopulated. It describes simply and competently the demographic trends in the world, and goes on to explore the controversial issue of resource adequacy and the constraints that population expansion poses for growth and development.

The author concludes that fears of an explosion of world population and of hunger catastrophies and misery are exaggerated and unjustified. He accepts that in the short run, population expansion could pose a constraint to growth for some developing regions. However, in the long term, population expansion could be a spur to economic development.

In considering the demographic trends, the essay makes some very useful contributions. It shows how the steep mortality decline in the 1950s and 1960s in the developing countries, which came before the weaker fall in fertility, was a substantial factor in the fast expansion of their population in the postwar period.

The essay also deals interestingly with the historical differences in demographic trends between developed and developing countries. A significant factor in the higher peak fertility rates in the developing countries was marriage customs -- the earlier age of marriage and its higher incidence. Whether such customs were related to economic

factors is not made clear and the claim by the
author that seventeenth and eighteenth century
Europe had effectively checked fertility
through a network of rules, customs, and social
pressure would seem to associate cultural
factors directly with a fertility objective.

The author recognizes the great change
that has taken place in fertility in developing
countries. However, this fall is not given its
true significance in terms both of the
unexpectedness of the achievement and its full
consequences for the future. That the poor of
the world have been so ready to accept advice
on family planning, sometimes even before the
modernization process had begun in their
societies, is indicative of the potential that
still exists to reduce fertility further in the
third world. And the achievement is not fully
reflected in birth rates since the young age
structure conceals the full extent of the fall
in fertility. These points needed greater
emphasis in the chapter. Incidentally, the
substantial fall in mortality is seen in the
chapter too much as indicative of improvement
in the quality of life in the developing
countries. The role played by improvements in
medicine is given no credit.

Regarding the population/resource
question, the author advances convincingly the
case against regarding the world's resources as
finite in an economic sense. He supports fully
the view which the editor of this book, Thomas
DeGregori, has been advancing for some time now
-- that resources and their value depend on
technology, and what is a resource today may
not be so tomorrow because of technological
change. Whether resources remain adequate to
support an expanding population therefore
depends not only on quantities available but
also on technological possibilities. The

crucial question therefore becomes the scope
for such possibilities. Here the author takes
an implicitly sanguine position.

I fully agree with these views and greatly
welcome them since so much thinking on the
population issue is still informed by views
which do not reflect adequately this strong
connection between technology and resource
availability.

But while I share the view that current
circumstances do not justify concern with
resource depletion, this global view does not
mean that for individual countries, population
growth does not require significant attention.
The author concedes such a possibility but only
in the short term. According to him, where
there is a long-term problem it is only because
human efforts and technical progress are being
thwarted by the political and social system.
This is an extreme position. In some densely
populated countries, the pressure of population
on resources is evident especially on
agricultural resources, on which there is
usually much dependence, and the fact that
migration opportunities are limited for third
world countries adds to the problem. There is
no doubt that both South Asia and Canada or
South Asia and Australia could all benefit from
shifts of population. But racial attitudes
intervene to prevent needed migration. This is
not often openly recognized, however.

The essay does not develop adequately the
distinction it makes between the short-term and
long-term effects of population growth. The
fact is that for many developing countries, the
savings ratio is much less than the investment
ratio required to achieve GNP growth above the
population increase. It would not be enough to
argue that this need not be the case with good
economic management, as the author seems

implicitly to do. Are the levels of management
and the development of political and social
systems not dependent on the level of economic
development?   But aside from this argument, it
would   be   difficult   to   expect   low-income
countries, a category which comprises a large
proportion of the population of the third
world, to generate adequate domestic savings
for reasonable growth rates.   The issue of the
availability   of   financial   resources   for
adequate   investment   is   not   raised   in   any
explicit way in the chapter.

     If savings are made inadequate or already
inadequate savings are made more so by the
consumption requirements, including health and
education   needs,   of   a   rapidly   expanding
population, then fast population growth could
not be viewed in so complacent a manner.   And
if such constraints are recognized for the
short run, then I fail to see how they will not
continue to affect the longer run.

     The arguments put forward by the author
for different long run effects are based on the
impact of population pressure on technological
choice and on the creation of new knowledge.
In these areas, the author sees advantages and
positive effects from population pressure, and
he cites in support studies by Kuznets, Arrow,
and Boserup.   However, there is larger support
in the literature for negative impacts from
rapid population increase through adverse
effects on savings and resource availability.
While larger populations will increase the
possibility of having outstanding people, if
the short run effects of rapid population
growth are negative, then deteriorating
education and social facilities will not be
conducive to the blooming of any inherent
qualities the additional people may possess.

The chapter shows clearly that there are no resource constraints to developing countries producing many times their current food output. Even with a low level of technology, Africa could feed adequately three times its 1975 population and nearly twice its population projected for the year 2000. At high levels of technology currently available, Africa could sustain over 16 times its population projected for the year 2000.

These figures are very useful in showing that sub-Saharan Africa has a very hopeful future. Biotechnology, which is not mentioned in the essay, could increase the potential further. However, inadequate attention is given to the setbacks of recent years in realizing Africa's potential. There is also the issue of desertification, deforestation, and soil erosion which are destroying valuable agricultural resources. The last decade has seen recurring famines, and the statistics provided indicate declining per capita food output in many African countries.

These cannot be regarded as just temporary problems. Poor economic management has been a significant cause of economic distress in sub-Saharan Africa. There is much effort at policy reform, but improved policies are far from being the only requirements for rehabilitation. The external environment remains adverse. Low commodity prices persist, and these countries have a great dependence on exports of commodities for their foreign exchange earnings.

A substantial adverse development for sub-Saharan Africa, and one that is becoming worse, is the sharp decline in its net resource inflows because of indebtedness and continuing poor export prospects.

A particular weakness of the chapter is neglect of how these developments can affect economic prospects and lead to a continuing impairment of living standards. The situation cannot be examined in terms of the potential for food production alone. There is no doubt that the potential is there. But in the absence of adequate investment and resources to assist in the whole economic rehabilitation process, the fast population increase could add to the present vicious circle, which could take a long time to break, and could lead to recurring famines and the continuing danger of economic collapse.

On the whole, the author's sanguine position on the consequences of population growth seems to be related to a treatment which is too global in its approach. The macroeconomic position for countries with 3 to 4 percent growth in population, taking into account savings and investment ratios, population dependency ratios, increases in the labor force, etc., is given very inadequate attention.

In making a case against resource depletion prospects, the author cites Julian Simon who argues that the human imagination coupled with the human spirit is the ultimate resource. This is a powerful point. In terms of human capacity in a global sense, current levels of world population and even its current rate of growth should pose no problem. But the world is not organized to deal with these problems in a cooperative way. The chapter's optimism in man's ability to cope with population expansion would have been justified if global resources of brain power, capital, and technology could be brought to bear on the problem. But this is not happening, nor has the paper recognized its need.

Optimism would be justified if the international community were recognizing the need to deal more seriously with the development problem. Current thinking, especially in the developed countries, does not lend much support to global cooperation to deal with the problems of development and the constraints imposed on it by population expansion. Yet there is an excellent case for such an approach. Its rationale could be based on the fact that in terms of current technology each person added to the world's population has the mental capacity and production potential to produce many times his/her basic requirements. If we could view the brain power of the newborn of the third world as resources which could yield high returns to investment in them (the difference in labor productivity between developed and low-income developing countries indicates the potential), then the expanding population of the world could be a means of increased living standards for all, less because of expanding markets than because of the dormant and stultified brainpower which would thereby be unleashed. In such circumstances, development generally and science and technology, skill development, and entrepreneurial endeavor would take place on a wider basis, with dynamic consequences for growth all over the world. And the quality of life would improve further because of the flowering of artistic talent in all its variety.

Population growth is much more of a problem than the author makes it out to be. Like him, though, I believe it is a surmountable problem. More attention to population control could help many developing countries to overcome their development problems.

4 STRATEGIES OF DEVELOPMENT: A SURVEY

Kenneth P. Jameson

James H. Weaver

Charles K. Wilber

INTRODUCTION

The 1950-1980 period witnessed economic development unprecedented for its rapidity and for its extension to virtually all of the peoples of the world.[1] There was rapid growth in per capita gross national product (GNP), growth in international trade, increased investment, and increased industrialization. More importantly, there was significant improvement in literacy, life expectancy, infant mortality, access to education, health services, and potable water.

Certainly problems remained; and, as Paul Streeten put it, "Every solution creates its own problem." Unequal income distribution, continued rural poverty, massive urban migration, industrial inefficiency, growth of bloated and corrupt governments all were signs that this was a period of mixed results and that the development process would be a long one.

The good performance of this period was aided by the combination of three factors.

137

First was the set of objective economic conditions that characterized the world. The Bretton Woods institutions -- the International Monetary Fund (IMF), the World Bank, and the United Nations -- combined with the end of imperialism, the movement to freer trade, efforts to stabilize commodity prices, technological breakthroughs in agriculture, a willingness to augment poor country resources through foreign assistance, and the internationalization of capital markets all provided a context that nurtured and supported the development process.

Second was the long postwar boom in the industrialized capitalist countries that provided a rapidly expanding market for poor country exports and generated a flow of private foreign investment for industrialization in the poor countries.

Third was the formulation of coherent strategies of development based on historical experience and on a growing understanding of economic processes. These strategies, the main focus of this chapter, were important because they provided a set of tactics or policies to guide and accelerate the development process.

By 1980, that same process had changed dramatically, as seen in table 4-1. With the exception of China and India, every grouping of countries shows lower growth rates in the 1980-1985 period. In sub-Saharan Africa and in many of the middle-income Latin American countries, there is an actual decrease in gross domestic product (GDP). Of course, per capita performance would be even worse. Trade, investment, and industrial output also performed poorly. Malaysia, South Korea, Taiwan, Japan, and China, India, Jordan, Cameroon, Congo were exceptions. But even in these cases, growth was generally lower.

Table 4-1.   Annual Growth Rates of GDP

	1965-80	1980-85
China and India	5.3	8.3
Other Low Income	3.2	2.8
Middle Income	6.5	1.7
Lower Middle Income	6.3	1.6
Upper Middle Income	6.6	1.7
Developing Economies	6.0	3.3
Oil Exporters	6.8	1.0
Manufacturing Exporters	6.7	5.5
Highly Indebted	6.4	0.1
Sub Saharan Africa	5.3	-0.7
High Income Oil Exporters	7.5	-2.2
Industrial Market Economies	3.7	2.3

Source: IBRD, World Development Report 1987,
          New York: Oxford University Press,
          1987.

Indicators of human welfare have not
deteriorated as dramatically, though gains in
life expectancy, infant mortality, literacy,
and school enrollment have slowed and, at least
in Africa, may have reversed.[2] It is also
clear that access to public services and the
resources spent on human resource services have
generally declined, that wages, income, and
consumption have fallen in many countries,
while employment has stagnated. This will show
up in the data on human welfare over the next
decade (IBRD, 1986).

The investigation of the causes of this
debacle will occupy researchers for many years.
Certainly a good part of it was a change in the
objective economic conditions in the world:
economic growth declined in the industrial
countries, the Bretton Woods system was altered
in response to a build-up of pressures, and
trading relations became more tense and less
buoyant. Commodity prices became highly
unstable, and, in cases such as tin, the market
literally disappeared. Foreign assistance from
many countries stagnated and changed its nature
dramatically. Capital markets served to
transmit instability, most clearly in Latin
America which first sustained an overheated
debt-led growth in the late 1970s and then
experienced a financially generated depression.

One stimulus to all of these changes was
the desire and ability of the OPEC countries to
claim a much larger share of the world
resources following 1973, and the U.S. reaction
to this step which led to inflation, then
rising interest rates, and finally culminating
in worldwide recession.

These changes in economic conditions and
the reversal of development performance have
affected thinking about the strategies of
development and about the policies or tactics

of development. So far, there has been no new
insight into a revised strategy for
development. As John Lewis (1986) put it in a
book reconsidering development strategies, "The
authors do not come up with any "eureka"
visions of brand-new development departures."[3]
Similarly, the disarray in strategic thinking
has called into question the traditional
tactics and policies of development. The task
of this article is to examine the issue of
development strategies, and implicitly the
tactics they suggest, to cut into the disarray
that presently reigns. It might help to use
the metaphor of the circus.

THE CIRCUS OF DEVELOPMENT

The current debate over development
strategies can be characterized as a three-ring
circus, with some interesting sideshows.
In the center ring, the emphasis is on
policies or tactics to improve economic
performance and social welfare. The act varies
by country, the roles are played by World Bank
technicians, politicians, socialist planners,
and by business people. At the present, in the
center ring, we find economists working on
installing or removing price controls, on
agricultural mechanization or debt
restructuring, structural adjustment,
technology transfer, or on project evaluation,
all the time oblivious to the two side rings
where other economists are debating strategies.
In one of the side rings, mainstream economists
expostulate on the working of markets, the
efficacy of export promotion, the success of
the Gang of Four, the desirability of growth
versus basic needs, and the centrality of
freedom. They keep their eye on the center

ring, claiming that the performers in the
center ring, be they capitalists or socialists,
need their guidance.

The other side ring is dominated by
political economists, united only in their
rejection of mainstream economics and a belief
in the importance of history. Their concerns
are planning and planning models, the role of
the peasantry, gender and development, surplus
value, social articulation, accumulation,
classes, and the transition to socialism. They
also have their eyes on the center ring, hoping
that their strategies will be heeded by either
the socialist planner or by the popular
movements dissatisfied with the capitalist
economy.

There are a variety of sideshows which are
peripheral to the global strategies of
development. One redefines or rejects the
accepted definitions of development, another
concentrates on decentralized or grassroots
development, while a third view considers
changes in international power relations.
Since one of them may move to the main tent in
the future, they bear consideration as well.

The other essays in this book focus on the
center ring, especially on the nonsocialist
acts. We shall concentrate on the two side
rings and their relation to the center ring.

Our basic claim is that, given the
external conditions prior to 1975, the
strategies played out in the side rings did
indeed contribute to the show in the center
ring, and were an important element in the
successful development performance of both
socialist and capitalist developing countries
during the period.[4] However, the disruption in
external objective conditions has broken this
neat and productive link. Strategists are
simply replaying old themes, performing dated

acts, while the tacticians and policy makers are using the same tactics to much less effect. There are two major exceptions. The first are the Gang of Four Asian countries. The second are the socialist tacticians who are borrowing from the mainstream strategists in developing new policies for their economies, with seeming success. China is the prime developing country example. Aside from these cases, it seems likely that the new departures in development are being prepared in side shows to the main circus and are likely to be important factors in the development process in future years.

We turn now to the mainstream ring to examine the strategy being discussed there and the tactics that it suggests for the center ring. It remains important to contrast the earlier successful performance of this strategy-tactic with its current difficulties.

THE MAINSTREAM RING

The problem of economic development surfaced as an important public issue in the 1950s when the mainstream Western economic paradigm consisted of an uneasy marriage between neoclassical microeconomics and Keynesian macroeconomics. A fundamental point of the former was its opposition to government interventions in the market, while in the latter, understanding and improving such intervention was the main focus.

Development economics relied heavily upon the interventionist side of mainstream economics, though at no point was the noninterventionist side completely absent.[5] There was an ongoing debate between the two wings which resulted in an amalgam that provided the basic strategy of development.

The starting point for virtually all
participants was the microfoundation of the
mainstream paradigm: development will be
promoted best by relying as far as possible on
market forces, with government limited to
facilitating those market forces.

This view grew out of the model of
competitive market capitalism.   Since an
uncoerced person can be depended upon to act
rationally to maximize his/her individual self-
interest, an automatic, self-regulated
mechanism to manage economic affairs naturally
emerges in the course of history.   These free
choices should overcome scarcity and result in
progress through the automatic adjustments of
free exchange in markets.   The forces of
competition ensure that the economy produces
those goods which people desire and that
maximum output is produced in the most
efficient manner.

To this model the interventionists added a
series of modifications.   First they pointed
out that there may be obstacles which could
block the workings of this development process
because of a country's low level of development
and its attendant market imperfections.
Hirschman identified two such factors: rural
underemployment and late industrialization
(Hirschman, 1981).   The former led to
interventionist schemes to utilize
underemployed manpower and to accelerate
capital accumulation.   The latter led to
economic planning and an activist state to
overcome the obstacles of late
industrialization.

These steps were reinforced by the closely
related problem of external economies.[6] In an
economy with poorly developed markets, current
market prices and profit maximization are poor
signals for investment decisions, and the

presence of potential external economies makes preplanned coordination among development projects highly desirable.

The strategy that emerged in the mainstream ring provided ample activity in the center ring: the tactics of mainstream development. Project analysis, investment criteria, price controls, credit allocation, import substitution, industrialization, export promotion, agricultural extension, the effort to create a domestic capitalist class, all these and many other activities were on the stage, growing out of the mainstream strategic understanding that had developed.

However, the tension within the mainstream approach continued and was displayed analytically in the debate between Latin American structuralists and monetarists.[7] Monetarists would have reduced the role of government to setting the money supply in a noninflationary fashion to facilitate the natural growth process of the free market economy, or even better to following a rule for money supply creation. Structuralists, on the other hand, took the interventionist approach to an extreme that bordered on political economy. Their view that market forces operated to the disadvantage of third world countries by keeping them in low productivity activities and extracting monopoly rents led to efforts to alter completely the underlying structures of economic interaction. This led to a heavy emphasis on import substituting industrialization, to efforts at economic integration in Latin America, and finally to demands for a new international economic order, all in an effort to change the system and its effects on development.

This, then, was the strategic basis for the 30 years of development effort. In his presidential address to the Development Studies Association in 1982, Amartya Sen isolated four elements that grew out of this strategy and underlay the performance of that period: (1) industrialization; (2) rapid capital accumulation; (3) mobilization of underemployed manpower; and (4) planning and an activist state (Sen, 1983, p. 746).

Any assessment of the current state of the mainstream paradigm would highlight that the noninterventionist version has grown to prominence in mainstream development economics, paralleling its general resurgence in the Western industrial countries.[8]

Skirmishes are fought over obstacles to growth such as low level traps, export instability, terms of trade, economies of scale, or monopoly. But the central thrust of the noninterventionist resurgence is the direct critique of government intervention, of what Deepak Lal terms the dirigiste dogma.[9] If there are problems with the functioning of the economy, such as monopoly, responsibility is laid at the doorstep of the government. He argues that the interventionists went from the obvious fact that there were market failures in less developed countries to the conclusion that governments could act to overcome these market failures. However, he makes the case that "none of the feasible instruments of policy allows a net improvement in welfare compared with the market outcome. From the experience of a large number of developing countries in the post-war period, it would be a fair professional judgment that most government interventions attempting to supplant the price mechanism (by direct controls) have done more harm than good -- even compared, possibly, with laissez-faire" (Lal, 1983, p. 77).

Noninterventionists find that governments in less developed countries have intervened in all aspects of the economy. They have reduced producers' incentives by setting low prices for agricultural goods, distorted labor markets by establishing minimum wages, contributed to inflation by engaging in deficit financing and massive borrowing from the central banks, subsidized inefficient state-owned enterprises, discouraged exports by overvalued exchange rates, protected inefficient industry through tariffs and quotas, discouraged industrial investment through myriad licenses and regulations, etc. The antidevelopment bias of much government intervention is clear to Lal; it leads to political rent-seeking activity (trying to get import quotas, licenses, etc., through bribes and corruption) rather than to productive activity (Krueger, 1974). In this sense, the interventionists have a poor theory of politics. And Lal argues that the detrimental aspects cannot be overlooked; action must be taken. Government interference must be curtailed, and the size of government deficits must be cut drastically.

This has led to an interesting reversal. Now the noninterventionists are the ones asking for structural change in the developing world, a likelihood suggested by Albert Hirschman as long ago as 1963.[10] For one of the tactics suggested by the neononinterventionists is "structural adjustment," economic reforms in developing countries which limit the role of government and restore the role of markets. The World Bank has been most active in the center ring with this tactic, with over 50 loans for structural adjustment, though the IMF is becoming involved and the two are mandated to cooperate. The United States Agency for International Development (USAID) tries to enter the ring with its "policy dialogue" as well. As a result, tax reforms are implemented to deal with fiscal deficits and tax incentives, effective protection studies suggest wholesale restructuring of tariffs, public enterprises are evaluated and usually found to be inefficient when compared with a privatized operation, etc. Intervention in the name of nonintervention is the main show in the center ring.

It is not at all clear that the success of this newly resurgent strain is assured. The experience since 1980 certainly gives no evidence of it, and evaluations of structural adjustment efforts show them to be loosely formulated, poorly evaluated, and in need of constant tracking and adjustment (Michalopoulos, 1987, pp. 7-10; Addison and Dohery, 1986).

Nonetheless, one of the contributions of the attack on the interventionist wing of the mainstream economics paradigm by the noninterventionist wing has been to place at the center of the debate the question of the proper role of the state in the development process. These attacks have resulted in a shattering of the earlier interventionist consensus and have shown a clear weakness in its stance, the inability to differentiate among types of "governments." In the interventionist analysis, policies undertaken by Ferdinand Marcos or Anastasio Samoza have the same developmental impact as similar policies undertaken by a freely elected social democratic government. This is patently incorrect and quite justifiably led to questioning of the interventionist approach.

However, it is not clear that the noninterventionist tactic of reducing government activity is any better. They are guilty of the opposite sin. The interventionists thought any market failure could be cured by government action. Noninterventionists claim that any example of government failure can be solved by the market. Both views are simplistic.

Noninterventionists have tried to strengthen their attack by a series of empirical studies demonstrating that minimalist states outperform interventionist states, that economies in which governments distort prices tend to grow more slowly than those economies in which governments permit prices to reflect scarcity values.[11] But there is ample reason to question this formulation of the debate. The empirical evidence is weak and ambiguous at best (Landau, 1983; Rubinson, 1977; Ram, 1986). The clearest, noncity-state noninterventionist program with any longevity, that of General Pinochet in Chile since 1973, has been far from a success story, e.g., there has been a 1.1 percent annual decline in GDP since 1980.[12] Even more importantly, both interventionists and noninterventionists point to the same group of countries as evidence for their position, e.g., Korea, Taiwan, Singapore, and Hong Kong, the Gang of Four. Market economists argue that the success of the Gang of Four has come about because these countries got their prices right and followed an "outward-oriented" strategy based on exporting products in which they had a comparative advantage. Others note that the governments of these countries intervened in these economies in a most decisive way, planning and carrying out allocation of resources, stimulating exports of certain industries with government subsidies, etc., and that these interventions have been responsible for their success. In addition, all these countries, except Hong Kong, pursued successful

import substitution policies that paved the way
for the present export promotion policies.

So the question may better be formulated
not as more or less government intervention but
rather to what ends government intervention is
directed, i.e., whether we can differentiate
governments in terms of their
developmentalism.[13]

This is certainly a preferable formulation
to the Reagan administration's stance of
private sector versus public sector, which
generated their major initiative in foreign
assistance, the private sector initiative.[14]
Certainly the private sector must take an
important role in any development process, but
the key to success is finding a synergy between
government and the private sector. This has
been the basis of the Asian success, and it may
be the basis for future success in the
socialist countries.

In any case, the top billing in the
mainstream ring goes to the latest remake of
that old classic: the invisible hand of
markets versus the visible hand of the state.
However, international interventions are now
taken in the name of nonintervention. It is
interesting to note that, despite the
inconclusiveness of the empirical evidence, the
neononinterventionists are winning the debate,
and the Keynesian developmentalists are
becoming less interventionist, though the
debate continues.[15] Since both groups hold the
same microeconomics, differing over the degree
of market failure, the burden of proof is
always on the developmentalists to show why
government intervention is needed. This forces
developmentalists to take a more conservative
stance. More and more they are calling for
government deregulation, the use of market
incentives for government programs, less

activist fiscal and planning policies, and so forth, all without convincing empirical evidence but certainly in harmony with the suggestions of neoclassical microeconomics. Thus, the obstacles to the efficient operation of markets due to low levels of development, originally emphasized by interventionists, have been displaced by the obstacle of government intervention itself.

So the center ring act offered by mainstream strategists is simple and repetitive: reduce the scope and level of government activity. This uniform rejection of government action and espousal of the market is the reverse side of the uniform interventionist acceptance of government activity. It provides an apt contrast with the political economy ring. And it may point to a strength that has been unnoticed in the dependency and Marxist schools who have not been taken seriously because they do not share the belief in the efficacy of markets. Let us turn now to that ring.

THE POLITICAL ECONOMY RING

Proponents of political economy approach development as the unfolding in human history of the progressive emancipation of peoples and nations from control by nature or by other peoples and nations. Key building blocks in the analysis are an economic interpretation of historical processes, the primacy of the production process, the importance of class relations, a dialectical method which finds the determinants of change within the processes themselves, and the expectation that change will be qualitative as well as quantitative.[16]

The economic or social surplus is a central concept. It is viewed as a residual factor -- that which remains after necessary consumption has been subtracted from total output. Political economists argue that control of this economic surplus determines the nature of the development process. If a landed aristocracy controls the surplus, one particular style of development will occur; if the middle class controls it, there will be a different style. The degree of foreign control of the surplus also will shape the strategy of development.

A major task of development theory is to explain why the productive use of the surplus has progressed much more in some cases than in others. At this point within the political-economy paradigm, there emerge two major schools of thought -- Marxist and dependency theorists. Their key difference resides in the identification of the locus of power and of the control and use of the economic surplus of society, which is the key to development. Marxists focus on the class structure internal to a given nation as the key to understanding control of the economic surplus. Dependency theorists focus on relationships between nations. However, this may be primarily a matter of emphasis. Marxists have always been concerned with the connection between the internal class structure and external dependency. But the different emphasis is important in understanding the political-economy paradigm.

For Marxists, the key to a strategy of development beyond capitalism is the socialization of the society so that the surplus can be used in a socially productive manner. For dependency theorists, the issue is one of changing the rules of the international game so that the social surplus generated in the developing countries can be utilized there for development purposes.

Just as with the mainstream strategists, the 30 years after 1950 have been a period of successful development when viewed through Marxist or dependency eyes. There was a substantial increase in the number of countries who termed themselves socialist, with China the leading example. Gurley (1979), writing from a Marxist perspective, counted 24 countries, most of which had become Marxian socialist after the Second World War. Dependency theorists could point to a whole series of changes in international relations which appeared to guarantee third world countries more control over the surplus: licensing and control of technology transfer, restrictions on foreign investment and profit repatriation, local content requirements, common market arrangements, commodity stabilization agreements, and the outlines of a new international economic order.

And again both strategies provided ample guides for tactics or policy to the center ring. While revolutionaries attempting to establish a Marxist regime might be loathe to leave the rice paddies or the jungle for the center ring, others were working with laborers, farmers, and the landless to transform their economies. And the dependency activists were quite visible in the United Nations Conference on Trade and Development (UNCTAD), the Junta of Cartagena, the Lome negotiations, and a host of other international events.

Even from the narrower perspective of economic growth, the development performance that resulted from these efforts was quite positive. Gurley found growth and performance on social indicators in the Marxian socialist

countries quite comparable to the successful
development performance in other countries.
Many analysts noted that significant increases
in efficiency and growth were achieved when a
socialist government and planning replaced an
inefficient and usually corrupt government.[17]
And dependency theorists had to deal with
"dependent development," i.e., the relatively
rapid growth despite heavy dependence on an
outside country which occurred in a number of
countries.

But the period after 1980 has been no more
kind to political economy strategists than to
the mainstream. There have been few additions
to the socialist camp; perhaps Nicaragua would
be an example, but the continued dominance of
its economy by the private sector causes some
doubt. Chile was turned back to capitalism,
and Guyana or a Somalia seem doubtful examples
of socialism. Economic performance in
Mozambique was disastrous, and in Ethiopia and
many of the other socialist countries it
deteriorated notably (IBRD, 1987).[18]

The dependency strategy has had similar
problems. The movement to any reformation of
the international economy has been reversed.
Virtually all of the commodity agreements are
far weaker or even in collapse; restrictions on
foreign investment such as the Andean Pact's
Decision 24 have been repealed, and
transnational corporations are certainly
stronger in their bargaining and are
collaborating with the banks in debt for equity
swaps which may shift important segments of
many economies to foreign ownership. In
addition, a whole new nexus of dependency has
been established in many countries, debt
dependency, and its negative impact on
development is clear from Latin American
economic performance.

This points out one key element of both
dependency and Marxism: their theories of
underdevelopment are far more carefully
elaborated than their theories of development.
          What is to be done after the revolution?
Political economists, Marxists and dependency
theorists alike, have not developed theories of
development.   Rather Marxists and many
dependency theorists have drawn empirical
generalizations from the historical development
experience of the Soviet Union and China.
Until recently the Soviet model of development
was looked to for guidance in development
strategies.[19]   Then Marxists and dependency
theorists turned to the Chinese experience as
an alternative to the Soviet model of
development.   Many factors played a role in
this shift in allegiance: the Soviet obsession
with growth that relegated people's values to a
secondary position, the concentration of power
in the hands of the Communist party at the
expense of the mass of people, the focus on
industrialization to the neglect of
agriculture, and so on.
          To many political economists, China seems
a more appropriate model of development.[20]   A
great deal of work has been done on the
accomplishments in China, some indications of
which are seen in table 4-2.   A review of this
literature finds extensive and numerous
treatments of China's gains in health care,
sanitation, worker organization in industry,
rural development, and rural mobilization.
          The general strategy drawn from Chinese
experience was that self-reliant development be
pursued with an emphasis on fulfilling people's
basic human needs (food, shelter, health,
education) and on providing institutional
structures (brigades, communes, etc.) that
enable people to exert control over the

Table 4-2.   China's Development Performance

	Growth rate GNP Per Capita (1965-85)	GNP Per Capita (1984$)	Life Expectancy	Infant Mortality Rate
China	4.8	310	69	35
Large LDCs	.4 - 4.8	130 - 2060	49 - 69	35 - 132
Large LDC Ave.	2.8	838	58	69
India	1.7	260	56	89
Brazil	4.3	1640	65	67
Low income LDCs	2.9	270	60	72
Middle income LDCs	3.0	1290	62	68
Japan	4.7	10,390	77	7
Nigeria	2.7	770	49	113
Egypt	3.1	720	58	102

Sources: IBRD, World Bank Atlas, 1987 and
            World Development Report, 1987.
            Large LDCs includes Bangladesh,
            Brazil, Egypt, India, Indonesia,
            Mexico, Nigeria, Pakistan,
            Philippines, Thailand, Turkey.

conditions in which they lead their lives. Most dependency theorists were more circumspect about citing China as their model of development (Cardoso and Faletto, 1967).

To many, the show in the "left" ring is getting stale, boring, and irrelevant. New ideas are needed but not forthcoming. The spectators are getting restless and are frequently seen trying to watch what is going on in the center ring.

The arguments of the left seem particularly weak when socialist countries such as the USSR and China are rushing to introduce markets, international trade, foreign investment, and other elements of capitalism into their economies to invigorate them with the dynamism that characterizes capitalist countries such as Japan and Korea. No major less developed country looks to the USSR or China as the model. Countries that have opted for socialism, such as Vietnam and Angola, are trying to make their peace with the developed capitalist countries of the West. It is these countries, not the USSR and China, that have the capital, technology, and success in international markets that the less developed countries need. The socialist appeal is mainly fueled by the disastrous effects of U.S. economic policy on the third world, e.g., the worldwide inflation triggered by U.S. spending for both "guns and butter" in the 1960s and early 1970s, the collapse of the Bretton Woods system triggered by the outflow of gold from the United States as it spent abroad to pursue the Vietnam War, the monetarist onslaught of the 1980s which brought high interest rates and a global depression, low commodity prices and the debt crisis, and the fact that the United States has moved from being the world's largest creditor country in 1980 to being the world's

largest debtor country in 1985, and is now a
net importer of capital.

And yet when compared with the mainstream
strategy, it is conceivable that many of the
socialist countries may be better poised to
renew their development than the countries
following the mainstream approach. The
impressive performance of the Chinese economy
has grown at an astounding 9.8 percent per
year. One reason is that the issue of
government in China has been solved; the state
is clearly going to set the direction for that
economy of 1 billion people, 20 percent of the
total population of the world. And the state
is clearly dedicated to development, to
increases in the material welfare of all of the
population. Having solved that central
problem, it is possible to pick those
techniques and institutions which can
contribute most effectively to development. In
this case, the introduction of markets and of
foreign influences are the chosen innovations,
in the usual two steps forward one step
backward fashion of China. Thus, rather than
taking an a priori stance that markets must
completely replace government activity or that
the private sector must struggle with the
corrupt and inefficient government, China, the
Soviet Union, and other socialist countries are
able to search for that balance of public and
private, always in the context of a
developmentally oriented state. It remains to
be seen whether other developing socialist
countries will be able to learn the lessons
from China and whether their performance in the
next decade will surpass that of the mainstream
developing countries.[21]

While it is possible that the socialist
countries may have a more successful stint in
the center ring in the future, there is a

nagging feeling that what may finally takeover in the center ring is a transplant from the sideshows, the less coherent and pretentious efforts to understand and develop a strategy of development. Let us give them their due.

SOME SIDESHOWS OF DEVELOPMENT

There are a number of incipient strategies that could affect the direction of development in the future. We have chosen to mention three at this point: the redefinition of rejection of commonly defined development; decentralized grassroots development; and the evolution of the international structure into separate spheres of influence. One of these may move to the main development agenda in the future, so completeness requires treatment. Let us look at each in turn.

Redefinition and Rejection of Traditional Development

The starting point for thinking about development is usually some conception of history. One sideshow claims that we must be wary of the accepted conception of history and avoid assuming the view of historical progress which is common to both mainstream economics and political economy. History as we live it simply does not seem to be moving in that direction. The parable of historical progress common to both the mainstream and political-economy paradigms is a metaphor that may be useful in studying an abstraction-- civilization or socialism -- but it is misplaced in studying the actual development of Peru or Uganda.

Nisbet   summarizes   the   difficulty
succinctly and elegantly:

> The relevance and utility of the
> metaphor   of   growth   are   in   direct
> proportion to the cognitive distance
> of the subject to which the metaphor
> is applied. The larger, more distant
> or   more   abstract   the   subject,   the
> greater   the   utiltiy   of   metaphor-
> derived attributes . . . .
> It is something else entirely,
> however, when we try, as much social
> theory   at   present   is   trying,   to
> impose   these   concepts   of
> developmentalism upon, <u>not</u>
> constructed entities, but the kind of
> subject matter that has become basic
> in the social sciences today: <u>the
> social behavior of human beings in
> specific   areas   and   within   finite
> limits of time</u>.   Efforts to extract
> this   further   from   the   metaphor   of
> growth are . . . wholly unsuccessful
> (1969, pp. 267-268).

There   is   no   simple   march   of   progress.
There are no general paths to development just
as   there   is   no   general   definition   of
development.   Each people must write its own
history.   As Denis Goulet says regarding the
strategy   of   development   pursued   by   Guinea-
Bissau: "Paradoxically, the lesson of greatest
importance   is   that   <u>the   best   model   of
development is the one that any society forges
for itself on the anvil of its own specific
conditions</u> (1978, p. 52).[22]
What does this mean for the development
economist?   There is an interesting parallel in
modern   medicine   in   a   tension   between   the

"scientific" explanation of a disease and the
diagnosis a clinician makes for a particular
patient.[23]   This is well described by Tolstoy
in War and Peace:

> Doctors came to see Natasha,
> both separately and in consultation.
> They said a great deal in French,
> German and in Latin. They criticised
> one another, and prescribed the most
> diverse remedies for all the diseases
> they were familiar with.   But it
> never occurred to one of them to make
> the simple reflection that they could
> not understand the disease from which
> Natasha was suffering, as no single
> disease can be fully understood in a
> living person; for every living
> person has his complaints unknown to
> medicine--not a disease of the lungs,
> of the kidneys, of the skin, of the
> heart, and so on, as described in
> medical books, but a disease that
> consists of one out of the
> innumerable combinations of ailments
> of these organs.

While Tolstoy's depiction of every illness
as a unique event may no longer be justified,
economic development is even more of an art
than medical diagnosis. Economic theorists can
scientifically explain the results of
underpricing capital regardless of country or
time.   Development economists, on the other
hand, are diagnosticians of the particular
illnesses of particular countries at specific
points in time. They are forced to transcend a
specific scientific paradigm to become artisans
of the particular.

And in much of the Islamic world, the
rejection of both paradigms is even more
complete. The definition of development is
rejected, the process by which it has been
pursued is rejected, and the institutions that
have been part of either the capitalist or
socialist approaches are rejected. The society
will be organized along the dictates of the
Koran, including institutional changes such as
interest free banking.[24] Of course, Iran has
gone furthest in this regard, but Pakistan and
a number of other countries are moving in the
same direction. And there is a strain in the
Western economies that desires the same
approach, but in this case based upon
Christianity.[25]
So over time these concerns may move to
the forefront and, along with ethnic and
regional vindications, dominate the process of
development in many parts of the world.

Decentralized, Grassroots Development

During the 1970s, when concerns with
issues of income distribution grew, a great
deal of work both in strategy and actual policy
was undertaken to foster basic human needs.
With the collapse of world growth rates such
concerns have also lessened; yet there is an
active interest in elements of this approach.[26]
It is now undertaken primarily by the private
voluntary organizations and is focussed on the
many small scale development projects, often at
a rural village level, whose purpose is to
provide both an increase in well-being and an
empowerment of local persons and groups. The
successes are described in organs such as
Grassroots Development, a publication of the
Interamerican Foundation in Washington, D.C.

And there are very real successes, e.g., in
increasing yields by working with villagers to
adopt new agronomic practices such as seed
spacing and row distances and the use of
nitrogen fixing plants interplanted with corn.
Of course, at a macro level these effects may
hardly be noticeable, and macro influences can
cancel many of them out.[27] But in a broader
perspective of development as the gradual
empowerment of large numbers of people, they
may have a major impact on a country. Denis
Goulet has provided a number of examples of
small scale projects that have had important
multiplier effects.[28] Also the responses to
the initial critiques of basic needs approaches
make a strong case for the efficiency of
locally based and targeted development efforts.

Reorganization of the World Economy

There has been a clear movement toward
international integration of the world economy,
especially since the 1960s. However, the
current malaise may forced this movement to
change directions. Though it is difficult to
predict, increased control over economic
processes by governments or institutions seems
likely. One movement that may become more
prevalent over time is the growth of spheres of
economic influence. Japan has developed a
significant and highly pervasive influence
throughout Asia, has created in a modest form
the co-prosperity sphere that had been its aim
before 1940, though not without tensions and
resentments. China is likely to challenge
Japan for leadership. France has continued
with its sphere of influence in the former
French colonies, seen most clearly in the CFA,
a currency area of African countries linked to

the French franc at fixed exchange rates since
1948.   This allows France substantial control
over macroeconomic policy in the 13-member
countries.

     The USSR continues to exert substantial
control over the East European allies through
the Council for Mutual Economic Assistance
(CMEA), and if reforms dynamize its economy,
that influence is likely to grow.

     The case can be made that the United
States exerts a similar influence in Latin
America through its importance in trade and now
through its claim to Latin American resources
as represented in the debts that are
outstanding.   One can usefully view this
relation as a new "dollar area" where the
financial influence of the United States is
dominant.[29]

     It is possible that these groups may grow
in importance as the world economy begins to
revive and to adjust to the imbalances of
recent years.   If so, the key questions in the
center ring will be how to make these spheres
function in an effective manner to the benefit
of all their members, and how they can be used
to increase the development of those members.
This is certainly a different set of questions
from those that are in the center ring at this
point.

     There are other candidates for entry into
the center ring of development, and we are
likely to be surprised at what appears there
during the rest of the century.   In any case,
we can all hope that the context will be more
like that of the first 30 years of the
development experience than of this decade.   In
any event, it is clear that experience will
continue to be conditioned by three factors:
the objective economic conditions, the dynamism

of the advanced countries, and the strategies of development with the tactics they suggest.

The objective economic conditions can only improve over what they have been since 1979, which is some grounds for hope. There are signs that the lessons of the Gang of Four have been taken to heart and that the pragmatism of the socialist countries in introducing market signals will have positive results. Certainly there will be few ideological capitalist programs such as Chile's and so a viable strategy may be fashioned in the capitalist developing world as well.

When the leaven of the three sideshow elements is added, there is reason to feel that the positive momentum of 1950-1980 may be regained, that as John Lewis (1986, p. 23) put it, "There is no grounds for quitting."

NOTES

1. Morawetz (1978) summarized this performance to 1975. See Appendix 1 for regional detail on growth in production, population, and production per capita.

2. See James (1988) for a treatment of these effects in Bolivia.

3. Lewis' reconsideration brought together "mainstreamers from the development promotion community," omitting the political economist strain of thought and perhaps skewing the treatment toward the role of foreign assistance.

4. Gurley (1979) has made a persuasive case that growth rates were quite comparable between socialist and capitalist countries and that

income   distribution   favored   the   socialist
countries.

5.   See Bauer and Yamey (1971).

6.   See   Scitovsky   (1958,   pp.   295-308),
Rosenstein-Rodan   (1958,   pp.   245-56),   Dobb
(1960, pp. 5-13), and Myint (1964, pp. 118-
125).

7.   See Baer (1967, pp. 3-25) or Caceres and
Jimenez (1983, pp. 1019-1042).

8.   See Lal (1983), Balassa (1982), and Little
(1982).

9.   P. T. Bauer has reentered the fray with
his tried argument and an "I told you so," in
Reality and Rhetoric: Studies in The Economics
of Development (1984) and Equality, The Third
World and Economic Delusion (1983).

10.   See   Jameson   (1986,   pp.   223-232)   for   a
treatment of this structuralist reversal.

11.   Many studies have been done by the World
Bank   and   their   use   can   be   seen   in   the
"distortion index" in its World Development
Report, 1983.   Colin Bradford (1987, pp. 299-
316)   reexamined   this   issue   and   found
diametrically different results, e.g., that
growth   in   NICs   was   greatly   aided   by
underpricing investment goods and that there
was little difference in distortion between
outward and inward oriented countries.   He
concluded that "policies matter for growth,
though not only policies" paraphrasing the
Bank's use of "prices."   Nigel Harris (1987)
finds the key to NIC success in their ability

to repress labor, thereby distorting wages, one element of the price matrix.

12. IBRD, <u>World Development Report, 1987</u>, Table 2, p. 205; see Foxley (1982) for a treatment of this model and its early performance.

13. This is the thrust of Colin Bradford's evidence in "Trade and Structural Change." See also Hofheinz and Calder (1982), Johnson (1982), and Jones and Sakong (1980).

14. Assessments of private sector initiatives have shown them to be only minor contributors to development. See Robbs (1987, pp. 27-31) or U.S. AID (1985).

15. See Sen, "Development: Which Way Now?"; Stewart (1985, pp. 282-292), Streeten (1985, pp. 14-16).

16. On these issues and the political economy approach to development see Griffin and Gurley (1985, pp. 1089-1143).

17. See Boorstein (1969). Sutcliffe (1984, pp. 121-133) provides an interesting assessment of industrialization which is a nice political economy complement to Sen's views noted above.

18. It is of interest that data for many of the socialist countries are no longer reported in these publications.

19. For a full treatment see Wilber (1969).

20. For the classic statement of the Chinese model see Gurley (1983). See also Gurley (1979) and IBRD (1985).

21. Jan Prybyla's "skeptical" about the
possibilities of this new amalgam for making
fundamental changes in the socialist countries;
see "Chinese and Soviet Reforms Fail the Acid
Test" (1987).

22. For a summary of rejections of Western
development models and the search for
indigenous models see Wiarda (1983, pp. 433-
452).

23. The following is based on the discussion
of a related issue taken from Hauerwas,
Burrell, and Bondi (1977).

24. See Khan and Mirakhor (1986, pp. 32-36).

25. For a discussion and critique of the
writings of Rushdony, North, Bahnsen, Jordan,
and Tilton, the postmillenialists, see Neuhaus
(1987, pp. 2-3).

26. An updating of the issues of basic needs
is provided in Stewart (1985). One reviewer
says "What is missing, however, is a discussion
of why this approach . . . has passed so
quickly from the scene." It may return.

27. There is currently a good deal of interest
in linking these local successes into a macro
framework. For example, see Annis (1987, pp.
24-29).

28. See, for example, Goulet (1981).

29. See Jameson (1987).

REFERENCES

Addison, Tony, and Dahery, Lionel. Poverty Alleviation Under Structural Adjustment, London: Overseas Development Institute, 1986 (mimeo).

Annis, Sheldon. "The Next World Bank: Financing Developing from the Bottom Up," Grassroots Development 11 (1): 1987, 24-29.

Baer, Werner. "The Inflation Controversy in Latin America: A Survey," Latin American Research Review: Spring 1967, 3-25.

Balassa, B. Development Strategies in Semi-Industrial Countries. Baltimore: Johns Hopkins Press, 1982.

Bauer, P. T. Equality, The Third World and Economic Delusion. Cambridge: Harvard, 1983.

Bauer, P. T. Reality and Rhetoric: Studies in The Economics of Development. Cambridge: Harvard, 1984.

Bauer and Yamey. The Economics of Underdeveloped Countries; Bauer, P. T., Dissent on Development. London: Weidenfeld and Nicolson, 1971.

Boorstein, Edward. Economic Transformation of Cuba. New York: Monthly Review Press, 1969.

"Chinese and Soviet Reforms Fail the Acid Test," The Wall Street Journal, August 20, 1987.

Bradford, Colin. "Trade and Structural Change: NICs and Next Tier NICs as Traditional Economies," World Development 15 (3):   1987, 299-316.

Caceres,   Luis,   and   Jimenez,   F. "Estructuralismo, monetarismo e inflacion en Latinoamerica," El Trimestre Economico, April-June 1983, 1019-1042.

Cardos, Fernando Henrique, and Faletto, Enzo. Dependencia y Desarrollo en America Latina. Santiago: ILPES, 1967.

Dobb, Maurice. An Essay on Economic Growth and Planning.   London: Routledge & Kegan Paul, Ltd., 1960.

Foxley, Alejandro.   Latin American Experiments in Neoconservative Economics.   Berkeley: University of California Press, 1982.

Goulet, Denis.   Looking at Guinea-Bissau: A New Nation's Development Strategy, Occasional Paper no. 9, Overseas Development Council, March 1978.

Goulet,   Denis.   Survival with Integrity: Sarvodaya at the Crossroads.   Colombo, Sri Lanka: Marga Institute, 1981.

Griffin, Keith, and Gurley, John.   "Radical Analysis of Imperialism, The Third World, and the Transition to Socialism: A Survey Article," Journal of Economic Literature 27: September 1985, 1089-1143.

Gurley, John.   "Economic Development: A Marxist View."   In Kenneth P. Jameson and Charles K. Wilbur (eds.), Direction in Economic

Development. Notre Dame: University of Notre
Dame Press, 1979.

Gurley, John. "Maoist Economic Development:
The New Man in the New China." In C. K. Wilbur
(ed.), Political Economy of Development and
Underdevelopment, 3rd edition.   New York:
Random House, 1983.

Gurley, J. "Rural Development in China, 1949-
1975 and the Lessons to be Learned from It."
In N. Maxwell, China's Road to Development.
Oxford: Pergamon, 1979.

Hauerwas, Stanley, Burrell, David, and Bondi,
Richard. Truthfulness and Tragedy: A Further
Investigation in Christian Ethics, "An
Alternative Pattern for Rationality in Ethics."
Notre Dame, IN: Notre Dame Press, 1977.

Harris, Nigel. The End of the Third World:
Newly Industrializing Countries and the Decline
of an Ideology. New York: Penguin, 1987.

Hirschman, A. O. Essays in Trespassing:
Economics to Politics and Beyond. Cambridge:
Cambridge University Press, 1981.

Hofheinz, Roy, and Calder, Kent. The East-
Asian Edge. New York: Basic Books, 1982.

IBRD. China: Agriculture to The Year 2000.
Washington, D.C.: IBRD, 1985.

IBRD. Poverty in Latin America: The Impact of
Depression. Washington, D.C.: IBRD, 1986.

IBRD. World Development Report, 1987, Table 2,
p. 205.

James, Kenneth. "Varieties of Austerity: The Case of Bolivia." In Howard Handelman and Werner Baer (eds.), _Paying the Costs of Austerity in Latin America_. Boulder: Westview, 1988.

Jameson, Kenneth. Latin America: A New Dollar Area, 1987 (mimeo).

Jameson, Kenneth P. "Latin American Structuralism: A Methodological Perspective," _World Development_ 14 (2): February 1986, 223-232.

Johnson, C. _MITI and the Japanese Miracle: The Growth of Industrial Policy, 1925-1975_. Stanford: Stanford University Press, 1982.

Jones, L., and Sakong, L. _Government Business and Entrepreneurship in Economic Development: The Korean Case_. Cambridge: Harvard University Press, 1980.

Khan, M., and Mirakhor, A. "The Framework and Practice of Islamic Banking," _Finance and Development_ 23 (3): September 1986, 32-36.

Krueger, Anne. "The Economics of the Rent-seeking Society," _American Economic Review_: June 1974, 291-323.

Lal, Deepak. _The Poverty of Development Economics_. London: Institute of Economic Affairs, 1983.

Landau, D. "Government Expenditure and Economic Growth: A Cross Country Study," _Southern Economic Journal_, 1983.

Lewis, John P. "Development Promotion: A Time for Regrouping." In John P. Lewis and Valeriana Kallab (eds.), Development Strategies Reconsidered. New Brunswick, NJ: Transaction Books, 1986.

Little, I.M.D. Economic Development: Theory, Policy, and International Relations. New York: Basic Books, 1982.

Morawetz, David. Twenty-five Years of Economic Development: 1950 to 1975. Baltimore: Johns Hopkins, 1978.

Michalopoulos, Constantine. "World Bank Structural Adjustment Loans," Finance and Development 2442: June 1987, 7-10.

Myint, Hla. The Economics of the Developing Countries. New York: Frederick A. Praeger, Inc., 1964, 118-25.

Neuhaus, Richard. "The Theocratic Temptation," The Religion and Society Report: May 1987, 2-3.

Nisbet, Robert A. Social Change and History: Aspects of the Western Theory of Development. New York: Oxford University Press, 1969, 267-268.

Ram, R. "Government Size and Economic Growth: A New Framework and Some Evidence from Cross Section and Time Series Data," American Economic Review: March 1986.

Robbs, Peter "Privatization in Africa: Neither Pox nor Panacea," Development International 1 (2): March/April 1987, 27-31.

Rosenstein-Rodan, P. N. "Problems of Industrialization of Eastern and South-Eastern Europa." In A. N. Agarwala and S. P. Singh (eds.), The Economics of Underdevelopment. Oxford: Oxford University Press, 1958, 245-256.

Rubinson, R. "Dependency, Government Revenue and Economic Growth: 1955-70," Studies in Comparative International Development: Summer 1977.

Scitovsky, Tibor. "Two Concepts of External Economies." In A. N. Agarwala and S. P. Singh (eds.). Oxford: Oxford University Press, 1958, pp. 295-308.

Sen, Amartya. "Development: Which Way Now?," Economic Journal 93: December 1983, 745-762.

Stewart, Frances. Basic Needs in Developing Countries. Baltimore: Johns Hopkins University Press, 1985.

Stewart, Frances. "The Fragile Foundation of the Neoclassical Approach to Development," The Journal of Development Studies 21 (2): January 1985, 282-292.

Streeten, Paul. "A Problem to Every Solution: Development Economics has not Failed," Finance and Development 22 (2): June 1985, 14-16.

Sutcliffe, Bob. "Industry and Underdevelopment Reexamined," Journal of Development Studies, 21 (1): October 1984, 121-133.

U. S. AID. <u>A Review of AID's Experience in Private Sector Development</u>, A.I.D. Program Evaluation Report #14, Washington, D.C.: AID, 1985.

Wiarda, Howard J. "Toward a Nonethnocentric Theory of Development: Alternative Conceptions from the Third World," <u>The Journal of Developing Areas</u> 17: July 1983, 433-452.

Wilber, Charles K. <u>The Soviet Model and Underdeveloped Countries</u>. Chapel Hill: University of North Carolina Press, 1969.

World Bank. <u>World Development Report, 1983</u>. New York: Oxford University Press, 1983.

Appendix 1. Growth of World Product and Population 1950-1980

| | 1980 LEVELS | | | | | Growth Indexes 1980 (1950 = 1.00) | | |
	Production (Billion 1980 US$)	Percent of World	Population (Million)	Percent of World	Production Per Capita (1980 US$)	Production	Population	Production Per Capita
World	11,269	100.0	4,488	100.0	2,511	3.83	1.78	2.16
Americas	3,649	32.4	613	13.7	5,953	3.07	1.86	1.65
USA	2,557	22.7	228	5.1	11,231	2.67	1.49	1.78
Canada	237	2.1	24	0.5	9,875	3.85	1.75	2.21
Latin America	856	7.6	361	8.0	2,371	5.06	2.20	2.30
Brazil	327	2.9	122	2.7	2,687	8.13	2.28	3.57
Mexico	179	1.6	67	1.5	2,657	5.71	2.53	2.26
Europe	4,358	38.7	796	17.7	5,475	3.67	1.34	2.74
Germany W.	643	5.7	61	1.4	10,487	4.50	1.23	3.67
France	505	4.5	54	1.2	9,420	4.03	1.28	3.15
Italy	303	2.7	57	1.3	5,308	4.05	1.21	3.33
U.K.	298	2.6	56	1.2	5,323	2.07	1.11	1.86
Spain	116	1.0	38	0.8	3,097	4.46	1.34	3.33
USSR	1,280	11.4	266	5.9	4,822	3.96	1.47	2.69
Poland	125	1.1	36	0.8	3,511	3.47	1.43	2.42
Africa	455	4.0	472	10.5	963	3.91	2.15	1.83
Nigeria	87	0.8	77	1.7	1,126	8.33	2.32	3.59
South Africa	62	0.6	28	0.6	2,196	3.75	2.09	1.79
Egypt	53	0.5	42	0.9	1,261	3.77	2.05	1.84
Oceania	161	1.4	22	0.5	7,318	3.31	1.81	1.79
Australia	133	1.2	15	0.3	9,156	3.44	1.76	1.95
New Zealand	18	0.16	3	0.07	5,834	2.30	1.64	1.41

Appendix 1. (continued)

	1980 LEVELS					Growth Indexes 1980 (1950 = 1.00)		
	Production (Billion 1980 US$)	Percent of World	Population (Million)	Percent of World	Production Per Capita (1980 US$)	Production	Population	Production Per Capita
Asia	2,647	23.5	2,585	57.6	1,024	6.63	1.89	3.52
W. Asia	269	2.4	103	2.3	2,587	8.85	2.29	3.88
South Asia	387	3.4	887	19.8	436	2.88	1.89	1.52
India	302	2.7	680	15.2	444	2.77	1.84	1.51
Pakistan	45	0.4	86	1.9	526	4.05	2.19	1.85
S.E. Asia	299	2.7	360	8.0	831	7.00	1.97	3.54
Indonesia	139	1.2	151	3.4	918	13.17	1.81	7.29
E. Asia	1,692	15.0	1,233	27.5	1,372	8.83	1.83	4.81
Japan	955	8.5	117	2.6	8,163	10.39	1.40	7.44
China (PAC)	592	5.3	1,032	23.0	573	6.96	1.89	3.70
Korea, So.	55	0.5	40	0.9	1,387	7.83	1.88	4.17
Taiwan	42	0.4	18	0.4	2,373	11.05	2.23	4.95
Hong Kong	19	0.2	5	0.1	3,822	13.34	2.24	5.94

Source: Table prepared by W. S. Hunsberger based on Herbert Black, The Planetary Product in 1980, Washington, Dept. of State, Bureau of Public Affairs, Appendix Tables 1, 2 and 3.

COMMENTARY BY PETER DELP

"Strategies of Development: A Survey" provdes an interesting and entertaining survey of the theories of development economics using a metaphor of the three-ring circus. The image of economists competing for the limelight of center stage in the tasks of development planning, providing advice to both governments and donors and in scholarly pursuits does seem to be a fitting depiction, if not the clearest to follow. Here briefly is a summary. Adjacent to the center ring of the circus-- the arena of policies and tactics -- the authors describe two side rings which represent competing schools of economic thought: a mainstream ring shared by both interventionists and noninterventionists, and a third ring populated by political economists (e.g., Marxists and dependency theorists). The survey concludes by describing three sideshows to the main rings, which they believe could eventually set the agenda for future development strategies.

After reading the authors' treatment of the main branches of development economics, I suggest that a tree with diverging limbs is a clearer metaphor to characterize the growing body of thought and practice of development economics. There is no common trunk to the separate branches, however, only entangled

179

limbs searching for the light. The survey
fails to identify any common threads running
through the seemingly crazy quilt of
development strategies, only disarray. I
conclude this comment with a discussion of two
possible cross-cutting concerns.

The survey of development strategies
begins with disturbing trends in economic
growth and stagnation attributed to a tangled
"disarray in strategic thinking" that has led
to questioning of traditional tactics and
policies of development. The source of this
disarray is the dramatic shift in growth rates
around 1980, ending a 30-year boom in developed
and developing countries, and starting a
recession in all but a handful of countries.
The authors offer reasons for this "debacle,"
such as the change in the objective economic
conditions in the world, e.g., a decline in
growth in the industrial countries, stimulated
by the oil-rich countries "claim [to] a much
larger share of world resources." Apparently,
economic strategy hasn't adjusted to changing
economic circumstances.

The authors take on the task of
"examin[ing] the issue of development
strategies, and implicitly the tactics they
suggest, to cut into the disarray that
presently reigns." Using the metaphor of the
three-ring circus, the authors believe that the
change in objective economic conditions has
broken the link between strategists in either
side ring, who are "simply replaying old
themes," and the politicians and technocrats in
the center ring. (The newly industrialized
countries in Asia and the People's Republic of
China are cited as exceptions.)

The authors postulate that the future
departures in development strategy are likely
to come from the sideshows to the main circus.

To support their case, the survey's authors
treat each side ring in turn, describing why
the mainstream strategies performed
successfully at first but have current
difficulties; and why the political economists
have been frustrated by having "theories of
underdevelopment [that] are far more carefully
elaborated than their theories of development."
The show in the "left ring" of the circus has
become "stale, boring, and irrelevant." The
mainstream ring has become entangled with
interventionists in the market attempting to
correct its imperfections, noninterventionists
relying on individuals to maximize their self-
interest, and neononinterventionists promoting
"structural adjustment." As the authors put
it: "Intervention in the name of
nonintervention is the main show in the center
ring." Although the authors describe how this
has come about, the reader may be
understandably confused, and the circus
metaphor seems not much help. Tracing out the
mainstream branches on a tree diagram helps to
clarify the historical relationships.
     I agree that what will finally take over
on the main stage of policies and tactics will
very likely come from a "sideshow," rather than
the mainstream or the political economists.
The survey concludes with treatment of three
sideshows in development economics. The first
is redefinition and rejection of traditional
development -- a nonhistory approach. There is
no general definition of development, no
"simple march of progress." Quoting Goulet:
". . . the best model of development is the one
that any society forges for itself on the anvil
of its own specific conditions" (1978, p. 52).
Iran has gone the furthest in rejecting past
development definitions, policies, and
institutions. While the authors have raised an

interesting point, I doubt that "these concerns [whether based on Islam or Christianity] will move to the forefront . . . in many parts of the world."

A second sideshow described in the survey is "decentralized, grassroots development." Local development efforts, carried forward by private and voluntary development organizations, have important multiplier effects, yet "may hardly be noticeable" at the macro level of a country. I would include in this sideshow the past fascination with "appropriate technology" as both a means and an end. The empowerment of people and increase in well-being at the village level are lofty goals. Yet I am neither convinced from our own study of the progress of decentralization and of the appropriate technology movement or by the authors' brief comments that grassroots development and decentralization will reach center stage on their own momentum.

The last sideshow described is the reoganization of the world economy so that regional groupings and spheres of economic influence dominate issues for the politicians and tacticians in the center ring. The key question may be "how to make these spheres function in an effective manner to the benefit of all of their members . . . ." Or it may be how to maintain the structure of a globally integrated economy despite such groupings.

The survey is a stimulating account of development strategies as seen by economists. Not being an economist, I found little to fault in the description of competing approaches and philosophies. However, as a development practitioner, I suggest that a number of trends in the developed and developing world are having a considerable impact on development planning processes, and coincide with the dramatic shifts in growth rates between the last and current decades. Two such trends are (1) the politics and economics of food production and distribution, and (2) the worldwide impact of a continuing advance in information technology. Both represent changes in the objective technological conditions (to paraphrase the authors) and have implications for setting development strategy.

FOOD SYSTEMS AND DEVELOPMENT STRATEGIES

The development community has lived for decades with forecasts of food scarcities continuing and even becoming worse. Development strategy is concerned with the long view, and for most developing countries, the food situation seemed bleak. Strategists have been concerned with achieving self-sufficiency in food production to reduce food imports, while the industrialized countries have been concerned with disposing of agricultural surpluses generated by highly subsidized farm sectors. Today only the USSR is a regular importer of food grains, apart from mismanaged and drought-prone Ethiopia and one or two other countries. "Today we have a worldwide glut" (Bell, 1988, p. 133).

An issue for the macroeconomics advising many countries was the choice of goals: self-sufficiency in production of basic food grains versus food security. The latter goal, to garner sufficient foreign exchange through exports to be able to buy food stocks as needed from the more efficient producers, was much debated by economists in the early 1980s. This debate continues, and despite arguments of comparative economic advantage, it is often the political dimension of the issue that has

influenced economic planning.   There is general
agreement that within regions and countries the
food problem is not so much a production
problem, but one of uneven distribution brought
about by the inability of the lower end of the
socioeconomic spectrum to participate in the
marketplace.   Thus, malnutrition confronts many
population groups in the developing countries,
even though technological advances have largely
eliminated production shortfalls (DeGregori,
1985; Wortman and Cummings, 1978).

The authors could categorize the issue of
food as part of the continuing policy disarray
b e t w e e n   i n t e r v e n t i o n i s t s   a n d
noninterventionists.   Is it a question of
getting the price incentives right for
producers, middlemen, or consumers, or is it a
task of improving political institutions and
physical infrastructure, or both of these?
Development strategists will have the problem
of juggling food policies for many years to
come.

Timmer, Falcon, and Pearson (1983) make a
convincing argument for the interconnections
among   food,   nutrition,   agriculture,
macroeconomic policy, and trade regimes, and
offer a strategy for food systems planning.
They illustrate the complexities with a simple
example:

In many developing countries the
primary protection for poor consumers
against high food prices comes from
an overvalued exchange rate, which at
the same time is an important factor
in keeping those consumers poor.
Overvalued exchange rates slow
economic growth and lower incentives
for agricultural production; the

combination reduces the demand for unskilled labor (p. 10).

Because of these systemic linkages, food policy analysis extends beyond the "traditional boundaries of agricultural or nutritional policy." It is thus a far-reaching, never-ending concern to development strategies.

INFORMATION AND DEVELOPMENT STRATEGY

The information revolution is a well-documented, popularized (Naisbitt, 1982; Ganley and Ganley, 1982), and a multifaceted concern to both industrialized and developing countries. Freer flow of information is one significant aspect of the advances in information technology. The instantaneous communications that enable global trading on an unprecedented scale have made the world's financial systems much more susceptible to instability. On a national scale, the freer flow of information relates to the efficiency of domestic markets as well as tying them to international trading. Centrally planned economies have substituted direction from on high for the signals of demand and supply from the marketplace, but how long with this continue? As information flows more freely in a society, both the political realms and economic realms are affected. This presents a challenge to development strategists and political and economic power brokers. Information can be both a centralizing and decentralizing force (DeGregori, 1985).

A developing country's economic management is intertwined with how it acquires and develops information management capabilities for planning and budgeting. The flow of information is facilitated by adoption and spread of new information technologies within a society and within government. However, the political dimension is often the determining factor in this process, at least in the short run. Experiences in Chile and Kenya illustrate.

One of the ironies of the early 1970s was the succession of interventions aimed at changing the direction of Chile's economy. The socialist government of Allende was in the process of instituting large-scale management information systems to aid centralized planning. These efforts were being resisted by factory managers and lower echelon officials. Subsequent events in Chile derailed the effort. A new regime, and a new set of advisors from a different school of economics, installed a monetarist economic policy. They could have just pulled the plug on the central computers.

Recent technological advances in telecommunications, in mini- and microcomputer hardware and memory storage, and -- most important -- in applications software, are forging a revolution in development planning. It is not so easy to pull the plug when computers are scattered in offices in different ministries or around the country.

The government of Kenya's experience with using microcomputers in economic planning illustrates the trend. Although the impact on development economists has yet to be fully felt, the people who must assemble the annual budgets, prepare sectoral ministry forward budgets and development plans, and account for what has been spent are now part of an information revolution. Instead of the audits of government's expenditures lagging the planning process by as much as a year, the accounts are updated in a time frame that

facilitates information-based planning. The
changes have been incremental thus far, but the
implications are far-reaching. The process was
immeasurably aided by the cabinet's political
decision to make significant moves to
decentralize government.

Development assistance provides a vehicle
for introducing information technologies to
many other countries through technical
assistance projects. In many instances, the
business sector has responded to the changing
technologies at a surprising pace, leaving some
governments vacillating between embracing and
severely regulating information and
communications changes.

Increased information flow is no panacea
for the ills of developing planning. "Garbage
in -- garbage out" still holds true for any
automated data collection effort. Our early
skepticism in the case of computer applications
to development planning was based on too many
experiences with management information systems
that promised far more than was ever delivered.
It is the microprocessor that enables
decentralized workstations, on-line processing,
and quick turnarounds that make the difference.
"Garbage" data input is quickly seen as
deficient, stimulating better data acquisition
and incentives for self-correcting operations.
User friendly software has been applied
successfully in custom designed agriculture,
education, and health sector planning models.
Trends now well underway in this country toward
greater utilization of expert inputs to highly
sophisticated but easy to use planning software
will surely be transferred to developing
country finance and development planning
bodies, where expertise is in short supply.

There is another dimension to the
information revolution which is linked to

international transfer of manufacturing
technology and trade.   Computer chip assembly
was first exported to developing countries to
take advantage of cheap, but increasingly
skilled labor.   Microchip production is,
however, a highly dynamic economic and
technology linked system.   Furthermore, the
information revolution is based on
technological processes that are increasingly
automated.   Countries such as Malaysia that
established a base in microelectronics assembly
have to respond to rapidly changing
technological conditions, where the product
life of current technologies is measured in
months, not years.   Countries such as Thailand
and Indonesia are looking for guidance on where
to jump into such dynamic enterprises, so as
not to be passed by in the information
technology revolution.   Yet their bureaucratic
mechanisms can doom ventures before ground is
broken because of the increasing pace of such
developments.   The rate of change in
biotechnological applications for health, for
agricultural productivity, and for improved
fertilization control raises a similar dilemma
to country planners.   These will be the
concerns of development planners in the 1990s,
alongside international debt, ideological
revolutions, and grassroots movements.

CONCLUDING THOUGHTS

The survey of development strategies was
presented as competing acts in a circus, with
the mainstreamers and political economists
competing for the center ring -- but with
outdated theories and strategies.   In our final
analysis the survey is quite entertaining, but
missing common threads.   The disarray of

strategies and tactics that characterizes the
economic fori of the 1980s have been more
clearly categorized. To add to this metaphor
of a three-ring circus with distinct sideshows,
I have touched on only two cross-cutting
issues. Food policy and information
technologies will continue to be the concern of
development planners for the future. Energy
policy is another concern. All raise similar
tactical and strategic issues: problems of
production, access, affordability, and
utilization in the context of changing
technological conditions. These concerns are
not limited to a particular ring or school of
economic thought, but rather raise issues
across the entire three-ring circus of
development strategies.

NOTE

1. The first application of the microcomputer
in Kenya was an attempt to use VisiCalc
software on the Apple IIe in the Ministry of
Agriculture to manage maize storage depots.
While this proved beyond the capacity of the
technology in 1981, it provided an entry point
for successful transfer of microprocessors in
the planning unit.

REFERENCES

Bell, Daniel. "Reviewing Planet Earth in
2013," Washington Post, January 3, 1988, p. B3.

Goulet, Dennis. Looking at Guinea-Bisseau: A
New Nation's Development Strategy, Occasional
paper no. 9, Overseas Development Council,
March 1978.

DeGregori, Thomas R.   A Theory of Technology.
Ames, Iowa: Iowa State University Press, 1985.

Ganley, Oswald H., and Ganley, Gladys D.   To
Inform or to Control? The New Communications
Networks. New York: McGraw Hill Books, 1982.

Naisbitt, John. Megatrends. New York: Warner
Books, 1982.

Timmer, C. Peter, Falcon, Walter P., and
Pearson, Scott R.   Food Policy Analysis.
Baltimore: John Hopkins University Press,
1983.

Wortman, Sterling, and Cummings, Ralph, Jr. To
Feed This World: The Challenge and the
Strategy. Baltimore: John Hopkins University
Press, 1978.

5 THE DEBATE OVER MONETARISM: MONETARY POLICY AND ECONOMIC DEVELOPMENT

Alan Rufus Waters

MONETARISM

Monetarism has several distinct meanings. In Latin America, for example, it stands for a set of political outcomes rather than an approach to the process of macroeconomic management. In other areas the debate over monetarism in the Less Developed Countries (LDCs)[1] parallels the debate in the United States but at many different levels. At whatever level the debate is conducted, and however dissimilar the protagonists may appear, there is a fundamental commonality that cannot be ignored. Monetarists are essentially capitalist and argue for market solutions.

> The revival of the quantity theory by neomonetarists is closely associated with their advocacy of laissez faire philosophy in policy matters (Eshaq, 1983, p. 73).

The monetarists make the case that only well-defined ownership and unfettered markets can effectively coordinate information flows, and ensure both economic success and social justice. They argue that money, through its

191

relative price, affects the real process of economic development.

The anti-monetarists bear no single label. They have lost the cohesion that once made it possible to call them Keynesians. However, whether structuralists in Latin America or socialists in Africa, the common thread is a conviction that markets do not produce benign outcomes. The anti-monetarists see money as just another means to social control. Monetary policy is merely another tool or instrument in the hands of those who will direct the economy and overcome its problems through altered financial signals (Uri et al., 1968, p. 4).

There is little of intellectual interest in the anti-monetarists' position. Their goals are as old as the vision of an aristocracy-of-merit and the anthropomorphic conviction that men (or at least a select group of men) can and should control economic destiny. Their vision has comforted apologists for 75 years of failed collectivist and dirigists experiments in our own century alone. Proponents of anti-monetarism encompass a wide range of interest groups (including many businessmen)[2] and they reject or ignore an unrelieved historical record of failure. The anti-monetarists continue to seek a more perfect system in which economic planning and control will be removed from the uninformed, unpredictable, and tasteless masses, and centralized instead in the hands of a thoughtful and benevolent natural elite. Theirs is the underlying case for every form of active macroeconomic policy.

The decline of the anti-monetarist camp into a collection of special cases for special interests has forced those facing the intellectual challenge of economic development to focus on another source of potential insight: Austrian economics. The Austrians in

the United States were driven to the outer
fringes of the economics profession and hence
forced to rethink and hone their approach.
They have, therefore, been ready with a viable
alternative thesis when the mainstream began to
fragment.   The Austrians focus on process
rather than state.   They recognized that
institutional arrangements are important and
hence accept the work done in public choice and
property rights analysis. They understand that
there is good evidence that individuals in
control of government power can do great harm
but much less evidence that they can do good.[3]
Furthermore, the great thinkers of the Austrian
tradition (Bohm-Bawerk, and the recent Nobel
Laureate F. A. von Hayek) were monetary
theorists, although not necessarily monetarists
(Machlup, 1976, pp. 13-59).[4]   The Austrian
approach has led men of common sense to review
their thinking on both monetarism and economic
development.
        The monetarists are interesting; they
offer testable hypotheses and they seek
statistical evidence in the historical record.
In doing so they are vulnerable.   The debate
can be shifted to technical issues where the
outcome depends on the quality of data or
econometric fashion, i.e., the form and length
of lags, the ever-present identification
problem, or the removal of "white noise" from a
time series.   The complexity of the techniques
frequently excludes the uninitiated and
generates its own rewards for the participants.
In the process, however, the fundamental
question is usually lost: does an activist
macroeconomic policy, and in particular an
activist monetary policy, lead to greater
economic success than does a competitive-market
alternative?

Is the debate over monetarism anything more than intellectual jousting? If not, then those who specialize in the study of economic development - the epitome of applied economics - would do well to ignore it. If, on the other hand, the debate over monetarism leads to explicit policy prescriptions, it must be of central interest. We must, therefore, first determine what monetarism involves and what policy prescriptions it offers.

Monetarism can be as confined as the study of the narrowest definition of the money supply or can be allowed to cover every aspect of a money-using economy.[5] Traditionally the anti-monetarists have chosen the broader definitions and the monetarists the narrower. In recent years, however, there has emerged the "neoliberal" approach which subsumes much of monetarism and emphasizes the necessary role of high real interest rates and the importance of financial deepening in the process of economic development.[6] Furthermore, while there have been a wealth of studies on the relation between inflation and the real demand for money, there has been little empirical work on the effect of inflation on investment and economic development (Vincenk, 1979). The few studies that have been undertaken suggest that the connection is between ill-conceived and poorly executed macroeconomic policy and malinvestment rather than between inflation and the quantity of investment (Sebastian, 1986).

Whatever definition of monetarism we select will contain some central recognition of a connection between the supply of, and the demand for, money as a central determinant of the price level. There will be an argument about how to define money, with even the narrow definition of M_1 (coin and currency outside the treasury and demand deposits adjusted for

interbank accounts) being called into question
if it is seen that cash and checking accounts
are not adequate substitutes for each other
under the institutional arrangements in some
LDC (Trescott, 1971, p. 21). The broader the
definition the more difficult it is to study
money empirically. As a rule, the supply of
money is taken to be amenable to control by the
government institution operating the usual
monetary monopoly. It must also be allowed
that there will be autonomous variations in the
supply of money in an open economy due to the
effects of foreign trade and investment on the
nation's reserve position.[7] This is not to be
confused with the popular and false assumption
that a fall in the rate of exchange of a
country will lead inevitably to domestic
inflation.

> The necessary floating of the peso,
> which brought it down to nearly 19 to
> the dollar compared with 8.5 to the
> dollar in mid-1983, has triggered a
> substantial rise in prices (Paine,
> 1985, p. 34).

> Jugoslavia's drastic 30% devaluation
> of its dinar .... First mooted last
> autumn, before the government got
> cold feet when it considered how much
> it would push up domestic inflation
> ...("Jugoslavia: Devaluation and
> After," 1980, p. 74).

There is nothing inevitable about the
result of a decline in the value of a currency
unless the group in charge of the government
seeks to avoid the political cost of pursuing
appropriate domestic economic policies. If the
money supply is allowed to expand so that the

adjustment to import substitutes is postponed
and the illusion of no change is purposely
sustained, the cost will be general inflation.

Whether it is a question of accommodating
to external forces by expanding the money
supply faster than the growth in demand, or
doing so for purely domestic reasons, the
effect is unequivocally the same. There are
good arguments for following a rational foreign
exchange policy (not overvaluing the currency),
and there are equally good arguments for
following a rational monetary policy (not
continually expanding the money supply as a
means to transfer control over assets to the
nonprivate sector), and there are certainly
sound arguments for coordinating the two
policies (Aghevli, 1987). There is not
justification for an LDC (or any other nation)
pursuing an irrational foreign exchange policy
and hoping to have the sophistication to be
able to offset its effects by a finely tuned
domestic monetary policy.

Since the issue is central to the
monetarist case, research emphasis has
concentrated on the issue of the stability or
instability of the demand for money.[8]
Nevertheless, although such studies may be
theoretically important for sustaining the
monetarist position, the practical significance
for the student of the LDC may not be great.
The weakness of the available monetary data and
the magnitude of the shifts that would occur on
the supply side provide adequate general
evidence that instability of the demand for
money in the LDC could only exacerbate an
already impossible policy situation. Arguments
in the learned journals center on the
appropriate definition of the assets to be
included in the definition of money, or the
role of expectations. We have a simpler

question: do any of the LDCs appear to
actually practice, or have any of them recently
practiced, its basic policy prescription?

Monetary theory leads us to expect that a
steady, and hence predictable, rate of increase
in the money supply will reduce uncertainty and
lead to lower nominal interest rates.[9] This
policy prescription is usually associated with
the work of Milton Friedman on the more
developed economies and the United States in
particular.   However, there is a long history
of advocacy of monetary stability in studies of
the LDC.[10] We cannot measure nominal interest
rates with any worthwhile degree of accuracy
for most of the LDCs due to varying degrees of
financial repression by the people in control
of the government. We could, however, see if
there is any resonance between variations in
the rate of growth of the money supply and the
rate of economic development.   The question
would be: does a more stable monetary policy-
a steady expansion of the money supply-
coincide with more rapid economic growth?
Though fascinating in itself, the answer to
this question lies beyond our present interest.
At this stage all we wish to do is to establish
whether or not there is any indication that the
LDCs do or do not pursue monetarist policies.
Before proceeding to the evidence, we should
say something about the anti-monetarist policy
alternatives.

The anti-monetarists offer a critique of
the individualist, market approach to the
problem of economic coordination.   The
opponents of monetarism espouse some form of
collectivist faith.   They are the outright
authoritarians, the seekers in the reemerging
pre-Marxist mist, members of that superbly
contradictory group the democratic socialists,
or of any one of a range of other groups with

similar beliefs. They do not offer concrete
policies other than the transfer of political
power to people who support their views and the
concentration of economic power where they
believe it can be used for the general good.
In the final analysis it is perhaps unfair to
call upon the structuralists and other anti-
monetarists to offer policy alternatives since
the debate is about monetarism and not its
alternatives. It is, however, reasonably clear
that all of the alternatives offered require
some form of direct intervention. As one
sympathetic scholar has it:

> The essence of the structuralist
> argument is that price stability can
> only be attained through selective
> and managed policies for economic
> growth (Thirlwall, 1977, p. 288).

Pierre Uri was correct about at least one side
of the debate when he said:

> ... the theories are not codified
> bodies of doctrines but are rather
> two general lines of approach pushed
> to more or less extreme consequences
> by their followers (1968, p. 6).

The key conclusion of monetarist analysis
- whether by Friedman or by Lucas and Sargent-
is that short-term (and in the Lucas-Sargent
model, long-term also) monetary policy actions
will have no effect on the real variables and
will merely result in inflation. The
monetarists, therefore, recommend a constant
real money stock, which is best approximated by
a constant rate of growth in the supply of
money over the business cycle. They argue that
a stable policy of this nature offers the best

means of facilitating economic success, and
that policies that attempt to adjust the supply
of money to the variations in other vectors-
such as some particular rate of interest - can
only have a perverse effect. The implication
for the LDC is clear: a constant rate of
growth of the money supply should also lead to
discernible improved performance in terms of
economic growth.
     There are two chains of causality linking
changes in the money supply to changes in the
price level, the rate of interest, and the
level of economic activity in general. First,
there is the direct price effect of a change in
the supply of money.   Second, there is the
indirect effect via changes in working money
balances as people adjust to the altered value
of money. The effect of these changes in money
balances works its way through the interest
rate to alter the opportunity cost of holding
money and hence the pattern of expenditures.
The two chains reinforce each other, and no
matter how much intervention is practiced by
the government (nonmarket imperfections) the
outcome with some delay will be the same: an
increase in the money suply will lead to an
increase in the price level.   Institutional
differences and varying degrees of intervention
in the system will produce distributional
effects and hence political stress in the
process of adjustment.
     By standard economic reasoning it follows
that the greater the uncertainty faced by the
participants in any economy the less successful
that economy will be in producing prosperity.
Uncertainty raises the cost component in
economic decisions under any regime of property
rights.
     Institutional rigidity and market
intervention are pervasive in many of the LDCs.

Such structures ensure that unanticipated changes in the money supply, and hence the price level, will have major distributional effects and will cause great political stress. The case for a stable money supply is even stronger for the LDC than for other economies. This makes it all the more surprising that our evidence indicates monetary stability has a low priority in the eyes of the central banks and treasuries of the LDC.

THE EVIDENCE

If an LDC pursues a monetarist monetary policy we would expect to observe, as a key component of that policy, relative stability in the rate of expansion of the money supply. To make the stronger case we would have to demonstrate that any observed fluctuations in the money supply were due to external forces beyond the immediate control of monetary authorities. Furthermore, we would have to demonstrate that the chosen definition of the money supply was reasonable and representative for each country. However, it can also be argued that for our purposes, the evidence of extreme fluctuations in the money supply defined as M_1 by the International Monetary Fund is itself sufficient indication that none of the LDCs examined have in the past decades attempted to follow a monetarist monetary policy. The following charts set forth the year-to-year rates of change in the money supply of a representative group of LDCs. The evidence is quite convincing and supports the conclusion that the supply of money has varied in a totally unpredictable way for the representative sample of LDCs we have chosen.

Not one LDC has been successful in attaining even the semblance of stable monetary growth.

It is possible to take each country independently and explain its monetary policy in terms of political events. An example would be a decision to increase the money supply in response to an external event such as an increase in the cost of a major import, rather than accept the inevitable adjustment to a lower standard of living. Similarly one can see the impact of other political choices such as Argentina's decision to go to war with the United Kingdom, or Ethiopia's choice of agricultural collectivization and a fight to the finish with the Eritreans. Even if we can explain every decision to deviate from a stable monetary policy in terms of political stress, we still have only a series of special cases and no general theory. Our argument is that no LDC has tried a stable monetary policy in the last two decades, and the evidence strongly supports our conclusion.

The evidence also demonstrates that although several LDCs have proclaimed from time to time that they were in the process of introducing a monetarist policy, they have either not understood what was involved or have been unable to carry through the policies they proclaimed, or they lied. We appear to have yet another example of the rule that it is what people actually do that should interest the social scientist, not what people say they will do.[11]

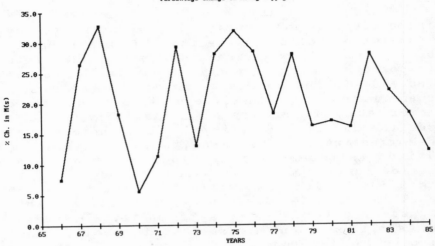

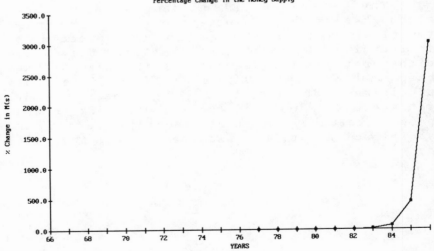

BANGLADESH
Percentage Change in the Money Supply

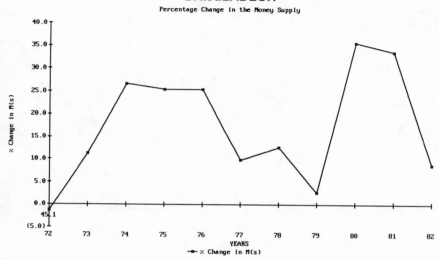

COLUMBIA
Percentage Change in the Money Supply

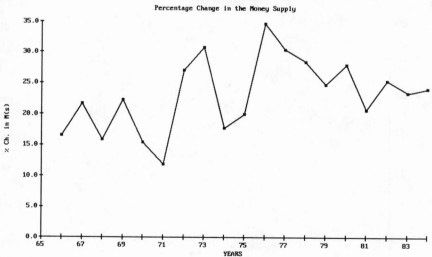

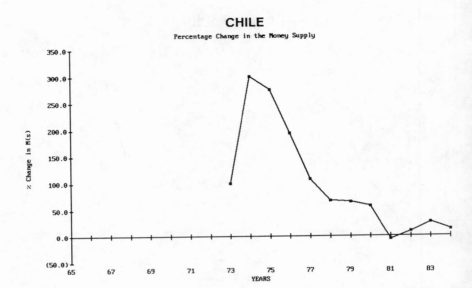

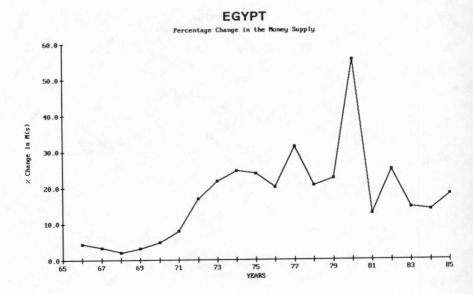

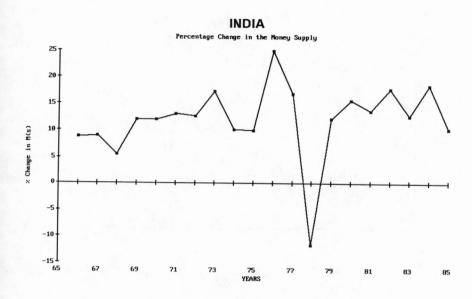

INDIA

Percentage Change in the Money Supply

INDONESIA

Percentage Change in the Money Supply

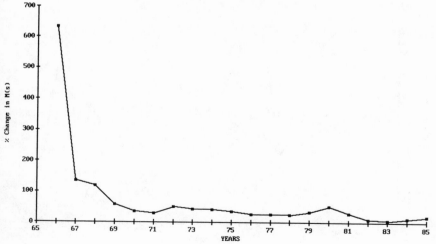

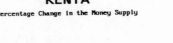

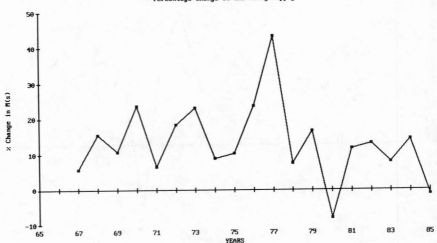

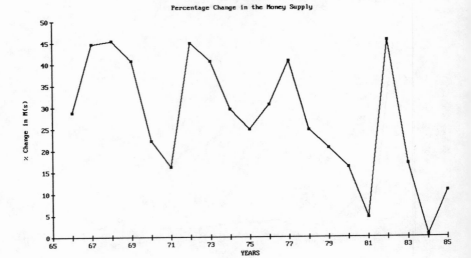

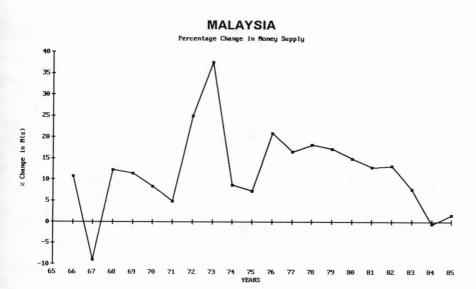

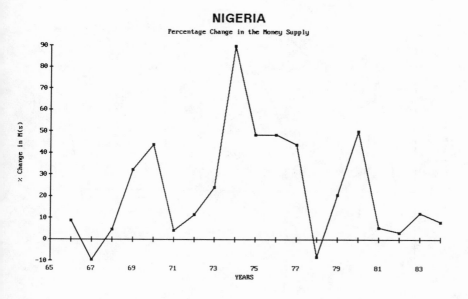

PAKISTAN
Percentage Change in the Money Supply

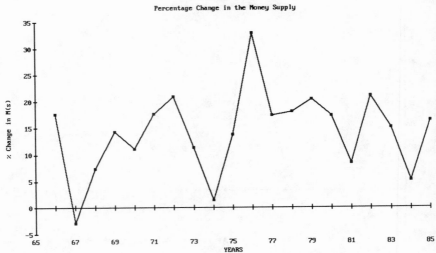

PARAGUAY
Percentage Change in the Money Supply

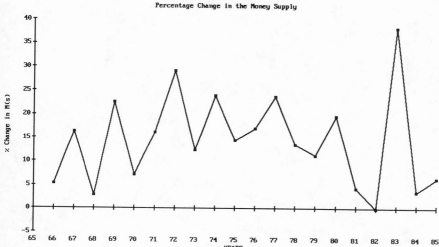

PHILIPPINES

Percentage Change in the Money Supply

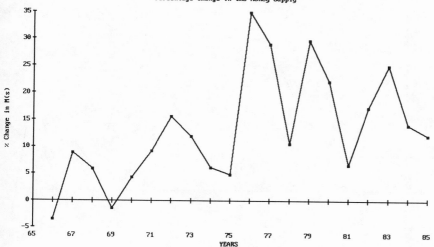

SRILANKA

Percentage Change in the Money Supply

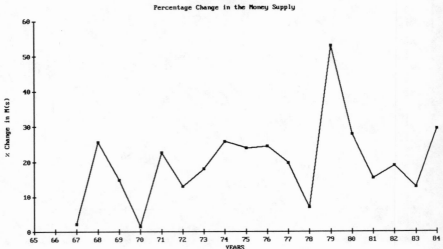

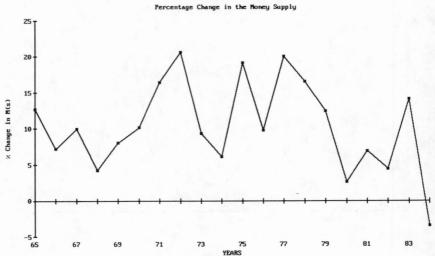

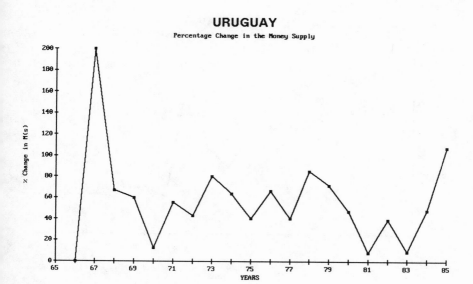

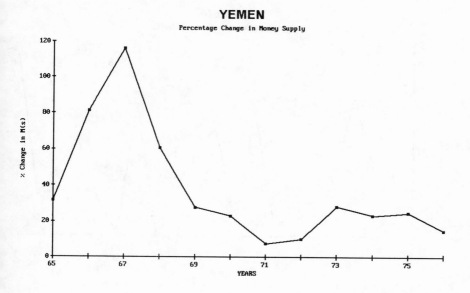

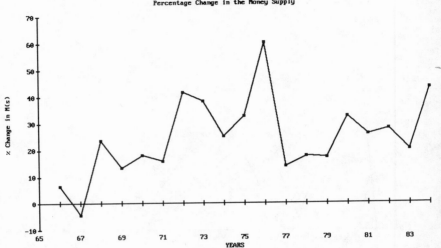

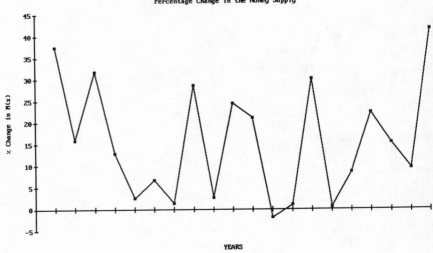

Monetary Institutions in the LDC

The plea for monetary stability has been made for both the industrialized and the LDCs (Woher, 1984, p. 115).[12] However, it has also been recognized that the institutional structure of a nation presents difficulties for detailed monetary policy in the LDCs.

> The outcome of any monetary action has always depended on the institutional structure in which the action takes place. T h e institutional structure of market economies has been and is now changing faster than ever. The impact of monetary actions is likely to continue to produce unstable and unpredictable responses (Dusenberry, 1986, p. 356)

It has been argued, with considerable force, that the recently created Central Banks of many of the LDCs have been a prime cause of much of the observed monetary instability (Ayau, 1987, p. 23). This view, which would have been considered ridiculous a short time ago, has substantial merit but is still not widely accepted (Todaro, 1985, p. 505).

In the early literature on economic development, both before and after World War II, much was made of the degree to which peasants in poor countries used money or were part of the monetary sector. This debate appears and reappears, although the evidence has consistently supported the view that the nonmonetary economy is merely an anthropological curiosa which is of little current economic significance anywhere.

Unfortunately, the debate about the existence or nonexistence of a segment of the economy which has not yet adopted the use of money is now part of the dualist rhetoric. Dualism is at best a static descriptive device. It has been rejected as a useful concept for the practical purposes of economic analysis. It is still, however, found as an explanation for continued economic failure and even as a justification for intrusive action by those in control of the government.

Of greater importance than the degree of monetarization of an LDC economy may be the degree to which rapidly changing institutional arrangements lead to instability of the monetary system.   However, the financial structures of the LDC are visibly rigid. Furthermore, there is a deep literature which records the existence and the effects of financial repression throughout the LDC.   It is, therefore, unreasonable to suggest that the observed fluctuations in the money supply have an institutional basis.

Monetary substitution, defined as the demand for foreign currenty by domestic residents, is widespread throughout the LDC (Ramirez-Rojas, 1986, pp. 35-38).   In some countries even domestic transactions are conducted in a foreign currency.   Currency substitution is a byproduct of high and erractic rates of inflation, and general monetary uncertainty.   The policy problems raised by currency substitutions are obvious: their solution requires tougher monetary measures than those which would have prevented the situation in the first place.

It has also been pointed out that the cost of currency substitution to those who practice it has been reduced by the same technical advances in communications and financial management that allow the transfer of funds at relatively lower cost than previously. Finally, there is the loss of seignorage revenue to the government that occurs where currency substitution is widespread and demand for the local currency thereby reduced.

A response to the inability of the people in control of the domestic money supply to provide a measure of disinterested restraint has been to peg the local currency to some more rationally managed currency of a major trading partner (Connolly, 1983, pp. 56-71).[13] Pegging their currency to the U.S. dollar has been tried with considerable success by those in control of some of the Latin American nations. Such pegs have worked well. Once committed to a currency peg, the risk - in terms of uncertainty and loss of confidence by the general public - of breaking a link may be considerable. Perhaps the strongest argument for a currency peg is that it is a clear signal of an intention to follow a more stable monetary supply policy in the future.

While present monetary policies continue in many of the LDCs, we will be forced to live with a situation best described in the Economist as part of a survey of the Nigerian economy:[14]

> ...smugglers get paid in cash, which is one good reason why there is so much smuggling (p. 7).

> On the broad view, Nigeria is much less seriously in debt than many other third-world countries. But the confusion of the accounts, and the inability of the ruling generals to understand accounts even if they were not confused, makes transactions with

the present regime particularly
ticklish (p. 7).

To buy dollars or sterling you need a
permit. Big orders are processed by
very senior bank officals, and
usually have to be approved by
government cabinet ministers.
Medium-sized orders pass through
the hands of middle-rank bank
officials, who may sometimes be
encountered discretely in Lagos
hotels and who happily accept cash in
plain brown envelopes. Small orders
are competed for by a swarm of market
women, commission agents and assorted
touts, shoving and jostling around
the Central Bank's street entrance
(p. 8).

Reforms are seen as a threat to those
who do very well out of the present
system (p. 11).

CONCLUSIONS

The debate about monetarism in the LDC is
a debate about the appropriateness of the
market approach to economic development. As a
practical matter the monetarist policy
prescription would require nations adopting a
monetarist strategy to follow a consistent
policy of increasing the money supply steadily
over the different stages of the business
cycle. The evidence from a representative
group of LDCs is that none have even tried to
adopt monetarism as a basis for policy.
Monetary stability is undoubtedly a desirable
condition for successful economic development.

Under the circumstances, central banks of the
LDCs may be operating perversely in their
present role, and it is reasonable to question
if their existence is necessary. If monetary
stability is to be found under present
circumstances, it may best be found in the
adoption of a system of pegging the domestic
money of an LDC to that of a major trading
nation which follows a stable policy.

NOTES

1.   We will use the acronym LDC which seems to
be the most accurate and long-surviving term
to describe the economically less successful
nations.   "Third World" is meaningless except
to include all the recipients for foreign aid,
and designations such as "poor" are politically
unacceptable.   Similarly, we will use the term
"economic development" instead of the older
terms such as economic progress, or economic
growth.

2.   "Oddly enough, among all those virulent
laissez-faire businessmen in Hong Kong it is
hard to track down any monetarist" (The
Economist, December 6, 1980, p. 24).

3.   A point being slowly recognized by
historians: Johnson (1983).

4.   See also: The Essence of Hayek, Edited by
Chiaki Nishiyama and Kurt R. Lube, with a
Foreword by W. Glenn Campbell (1984).   These
two volumes of collected papers presented at
Mont Pelerin Society Meetings represent an
excellent introduction to and synthesis of
Hayek's work.

5.   For an all-encompassing definition see:
Johri C.K. (1965, p. vii).

6.   The literature is extensive.   See, for
example, Galbis (1979).

7.   Whether a nation with a floating exchange
rate would or would not be able to pursue an
independent monetary policy in the face of
external forces has been discussed at length
since the early 1970s.   For our purposes the
issue is moot since the monetarists would not
in any case want a nation to pursue an
independent and activist monetary policy
because they see such a policy as being futile
at best and possibly damaging to the nation's
economic interests.   We will return later to
the possibility of a small country linking its
currency to that of a major trading nation and
hence accepting the monetary policies of its
larger partner.

8.   For example: Akhtar, M.A. (1974).   There
is an extensive literature on the subject.

9.   This follows from the Fisher definition of
the nominal interest rate as consisting of the
real rate plus or minus an element to account
for inflationary expectations.

10.   See Jucker-Fleetwood, (1964, pp. 26-27).

11.   The charts are based upon the percentage
change in the IMF definition of M_1 and data
from International Monetary Statistics,
Washington D.C., The International Monetary
Fund, various issues.

12.   Also see: Eshag (1983, p. 75).

13.   The argument on currency pegs follows much
of this article.

14.   See, for example: "Nigeria: Survey," The
Economist,   May   3,   1986,   pp.   7-24,   in
particular.

REFERENCES

Aghevli, Bijan B.   "Exchange Rate Policies of
Selected Asian Countries," Finance and
Development, June 1987, pp. 39-42.

Akhtar, M. A.   "The Demand for Money in
Pakistan," Pakistan Development Review: Spring
1974, pp. 40-54.

Ayau, Manual F.   "Who Needs Latin American
Central Banks? Good Question," The Wall
Street Journal, September 25, 1987, p. 23.

Connolly, Michael B.   "Optimum Currency Pegs
for Latin America," Journal of Money,
Credit and Banking 15(1): February 1983,
pp. 56-71.

Dusenberry, James S. "Financial Deregulation:
Micro and Macroeconomic Effects," Financial
Policy and Reform in Pacific Basin Countries,
edited by Hang-Sheng Chen. San Francisco: The
Federal Reserve Bank of San Francisco, 1986, p.
356.

Edwards, Sebastian.   "Monetarism in Chile,
1973-1983:   Some Economic Puzzles," Economic
Development and Cultural Change, 1986,
pp. 535-559.

The Essence of Hayek, Edited by Chiaki
Nishiyama and Kurt R. Lube, with a
Foreword by W. Glenn Campbell, Stanford,
California: The Hoover Institution Press,
Stanford University, 1984.

Galbis, Vicente. "Money, Investment, and
Growth in Latin America, 1961-1973," Economic
Development and Cultural Change: 1979,
pp. 423-443.

Johnson, Paul. Modern Times, The World from
the Twenties to the Eighties, New York: Harper
& Row Publishers, 1983.

Johri, C. K. Monetary Policy in a Developing
Economy, A Study of the Policies of the
Reserve Bank of India and Their Effects
on the Operations of the Banking System,
1956-65. Calcutta: The World Press
Private, Ltd., 1965.

Jucker-Fleetwood, Erin E. Money and Finance
in Africa, The Experience of Ghana,
Morocco, Nigeria, The Rhodesias and
Nyasaland, the Sudan and Tunisia from
the Establishment of Their Central Banks
Until 1962. London: George Allen & Unwin,
Ltd., 1964.

"Jugoslavia: Devaluation and After," The
Economist: June 14, 1980, p. 74.

Machlup, Fritz. "Hayek's Contribution to
Economics," Essays on Hayek, edited by
Fritz Machlup and with a Foreword by
Milton Friedman, New York: New York
University Press, 1976, pp. 13-59.

Paine, George. "Phillipines, Austerity Measures to Shrink the Total Import Market," Business America: March 1985, p. 34.

Ramirez-Rojas, C. L. "Money Substitution in Developing Countries," Finance and Development, June 1986, pp. 35-38.

Thirlwell, A. P. Growth and Development, with Special Reference to Developing Economies, 2nd edition, New York: John Wiley & Sons, 1977.

Todaro, Michael, P. Economic Development in the Third World, New York: Longman, 1985.

Trescott, Paul B. Thailand's Monetary Experience, The Economics of Stability, New York, Praeger Publishers, 1971.

Uri, Pierre, together with Nicholas Kaldo, Richard Ruggles and Robert Triffin, A Monetary Policy for Latin America, New York: Praeger Publishers, 1968.

Walter, Frank. "From Economic Miracle to Stagnation: The German Disease." In World Economic Growth, Case Studies of Developed and Developing Nations, edited by Arnold C. Harberger, San Francisco: ICS Press, 1984, p. 115.

COMMENTARY BY WENDELL GORDON

Professor Waters states that it is desirable that the money supply not fluctuate violently and that it increase at a reasonable pace over time. Surely those are defensible propositions. He also demonstrates, surely correctly, that there have been substantial fluctuations in the money supplies of many underdeveloped countries.

In these comments, the useful thing may be to discuss more specifically some of the implications involved in efforts to operate a policy designed to implement a constant percentage rate of increase in the money supply, the famous Milton Friedman proposal. In this setting, then, the discussion will center on problems involved in policy implementation rather than on questions concerning the desirablility of a certain state of affairs.

Friedman has alleged the desirability of a policy involving actually increasing the money supply by some percentage in the 3 or 4 percent range each year, a policy which would seem to call for some dirigisme. Professor Waters seems to oppose dirigisme, so comments about Friedman's proposal are not necessarily relevant to Professor Waters' position. However, both men seem to be in agreement in not having much use for central banks.

It is intriguing to speculate as to how the policy to effect the constant rate of

increase in the money supply would be effected,
especially if there were no central banks.   I
believe Milton Friedman once suggested, but I
cannot find the citation, that the appropriate
amount of money should be spread broadcast from
high-flying airplanes.   Perhaps it would be a
finance minister who would take the place of
the central banker and charter the high-flying
plane to distribute the money, the printing of
which would be financed by tax receipts.   It is
difficult   to   envisage   how   "well-defined
ownership and unfettered markets," the economic
arrangements Professor Waters advocates, would
handle the problem.   But it is worth a try.
      There   are   going   to   have   to   be   criteria
established   to   determine   who   will   be   the
primary   recipients   of   the   monetary   bonanza.
How   would   the   unfettered   market   handle   this
rationing problem?   Where would the rules come
from?
      Perhaps   governments   could   solve   the
problem by adopting a gold coin standard and
letting the gold miners be the beneficiaries of
the increase in the money supply.   But are we
really sympathetic with having South Africa and
the   Soviet   Union   reap   this   bonanza?   And
besides that, what natural law would assure
that the gold miners would develop new gold
production at a constant rate, even if fate
made them the beneficiaries of the process?
      Or,   in   another   scenario,   what   type   of
exercise   of   police   power   would   prevent
unfettered   businessmen   from   increasing   the
money supply freely, if money supply in the
important sense were taken to be purchasing
power? Purchasing power can be created without
a   by-your-leave   from   the   government   by   the
willingness of buyers and sellers to traffic in
IOU's.

In fact, there seems to be some historical basis for believing that paper money originally came into existence as much a result of pure private ingenuity as of government creation. Merchants with gold desposited the gold with goldsmiths for safekeeping and received receipts in exchange: gold certificates. And, depending on the credibility of the signature of the goldsmith, the gold certificates then circulated as money. But human ingenuity (goldsmith or banker ingenuity) developed a practice involving the issuance by goldsmiths of additional gold certificates (pieces of paper ostensibly representing claims on gold) to would-be borrowers in exchange for the promise of repayment of prinicipal plus interest. Of course, the goldsmith might be caught in a bind if all the holders of both types of gold certificates (those issued against deposited gold and those which were a by-product of debt creation) should present their claims on the inadequate gold supplies of the goldsmith at the same time. But if the goldsmith appraised the situation accurately enough and counted on the probability that everyone entitled to gold would not demand it at the same time, then the goldsmith could net some profit (interest) as a result of exercising the unfettered private initiative to create some increase in the money supply. The money supply was increased, business hummed, and perhaps the price lvel rose a little at the same time. Occasionally a goldsmith who overplayed his or her hand got caught and sent to jail. But historically, it seems, this did not happen often enough so that fear of being caught seriously inhibited the practice. But abuse did occur with enough frequency, so that the laments of the injured parties led to governmental regulation, some dirigisme.

Governments and kings and to-be central bankers
were happy to participate in the process and
provide the public with some protection against
private abuse. At the same time the kings and
central bankers frequently seem to have
arranged to profit from their participation in
the process, a process that occasionally saw
more money created than was desirable, and
there was consequent inflation and speculation.

     This way of viewing the matter, if there
is some substantial accuracy to it, puts things
in a somewhat different perspective. The cure
is a part of the problem. Private initiative
and unfettered markets helped create the public
regulation which is then revealed as having
some undesirable features. The ordinary
citizen, if there is such a thing, is caught
betwixt and between private business and public
behavior. Both the private and public sectors
are doing useful things, but, at the same time,
perhaps "profiting" unduly in the process, or
mismanaging the process in a manner that
untimately benefits nobody.

     For better or worse, it would seem that
unfettered private creation of the medium of
exchange is an arrangement that society will
not be, is not, willing to live with. The
reasonable response must be better regulation,
not no regulation.

     We are caught up in an ongoing learning
process, trying to work out reasonable
procedures for regulating the creation of money
and credit (medium of exchange, standard of
value, store of value, and standard of deferred
payment). And we have a long way to go, both
in the developed countries and in the
underdeveloped countries. But, however, it is
difficult to see how a system which left the
creation of money to private initiative could
work satisfactorily without some regulation.

And we have gone full circle and are back with the problem of dealing with the difficulties involved in regulation.

Let us try another approach. Money, that is to say purchasing power, is created in important degree by "private" commercial banks opening demand deposits against which borrowers can write checks. The private commercial bank is regulated to some degree, as to how much purchasing power it can create, by a central bank. The borrower may effectively use the borrowed money to expand production, in which case the creation of the new money has probably had a minimal inflationary effect and a considerable beneficient effect on the national product. On the other hand, the borrower may use the borrowed funds in an effort to corner the potato market in Arequipa, Peru. This activity will probably stimulate inflation and inhibit production. Which of these results follows depends on the interaction of the lending bank with its borrowers. If all banks over the world would effectively see to it that their loans finance useful production rather than speculation, it might be that such behavior would be enough to bring both the money creation and the inflation problems under control. Similarly those problems might be dealt with if the central banks would effectively regulate in a manner that compels commerical banks to be judicious.

Can we say more here than that this is the essence of the problem? And whether money is created with or without public regulation is not the essence of the problem. Private creation of purchasing power and government regulations can both, or either, perform their roles well or poorly.

Yet another approach: expansion of the money supply may occur because central banks

take the lead in creating a substantial
increase in the money supply without being
careful as to what the recipient of the money
will do with it. The quantity theory of money
works, and there is inflation, and the
regulatory authorities are properly blamed.
Or, out in the world of production and
business, wages may be increased as a result of
worker pressure, and the cost of raw materials
may increase for one reason or another. The
concerned producers and business people need
credit to see them through the production phase
until the goods can be sold at a profit. The
increase in the money supply may result from
banker and central banker appreciation of these
needs and their willingness to lend to help the
producers while production is going on. So, in
this case the expansion of the money supply is
not an activity conjured up by central bankers
because of their psyches but represents a
response to business needs.

Money supply increase may, on the other
hand (and this seems to be the standard
monetarist scenario), be initiated autonomously
for no good reason by central bankers, or it
may represent a response by bankers to the
needs of business. In either case the increase
in the money supply may have more or less
inflationary impact. But Milton Friedman and
Chicago monetarists seem blind to the existence
of two possibilities. For them, expansion in
the money supply is merely irresponsible,
spontaneous behavior by bankers, not a reasoned
response to the structural problems created by
the nature of the productive process.

At the end of his article Professor Waters
makes the recommendation, with regard to the
setting of foreign exchange rates, that this be
done by "the adoption of a system of pegging
the domestic money of an LDC to that of a major

trading nation that follows a stable policy."
This may well be a good idea, but it seems to
run counter to the call for dismantling
government controls, which has been one of the
author's major tenets.

For better or worse, the path that lies
before us involves an ongoing struggle to
obtain more socially responsible behavior from
both the private sector and from government
regulators. They are both going to be with us,
like death and taxes, whether we like it or
not. And it is appropriate and desirable that
it should be so.

6 DONORS, DEVELOPMENT, AND DEBT: THE ROLE OF EXTERNAL ASSISTANCE AND EXTERNAL INDEBTEDNESS

Peter Cashel-Cordo

Steven G. Craig

INTRODUCTION

Developing country (LDC) debt to the rest of the world grew at an annual rate of over 16 percent from 1973 to 1982. Debt grew as a percentage of aggregate Gross National Product (GNP) from about 18 percent to over 29 percent, representing a significant increase in the burden of debt on the developing economies. This rate of growth precipitated the international debt crisis, which has percolated continually since that time. Long-term debt of the LDC's was over $700 billion by 1985, and total debt including short-term obligations has now topped $1 trillion. Although there are many potential solutions to the debt problem, most require that the international aid agencies, such as the International Monetary Fund (IMF) and the World Bank, play a key role. Two avenues of international debt relief can be facilitated by these agencies. The most direct is that they are a source of low-interest concessional lending, thus reducing the debt service requirements of the mountain of debt. The second aspect of debt relief is potentially

of even more importance. The aid agencies may
be able to use the policy leverage available
from their lending programs to encourage LDC's
to adopt pro-growth policies. An increase in
economic growth would cause the existing debt
burden to be less onerous. If successful, the
avenue of growth would be the most desirable
solution to the debt crisis from virtually all
points of view. It is of paramount importance
to know whether the international aid agencies
are capable of fashioning a solution to the
international debt crisis. The answer to this
question depends crucially on the answer to a
second question: are the aid agencies capable
of altering the budgetary behavior of recipient
governments? Given the level of international
aid to date (it represents less than 25 percent
of the total LDC debt), it is only through
economic growth that the debt problem will be
fully resolved. Further, it is to LDC
governments that the solutions to the debt
crisis must look, as the public sector of the
LDCs has guaranteed repayment of over 80
percent of the outstanding long-term debt.
Thus the role of the aid agencies in
facilitating pro-growth policies of recipient
governments is crucial.

     This chapter examines the role of Official
Development Assistance (ODA) and its impact
upon LDC recipients. We show that an
assessment of the success or failure of ODA
depends crucially on its impact on the
recipient central government budgets. The
policy influence of the aid agencies is
determined through a detailed examination of
aid "conditionality." Conditionality is the
process by which the international aid agencies
impose policy changes on recipient governments.
The key to our assessment of the impact of aid
is that we carefully model how aid is

"filtered" through the central government budget. We demonstrate that aid may affect public sector expenditures, revenues, and budgetary surpluses or deficit. Our model is then applied to an examination of how ODA has affected the debt situation in the developing world.

Recent literature on the debt problem has primarily examined default risk and repayment problems of LDCs (see, for example, Edwards, 1984, and Hajivassiliou, 1987). One problem with this literature, however, is that debt flows are a result of other central government budgetary behavior. Some have argued, for example, that conditions imposed by the aid agencies on recipients is responsible for some of the existing debt and budgetary problems. Conversely, others have argued that only through the policy leverage represented by loan conditionality can the aid agencis guide recipients out of the mire of debt. Therefore, until the impact of foreign aid and debt on oher central government budgetary behavior is understood, little real progress can be made at fashioning workable solutions to the debt crisis. This chapter and the research we report upon here seeks to present a model that can be used to understand how the recipient central government "filter" processes aid and debt in order to ascertain the success of loan conditionality at altering recipient government behavior.

Another crucial aspect of understanding how the filter of recipient government behavior affects the impact of aid is in examination of the success of foreign aid at stimulating LDC growth (see, for example, Singh, 1985, and Mosley, 1980). These studies generally model growth as a function of government economic policies and aid. The true impact of foreign aid on growth, however, will be masked to the extent that recipient government budgetary behavior depends on foreign aid. In addition, aid conditionality varies as the proportion of aid from different donors varies, thereby affecting the degree of distortion from the omission of the important relationship. The conclusion, therefore, is that an understanding of how aid conditionality impacts recipient behavior is necessary before any analysis of the success of foreign aid can be undertaken.

Foreign debt for developing country governments is a whipsaw of good news and bad news. The advantage of foreign debt is that it alleviates some types of constraints on development, thus allowing more rapid economic growth. On the other hand, foreign debt can mortgage a country's future through debt repayments, and choke off further growth. Foreign aid loans on concessional terms are an attempt to get the good news without the bad. By making hard currency loans at favorable terms, it is hoped that growth can occur without the ensuing mortgage. From the donor's perspective, concessional aid has a further advantage which has been used to justify the economic cost to the donors. Access to resources at low interest rates may be used to obtain policy changes in recipient countries that, in the donor's view, will yield more rapid economic growth.[1] These policy changes represent the conditionality imposed by donors on recipients. Imposition of conditionality is perceived to be important by all of the major foreign aid donors, including the multilateral development banks (MDB), the International Monetary Fund (IMF), and bilateral donors participating in the Development Assistance Committee (DAC).[2] See table 6-1 for a summary of the aid donors.

The research we present here analyzes the impacts of loan conditionality on recipient LDC government behavior.[3]   We accomplish this through an analysis of how loan "strings," or conditions, alter budgetary behavior at the central government level.   In particular, we examine whether foreign aid resources supplement the public sector budget, or whether foreign aid enables the recipient to transfer its own funds from the targeted sector into other types of spending, such as defense.   A second tradeoff that may occur as a result of the receipt of loan funds is that taxes and other government revenue may drop as foreign aid funds replace local resource mobilization by the central government.   A third possible avenue of "fungibility" may occur if foreign aid loans replace hard currency loans from other sources.   If this is the case, total debt in the developing nations will not change, although interest rates may be somewhat lower. The final possibility we examine is that foreign aid actually may accomplish its purported goal.   If so, concessional terms may allow a recipient to undertake more projects and conditionality may assist recipients to redirect resources into targeted areas.   In this case aid would represent an increase in the total amount of resources available to recipients, but at a potential cost of increasing the debt burden.

The paradox of aid is that should we find that concessional foreign aid loans do represent additional resources to recipients, the total debt burden on LDC governments will increase.   Indeed, 1982 reflows to the World Bank's International Bank for Reconstruction and Development window (the "hard window")[4] have grown to such a degree that $6.4 billion in new lending disbursements only represents

$2.4 billion in net disbursements (World Bank, 1982).[5] The debt problems facing LDCs is leading some to call for a major change in the form of foreign aid. The World Bank, as well as the regional development banks, have traditionally provided project-oriented assistance where loan funds are targeted at a particular development project. In order to speed laon disbursement, some have advocated that project aid be replaced by quick disbursing program loans not tied to any particular project.[6] The analysis we present here allows a clear assessment of this policy recommendation that would considerably alter the existing form of aid conditionality.

The key to understanding what course policy should take is to determine the success of conditionality. Aid donors have long grappled with how to measure the impact of loan conditionality, with little success.[7] The basic measure continues to be anecdotal evidence, with which it is difficult to justify the considerable effort that project-oriented lending requires. Further, there has been little assessment of the budgetary impact associated with the conditionality imposed by IMF program lending. Given the furor that has accompanied IMF loan conditionality, this omission is in desperate need of redress. In this chapter we propose, for the first time to our knowledge, to measure the success of loan conditionality through an examination of the budgetary behavior of the central government of recipients.

In order to undertake an analysis of loan conditionality, we examine aid from each of the separate donors to account for differences in loan strings. The multilateral development banks (MDB's) primarily engage in project-oriented assistance (see table 6-1). Working through the government sector, project aid generally requires specific cost-sharing arrangements with recipient governments. We examine whether the cost-sharing provisions are successful at directing new resources into the targeted area. The second donor we examine is the IMF. While not engaged in development assistance exclusively, the IMF has been central at maintaining or restoring the creditworthiness of borrowers.[8] Of special interest here is that the conditionality usually imposed by the IMF is the opposite to that required by the MDBs, in that the IMF generally requires recipients to reduce spending and debt levels. The third group of donors we examine are the bilateral donors as a group. Aid provided by bilateral agencies is most often project assistance.[9] While the conditions imposed by bilateral donors varies widely, the cost-sharing and other requirements are usually less stringent than those of the MDBs.

The budgetary model we develop examines five avenues of aid fungibility, through an analysis of different aspects of central government budgets of recipients. The five equations we estimate are: nondefense central government expenditure, defense expenditure, taxes, revenue other than taxes, and other foreign debt flows. We determine the impact of aid on each of these categories of the public sector budget. This analysis determines how the aid strings, as they differ by donor, impact public sector behavior. An important attribute of this analysis is that the actual behavior may differ substantially from the professed behavior by recipients.

This chapter presents the model of the public sector budget. An important aspect of this model is the examination of aid as a resource transfer, and a model of how aid strings might be expected to impact the budget. The data we use in the empirical analysis follow in the section entitled "Data Description and Estimation Procedures." These data represent 40 countries over the period 1975-1980. The results of the analysis show that foreign aid strings are crucial in determining recipient response to aid. In particular, we find that project-oriented aid by the MDBs engender relatively large expenditure responses by recipients. Only highly constrained IMF aid, however, has been successful at reducing debt levels of recipients. We thus find that if aid donors alter the structure of the assistance they provide, the types of strings that accompany new aid will determine whether it is successful at achieving its objective.

A MODEL OF AID AND ITS STRINGS

Aid Strings and Fungibility

One of the central debates concerning foreign assistance is over the form of aid. Table 6-1 summarizes the structure of foreign aid. The choices facing the aid community are to offer project-oriented assistance, such as is typically offered by the MDBs, or to offer loans called "balance of payments support" or "structural adjustment." These latter types of loans carry very different types of strings attached to the use to which the loan funds may be applied. This chapter will not settle the debate about whether project loans or lump sum loans are preferable, but will offer important input into the debate by examining the budgetary impact of both types of assistance.

This section develops the theoretical expectations about what budgetary changes might be expected from the two forms of aid.[10]
In order theoretically to model the impact that loan strings might have on recipient governments, we use a model borrowed from the public finance literature on fiscal federalism (see Gramlich, 1977). The multilateral development banks (MDBs) primarily distribute project specific aid. In other words, aid is for specific development projects, and is only disbursed as the project is implemented. This type of aid corresponds to what is called closed-end matching aid. The recipient government is required, as a condition of the foreign aid loan, to contribute significant portions of the total project cost. The recipient is, therefore, required to match each dollar of foreign aid with a certain amount of contributed funds. The rate of the required match varies with the donor; typical rates are that recipients contribute about 50 percent of total project costs for IDA loans (a matching rate of 1 to 1), and about 25 percent of total project costs for IBRD loans (a matching rate of 1 to 3) (NAC). The reason the loan is closed-end matching is that the funds are matched only up to the total loan commitment.
Figure 6-1 illustrates the expected change in behavior by the recipient. The loan restrictions cause the budget constraint faced by the recipient government to have a "kink" at point A, where the matching funds are exhausted. Effectively, the recipient government must expend funds to reach this point to receive all of the committed loan funds. The question we wish to address is whether the change in targeted expenditure is greater than what would occur in the absence of project lending.

        The budget constraint shifts out, assuming
present   discounted   values,   by   the   "grant
element" (see IDA) of the loan after repayment.
In the absence of constraints caused by the
loan   strings,   expenditure   in   the   targeted
category   would   increase   by   only   an   amount
indicated by an income effect. If this amount
is   less   that   the   constrained   amount   as
represented by point B, the loan strings have
effectively   increased   recipient   government
spending in the targeted sector. On the other
hand,   if   the   pure   income   effect   would   have
increased targeted spending to a point like
point C, then the loan strings would not have
been successful at altering recipient behavior,
and   lump   sum   lending   could   presumably   have
accomplished   the   same   thing   at   less
administrative cost.

        This theory, however, does not completely
capture the entire story. Assume for a moment
that   the   loan   strings   would   normally   be
successful   at   altering   recipient   expenditure
patterns, that is, that the recipient would
most prefer a point such as point B even though
it   is   required   to   achieve   point   A.   The
incentive for the recipient is to attempt to
cause the loan funds to be "fungible."   That
is, if the recipient can fulfill the loan
covenants and spend less than its required
matching component, then the government could
achieve a spending pattern such as at B.   This
is only possible, however, if the recipient can
"fool"   the   donor   into   believing   that
expenditures that it would normally make anyway
are part of the required matching funds.   By
this bureaucratic ruse the recipient could
evade   the   matching   requirements   and   reduce
expenditure in the targeted sector, and instead
spend some of the now fungible funds elsewhere
in the budget. (See Craig and Inman (1982) for
an analysis of this process using federal to
state aid in the United States).

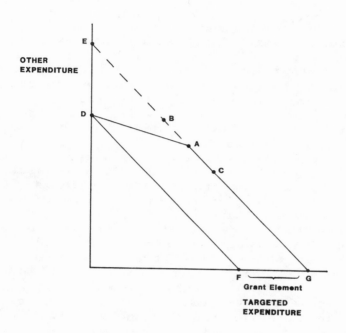

**OTHER
EXPENDITURE**

E

D

B

A

C

F   Grant Element   G

**TARGETED
EXPENDITURE**

**Figure 1: Closed–End
Matching Project Aid**

**DF–original budget constraint
DAG–closed–end matching funds budget constraint
EG–lump sum budget constraint**

The model we present in this chapter is
able to answer the bottom line question of the
efficacy of loan restrictions. In other words,
our budget model will measure the extent to
which loan proceeds are fungible in the
recipient budget. The source of fungibility
can be ascertained by examining the impact of
foreign aid funds in different sectors of the
central government budget. If the cause of
fungibility is successful evasion of loan
restrictions when desired expenditure is at a
point like point B in figure 6-1, then we will
observe that the now released foreign aid funds

find an outlet in other aspects of the central
government budget, such as defense expenditures
or tax relief.[11] On the other hand, if the
income effect of a loan is sufficient to move
desired expenditure beyond the minimum required
by the donor such as a point like C, then all
of the loan proceeds as well as the required
matching funds will be spent in the targeted
sector.   In this case, the cause of extra
expenditure may be somewhat clouded in that it
may be caused by implicit matching requirements
contained in sectoral policy reforms rather
than simply a desire by the recipient to
increase expenditure.[12]

     The budgetary model we present measures
fungibility through an examination of different
sectors of the central government budget.   In
particular, because the form of aid from
different donors varies, we can examine
alternative behavioral responses by the central
government recipient.   There are two general
classes of aid that generate recipient
response.   The model illustrated in figure 6-1
basically captures the expected impact of MDB
project-oriented lending.   A further important
behavioral relation is the impact of aid on
debt.   In particular, lending originated by the
IMF is, in part, targeted toward debt problems
and debt relief.   One expansion of the model
presented in figure 6-1 is to look for similar
behavioral response with regard to changes in
the level of debt.   If foreign aid is simply a
replacement for other sources of debt finance,
no debt relief will be provided.
Alternatively, if IMF aid is truly successful
(from the donor's perspective), a reduction in
debt levels will be observed.

     There are two types of MDB loans, direct
and bypass.   Direct loans are those made
directly to the central government.   Virtually

all lending from the soft loan window of the MDBs is direct lending. In addition, a significant percentage (about 40 percent) of hard loan lending also is direct lending. On the other hand, the bulk of hard window lending bypasses the central government, and is granted to local agencies such as state governments or autonomous government enterprises. Nonetheless bypass lending may have important central government budgetary impact, as the central government is fully informed about bypass lending due to the loan guarantee it must provide. Both direct and bypass loans have considerable explicit cost-sharing requirements on recipient governments.

Bilateral donors typically provide aid with considerably fewer strings than the MDBs (see OECD). This aid is country-to-country, and the structure of aid varies between donors. Some bilateral aid is direct and some is bypass. While the terms of bilateral lending also vary considerably between donors, bilateral grants comprise a large portion of bilateral aid, and allow us to examine the differential impact between loans and grants as to the ability of donors to alter recipient budgetary behavior.[13]

A final category of aid that we examine is debt service expenditure. Of course debt service is not aid, but represents repayments of interest and principal. Debt service expenditure is a form of negative categorical aid in the sense that it is expenditure dedicated to a specific target. Past decisions determine the level of debt service expenditure, so debt service is exogenous to current budgetary decisions. The budgetary impact of debt service expenditures is of crucial importance in examining how repayment difficulties affect other sectors of the

economy. Analyses of debt repayment problems
(Edwards, 1984; Hajivassiliou, 1987) have
ignored how debt repayments might alter
government behavior. Given the attention that
aid donors have paid to central government
recipient policies, this area appears to
deserve some attention. Further, examination
of debt service allows a test of how
categorical exogenous expenditure with no cost-
sharing requirements (as opposed to project-
oriented foreign aid) impacts governmental
expenditure.

The International Monetary Fund is the
other multilateral source of financing for
LDCs. Unlike the MDBs, IMF loans generally are
not tied to specific investment projects. IMF
loans on the surface do not require explicit
cost-sharing from recipients. There is a set
of conditions on IMF loan aid, however, in the
form of policy changes required of the central
government. The policy changes may involve a
significant restructuring of the public sector
budget. IMF aid is a form of closed-end
matching aid because to receive the fixed
amount of loan aid, the recipient may be
required to reallocate a certain amount of own
funds in addition to requirements on how the
IMF funds are used. The difference between
this form of aid and MDB lending is that
expenditure reductions may be required as a
means of relieving a debt problem. While
explicit matching requirements are not
available, an indication of the severity of the
matching requirements can be obtained from the
model. This is because the conditionality of
IMF lending varies depending on which "loan
facility" is the source of the IMF funds. The
sources of funding that are most restrictive as
to how recipients use the funds are the
supplemental financing facility and the

extended facility. Funds granted under ordinary tranche policies have lower conditionality attached to the release of the loan dollars. Special facilities, such as the oil and buffer stock facilities, may have special conditions attached and so the impact of these funds is tested separately (IMF Survey, 1979, 1985). In all cases, however, IMF aid goes directly to the central government. If the use to which funds from the different facilities are put varies, the degree to which recipient countries resist IMF terms can be determined.

THE BUDGETARY MODEL

Structural models of central government spending would be the most desirable method for examining the impact of foreign aid on central government expenditure and debt (see, for example, Shepsle, 1979). Indeed the major papers that have previously examined the impact of foreign aid (Heller, 1975; Mosley, 1987) use a structural model that explicitly states how government expenditure is determined. The process of how governments make budgetary choices, however, is not yet well understood. There is a broad array of models to choose from, but all have well-known disadvantages. In order to avoid these problems, we use a reduced form framework to model the budgetary process.

Existing structural models of government behavior start from a specified objective function. Heller, for example, assumes the government is maximizing the welfare of a typical individual. This procedure has several obvious problems. Even assuming a democracy, voters are not presented with the opportunity

to vote on every expenditure decision.
Instead, they are given an occasional choice to
vote for a representative in the governing
process. The objectives and constraints of
this representative are generally not
equivalent to what the voters would actually
desire. In the case of LDCs, moreover, many
countries do not use a democratic process to
even choose the participants in the governing
process. Even in a dictatorship, however,
different coalitions have some say over the
policies that eventually result. Similarly,
coalitions exist and may have disproportionate
power even in democratic societies. We,
therefore, use a reduced form model that
attempts to statistically capture some of the
factors that would influence the relative
strength of the various coalitions in the
ruling process. Craig and Inman (1986) develop
a model of how coalition strength may be
captured by a vector of economic structure and
demographic variables. The reduced form
framework, it should be noted, does not allow
specific meaning to be attached to any one of
the individual structural or demographic
variables. Instead, the vector of variables
hopefully will account for the relevant
differences in expenditure decisions. In
addition, however, we econometrically allow the
choice process in various countries to vary.

The variables that we use to capture the
forces that shape the level of central
government expenditures include: the per
capita income of the country, the structure of
the economy (such as the proportion of the
labor force engaged in agriculture or
industry), and the socio-demographic makeup of
the population. Inclusion of these factors is
consistent with models of preference
aggregation. In addition, however, public

expenditure depends on the level and form of outside aid that is available.

We specify the model of government expenditure to capture the differential effects of foreign aid loans and grants on the budgets of recipient countries. The model of debt determination is presented in part C below. Four equations capture the budgetary model, representing nondefense public expenditure (PUBEX), defense expenditure (DEX), tax revenue (TAX), and total own current revenue (REV). Each of these equations has as explanatory variables the economic structure of the economy, sociodemographic variables, population, a price deflator, and foreign aid from the different donors.

$$(6.1)$$

$$\left.\begin{matrix} \text{PUBEX} \\ \text{DEX} \\ \text{TAX} \\ \text{REV} \end{matrix}\right\} = \begin{matrix} f(\text{DIRECT, BY PASS, HIMF, LIMF, COMIMF,} \\ \text{BLOAN, GRANT, DSV, Structure,} \\ \text{Demographics, POP, DEFL)} \end{matrix}$$

where all expenditure variables are in per capita real dollars. DIRECT is the level of multilateral development bank loans made directly to the central government, BYPASS is the level of MDB lending that is made to lower level governmental entities, HIMF is IMF

lending with high conditionality, LIMF is IMF
lending with low conditionality, COMIMF is IMF
commodity aid, BLOAN is the level of bilateral
loans from DAC countries, and BGRANT is the
level of DAC country bilateral grants (see
Table 6-1). DSV is the level of debt service
payments and is treated as a negative grant.
The variables that comprise Structure are:[14]
the percentage of the population which works in
manufacturing (MAN), the percentage of the
population engaged in agriculture (AG) (with
services as the excluded sector), and the
percentage of the population that lives in
urban areas (URB). The variables which
comprise the socio-demographic variables are:
per capita real income (INC), the percentage of
the population under 14 years old (YNG), the
percentage of the population over 65 years old
(OLD), the population density (POPDEN), life
expectancy (LIFEX), the infant mortality rate
(INFM), the percentage of school age children
in primary (PRIM) and secondary (SECD) schools,
the labor force participation rate (LAB), and
the percentage of females in the labor force
(FEMLAB). Population (POP) is included to
capture potential scale effects, and the price
deflator (DEFL) captures potential price
effects.
        The marginal effect of an aid dollar
depends on the structure of the ODA loan.
Consider first the impact of the closed end
matching programs represented by DIRECT
lending. An increase of $1.00 in MDB Direct
loans potentially can cause much larger
expenditure changes than anticipated from
simply a $1.00 transfer directly to the central
government. This is because the government is
required to match the foreign aid with its own
funds, at the explicit matching rate m, in
order to qualify for the loan. Further, there

may be a required policy change as a condition for receiving the loan. This conditionality may generate additional expenditures, and constitutes an implicit matching requirement. Conversely, due to the potential fungibility of aid funds, there may be an offset of own resources the central government would otherwise have spent in the sector. This offset represents a dilution of the intended effects of aid, as funds which would have been spent in the target sector are moved elsewhere. The parameter β is defined to combine the two effects; the implicit matching requirement and the offset effect. If aid stimulates increases in government spending beyond m (low fungibility of aid), β will be estimated to be positive. On the other hand, if the offset effect dominates the implicit matching requirement (a high degree of fungibility), β will be negative. In the special case where aid has no impact on government expenditure, β will equal $-(1 + m)$, indicating that all of the aid dollars are fungible. The partial effect of Direct MDB aid on recipient spending is therefore:

$$\frac{\alpha PUBEX}{\alpha DIRECT} = \$1.00 + m + \beta \qquad (6.2)$$

where the \$1.00 is the direct receipt of the aid funds, m is the (closed-end) required matching funds, and β is the offset parameter.

The impact of bypass loans from MDBs is similar to that of direct loans, with the important exception that bypass loans are not received by the central government. Therefore the explicit matching funds, m, and any implicit matching funds must be supplied by the lower level governmental agency. This is because the lower level agency is the recipient of the foreign aid. The effect on the central government of bypass loans therefore reduces to exclusively the offset effect: $\partial PUBEX/\partial \beta ypass$ = β.   If the national government makes significant transfers to the lower level agency an offset may occur, because the national government will reduce its transfers when the lower level agency receives the foreign aid resources. Conversely, in order to assist the lower level agency in obtaining the needed matching funds, the central government may increase transfers to the lower level agency, resulting in a positive estimate of the offset parameter.

IMF lending has a similar impact to MDB lending, in the sense that there is an explicit and an implicit matching component to the loan program. Unlike the MDBs, however, the IMF does not make the explicit matching rate known. Thus while equation (6.2) describes the budgetary impact of an IMF program, we are not able to identify $\underline{m}$ from β. The estimates will, therefore, represent the combination of the matching and offset effects. Because high conditionality facilities, such as the supplementary and the extended fund facilities, have greater explicit matching requirements, recipients would be expected to be less willing to request loans from these sources. The IMF may therefore have greater leverage with the high conditionality facilities, as the recipients are willing to pay a higher "price" for the loan funds when they are requested. Our expectation therefore is that HIMF funds will exhibit a greater impact on the central government budget than will LIMF funds. In any case, the estimated budgetary impact will provide, for the first time, an estimate of the impact of IMF conditionality on central government fiscal behavior.

One important difference between MDB lending and IMF lending is that the direction of any implicit matching requirements may be different. This occurs because the IMF may impose austerity measures on the central government, requiring a reduction, rather than an increase, in expenditure. The question the empirical work can answer is where in the budget the IMF conditions manifest themselves. The relation described by equation (6.2) also exists in the other expenditure and revenue equations of the model. Thus we can estimate whether IMF lending causes changes in spending, revenue, or deficits and debt.

In using equation (6.2) to examine the impact of debt service, we will be able to estimate the implicit offset parameter that characterizes internal budgetary decisions. Since there are no matching requirements ($\underline{m}$ = 0), the question is where in the public sector budget are the needed funds for debt service obtained. The possibilities include decreases in public expenditure or defense, or increases in revenue.

THE SURPLUS DEFICIT MODEL

The impact of foreign aid on debt can be examined by using the budget constraint of the central government. The budget constraint relates revenue from all sources, including aid, to expenditures. The residual from the budget constraint is the budget surplus (or deficit). The composition of the deficit is of interest as it can be financed by international borrowing or from internal sources. The budget constraint is:

$$\begin{aligned}
\text{PUBEX} + \text{DEX} = \ & \text{TAX} + \text{ORV} - \text{DSV} + & (6.3)\\
& \text{DIRECT} + \text{HIMF} + \text{LIMF} +\\
& \text{COMIMF} + \text{BLOAN} +\\
& \text{BGRANT} + \text{SURP(DEF)}
\end{aligned}$$

where ORV equal other revenue, so that TAX plus ORV equals total own source revenue, REV. DSV is indicated as negative revenue consistent with our depiction of DSV as negative aid. As modelled in equation (6.2), the two expenditure variables (PUBEX and DEX) and the two revenue variables (TAX and REV) are the endogenous variables, while DSV and aid are exogenously determined. SURP(DEF) denotes the budgetary surplus or deficit that results after the initial budgetary allocations. We further model the choice of the central government in how the resulting surplus or deficit is financed:

$$\begin{aligned}
\text{DEBT} = \ & f(\text{DIRECT, BYPASS, HIMF,} & (6.4)\\
& \text{LIMF, COMIMF, BLOAN,}\\
& \text{BGRANT, DSV, Structure,}\\
& \text{Demographics, POP, DEFL})
\end{aligned}$$

where DEBT is the change in disbursed real foreign debt per capita, and the other variables are as defined previously. This equation has the exact same form as equation (6.1). The advantage of modelling changes in debt with this form is that we can assess the fungibility of aid on other debt flows in the same way as modelling the fungibility of aid on expenditure. This allows a test for whether foreign aid displaces borrowing from other sources, whether foreign aid represents additional resources to the recipient governments, or whether aid exacerbates the debt problems of LDC recipients.

DATA DESCRIPTION AND ESTIMATION PROCEDURE

The fiscal impact of foreign aid is estimated from revenue and expenditure data for a sample of 40 countries for the years 1975-1980 (see Appendix I for details). All financial data are converted to real U.S. dollars per capita. Foreign aid information was collected from three sources, which necessitated several modifications to the model presented in (6.1)

Multilateral development bank aid is divided into two components based upon how it is targeted internally within the recipient country. Bypass lending is primarily (over 90 percent) provided by the hard window of the MDBs. Lending directly to the central government is composed of about 60 percent soft window lending and with the remainder from the hard window (NAC).[15]

One problem with the MDB data is that hard and soft window lending is only available on a loan commitment basis, and not on a disbursement basis. In order to avoid potential simultaneous equation bias, as well as to better model actual financial flows, MDB commitments are therefore lagged six years.[16] The impact of a given loan can be discerned by adding the coefficients over the six lagged periods. Note that current commitments are omitted. The sum of these six coefficients represents the budgetary impact of about 90 percent of the total loan commitment, reflecting the fact that on average 90 percent of a loan is disbursed within six years of commitment.[17]

ODA loan and grant data from individual DAC countries to LDC recipients are available annually from the OECD (various). These data represent disbursements to a country, and categorize assistance as ODA if a loan has more than a 25 percent grant component.[18] This captures all concessional, or soft, aid. During the high interest late 1970s, however, some aid given as ODA was not classified as such by the OECD system. Thus it appears that bilateral aid more closely resembles soft loan multilateral aid, but it may contain some hard loan aid as well. Data on bilateral grants are also available, which include outright grants and local currency loans.

IMF loans are broken into three categories, based upon the degree of conditionality that the IMF imposes as a requirement for disbursing the loan. Drawings under the ordinary credit tranche policies of the IMF require the recipient to adopt certain economic policies that should alleviate relatively short-term balance of payments difficulties. These loans are primarily from the first credit tranche, and are classified as low conditionality (LIMF). Most drawings above the first credit tranche, however, require extended terms or supplemental resources. The goal of loans under the extended or supplemental facility are to stimulate fundamental policy reform to correct structural economic imbalances. IMF requirements are considered to be more severe than under ordinary IMF policies, and loans from these sources are therefore classified as high conditionality (HIMF). The oil and buffer stock facilities, as well as the compensatory financing facility, are considered as aids for temporary imbalances. Although these commodity facilities (COMIMF) have relatively low levels of conditionality, we separate them from LIMF because the problems to which these facilities

are targeted differ from those of the ordinary
credit tranche policies. All of the IMF data
are available from the IFS (annual) on a
disbursement basis.

The exogenous socioeconomic variables are
from the World Bank Atlas (1976, 1980, 1983),
as are the public expenditure data. As
discussed previously, the socioeconomic
variables cannot be expected to account fully
for the structural differences between
countries. Pooling test of the regressions to
test for statistical differentiation by region
and by time indicate that this supposition
holds. Therefore, Least-Squares Dummy
Variables (LSDV) is employed to estimate the
model. This regression technique uses a dummy
variable for each country and year in the
pooled regression to control for fixed effects,
and significantly improves the efficiency of
the estimates (Baltagi, 1981).[19]

ESTIMATION RESULTS OF THE BUDGET AND DEBT MODEL

Five equations are estimated using the
LSDV technique. Corresponding to the set of
equations in (6.1), there are two expenditure
relations: nondefense public expenditure
(PUBEX) and defense expenditure (DEX).
Additionally, we also estimate two revenue
equations: taxes (TAX) and total own current
revenue (REV). The difference between the two
revenue measures represents user charges and
transfers from other local agencies. Following
equation (6.4) we estimate changes in disbursed
foreign currency debt (DEBT) leaving internal
budgetary surplus and deficits as the residual
to be calculated through the budget constraint
presented in equation (6.3). The variable

definitions, means, and standard deviations are
presented in Appendix I.

The estimation results shed important new
insight into how foreign aid is filtered
through the public sector of the recipient
central government to determine expenditure,
revenue, and changes in debt levels. Table 6-2
presents the model estimates showing the impact
of aid on the public sector budget and debt
flows, while Appendix II contains the estimated
coefficients of the remaining variables. In
general, the parameter estimates from our model
show that the type and degree of conditionality
crucially determines the budgetary response to
the receipt of aid.

Table 6-3 uses the estimation results to
analyze the impact of aid on debt flows and
internal budget surpluses and deficits. In
general, the structure of foreign assistance to
LDCs is found to be the central component for
determining the ultimate impact on the public
sector budget. Thus there is a significant
degree of information provided to those who
would use these results to debate the merits of
aid conditionality. We first discuss the
impact of aid on central government
expenditures and revenues. The impact of aid
strings is discussed in more detail in Cashel-
Cordo and Craig (1987), and is only presented
briefly here. The remaining portion of the
discussion, therefore, focuses on the
behavioral impact of aid and debt service on
both internal and external debt levels.

AID IMPACTS ON EXPENDITURE AND REVENUES

Looking first at direct MDB aid, the
results in Table 6-2 show that a $1.00 increase
in direct aid causes a statistically

significant increase of $2.37 in public
expenditures. Allowing for the fact that the
six-year lag in commitments accounts for about
90 percent of loan disbursements, this implies
a $2.63 increase in expenditure over the life
of the loan. Since direct aid is composed 60
percent by soft loan aid and 40 percent by hard
loan aid, assume the explicit matching rate is
1.8, (the matching rate for soft aid is 50
percent, and for hard aid is 25 percent).
Using equation (6.2), we see that the total
increase in expected expenditure is $2.80
(equals $1.00 of aid plus $1.80 in recipient
matching funds). Thus all of the actual loan
funds plus $1.63 of local matching funds are
spent in the public sector budget. Only $.17
of the required expenditure is diverted into
other sectors of the public sector budget.
There is no significant increase estimated to
occur in public revenues, meaning that the
matching funds are not generated by local tax
efforts. The discussion below examines how
these matching funds are acquired through
public sector deficit accounts.

The estimation results concerning bypass
aid are somewhat different reflecting the
different degree and type of conditionality
attached to this form of aid. Bypass aid is
not granted to the central government, but to a
lower level agency. Nonetheless, the central
government is well informed about the level of
bypass aid since it is the guarantor of the
loan. Although imprecisely estimated, public
expenditure is found to increase by $1.59 for
each dollar of bypass aid granted to a local
agency. In addition, public sector revenues
are found to fall by $2.48 (primarily, at
marginal significance levels, through
reductions in taxes). Evidently, the central
government is attempting to provide the local

agency with the matching funds required as a
condition for receipt of the loan (see Cashel-
Cordo and Craig, 1987, for further discussion
of this issue).   If local agencies (such as
state governments) increase their taxes as the
central government lowers them, and if the
expenditure increase by the central government
corresponds to increased grants-in-aid, then
the total increase in funds to the lower level
agency is $4.07 (1.59 in grants plus $2.48 in
revenue).   Because bypass aid is virtually
entirely made up of hard window funds, the
matching funds required by the local agency are
$3.00.   Thus it appears that like direct aid,
bypass aid is successful at altering the
expenditure patterns of recipients.   The
primary difference, however, is that the
required expenditure is generated from public
sector revenue in the case of bypass aid, while
direct aid appears to leave the public sector
with a considerable revenue shortfall.
      Lending by the IMF has quite a different
impact on the public sector budgets of
recipients, consistent with the different
purported goals of the donors.   The base case
of IMF budgetary conditionality is represented
by lending under ordinary credit tranche
policies, LIMF.   The empirical results show
that an additional dollar of LIMF aid reduces
public sector revenues (at marginal levels of
significance) by $1.58, almost entirely
composed of cuts other than taxes.   The
estimated expenditure increase, while $.70, is
not significant.   Thus it appears that LIMF aid
is used to fund reductions in public sector
revenues without corresponding expenditure
reductions.   As discussed further below, LIMF
aid may be exacerbating recipient budget
difficulties by substituting foreign debt for
internally generated revenue.

HIMF lending, on the other hand, appears to contain significantly more strings on the uses to which it may be put. There is no estimated reduction in public sector revenues, but public expenditure is estimated to fall by a statistically significant $1.68. The stringent austerity programs that the IMF is famous for imposing on recipients is evident. The austerity program imposed by the IMF with HIMF funds is in stark contrast to the low conditionality funds as represented by LIMF aid.

The use of commodity aid (COMIMF) appears to be closer to that of LIMF consistent with the relatively low level of conditionality. The difference from LIMF is the COMIMF funds are found to significantly reduce public expenditures by $.77 for each $1.00 of aid. Public sector revenues, however, fall by a statistically significant $1.88 (composed mostly of tax cuts). While the public sector shrinks under a COMIMF program, IMF funds are still found to be used to fund public sector deficits. Only in this case, however, are defense expenditures also found to fall (by $.23). Thus the total public sector deficit that needs to be funded is $.88 (revenue reductions of $1.88 versus expenditure cuts of $.77 + $.23 in defense).

Bilateral aid is more difficult to categorize because of the heterogenous loan structure used by different country donors. The negative impact found on expenditures of $1.38 for BLOAN possibly indicates that a significant amount of bilateral loan aid bypass the central government. Under this interpretation, the central government is offsetting local agency receipt of aid with corresponding cuts in government transfers. No revenue reductions are estimated to occur,

indicating the central government has an
increase in funds at its disposal. The bypass
interpretation is consistent with the results
found for bilateral grants. No expenditure or
revenue changes are estimated to occur, meaning
bilateral grants serve as a substitute for
other sources of financing.

In order to emphasize the importance of
aid strings, we have also presented the
estimation results of debt service payments.
Debt service offsets other public sector
expenditure, where the point estimate is a
significant $1.03 reduction for each $1.00 in
debt service expenditure. Revenue is not
estimated to increase to pay for debt service.
Thus it appears that central governments prefer
to alter expenditure rather than revenue when
such a choice is possible. Further, the
defense expenditures appear to be relatively
isolated from other impacts on the central
government budget. Also of note is that debt
service expenditures are not found to decrease
public sector debt (the estimate of $.03 is
insignificant). Even before the debt crises of
the 1980's, LDC borrowers were not able to make
appreciable headway on their debt levels.

AID IMPACT ON PUBLIC SECTOR DEFICITS AND DEBT

Table 6-3 uses the estimates from the
model to examine more fully the impact of aid
on internal and external debt flows. The first
column summarizes the estimated impact on
expenditure and revenue using the point
estimates from table 6-2. For example,
expenditure is found to increase $2.37 for each
dollar of direct aid while defense expenditure
falls by $.09. This net increase in public
expenditure of $2.28 is offset by $.06 in

revenue increases, leaving the central
government with a shortfall of $2.22 (2.37-
.09 + .06). This value represents the budget
surplus (deficit) which either contributes to a
reduction (or an increase) in debt. The second
column of table 6-3 shows the expected change
in foreign debt disbursed as a result of
receipt of an additional dollar of aid. Note
that bypass aid is treated like direct lending.
This is because our debt measure is public and
public guaranteed debt. The third column
reports the estimated coefficients from the
debt flow equation reported in table 6.2. Note
that these estimates should include the change
due to official aid. Column four finds the net
change in borrowing from nonofficial sources
(or from governments where the loan is not
classified as ODA). The final column finds the
residual budget surplus or deficit that the
central government must finance from internal
sources.

Aid from the MDBs, both direct and bypass,
is found to offset to a large extent lending
from other sources. Direct aid reduces other
debt flows by $.89 per $1.00 of aid, while
bypass aid shows a $.78 reduction. In both
cases, significant internal deficits remain to
be financed. One implication of these results
is that changing the nature of MDB project
lending in order to provide loans with no
strings attached will not significantly alter
the debt picture, as most project assistance
appears to offset other borrowing. An
important caveat to this conclusion, however,
is shown by the impact of project assistance on
public sector internal deficits.

One of the important concerns that has
been expressed about MDB project aid in
particular is the problem of recurrent costs
(Jennings, 1983). The argument is that by

exclusively funding capital projects, the MDBs
cause budgetary problems later when recipients
attempt to finance operations and maintenance
after the construction phase. Evidence
pertaining to this point is provided by the
estimates in table 6.2 concerning debt service.
We find that debt service expenditures are not
financed by revenue increases, but exclusively
through decreases in public sector expenditure.
The analysis here does not completely address
the cause of the recurrent cost problem, but
does show that the attractiveness of MDB
project lending may lead recipient governments
to overextend themselves. Thus changing the
conditionality of project-oriented aid to forms
with less strings might alter the deficit
picture of LDC recipients. In any case,
however, the power of loan strings is shown by
the large changes in public spending patterns
in response to changes in foreign assistance.
The empirical evidence we present indicates
that the international aid community does have
significant policy leverage over LDC recipient
governments through loan conditionality.

Policy leverage is also evident in the
pattern of fiscal response to IMF loan
assistance as each of the IMF loan facilities
has different impacts on debt financing. LIMF
lending appears to be viewed as a source of
additional funds by recipients. Disbursed debt
rises by $.92 per dollar of LIMF loan funds.
The availability of this source of funds
appears to relax a borrowing constraint faced
by recipients. This econometric finding is
consistent with the results of Hajivassiliou
(1987) who also shows that borrowing
constraints are more important than loan terms
in predicting LDC debt levels.

The highly restrictive HIMF loan program,
conversely, is the only one that finds

significant   reductions   in   outstanding   debt
levels.   The $2.11   in   budgetary   surplus
generated   under   an   IMF   program   is   used   to
finance   significant   reductions   in   both   foreign
debt   and   internal   deficits.

COMIMF,   on   the   other   hand,   appears   to
provide   an   alternative   to   other   sources   for
foreign   borrowing.   The   budget   deficit   that
results   is   almost   entirely   an   internally
financed   deficit,   as   we   find   that   other   debt
falls   by $.92   for   each $1.00   of   COMIMF   loan
proceeds.   In   this   case,   the   IMF   is   either
providing   a   more   attractive   source   of   lending
than   available   alternatives   (in   contrast   to   the
LIMF   findings),   or   is   able   to   dictate   different
behavior   through   loan   conditionality.   The
strings   attached   to   this   lending,   as   discussed
above,   appear   to   be   somewhat   effective   at
reducing   the   overall   size   of   the   public   sector.

Bilateral   loans   represent   a   partial
relaxation   of   private   borrowing   constraints,   as
we   find   that   only $.41   of   other   debt   flows   is
replaced   by   each $1.00   of   bilateral   loan   aid.
Thus   the   debt   level   of   the   public   sector
expands   by $.59,   perhaps   reflecting   the   easy
terms   of   this   form   of   debt.

Bilateral   grants   appear   to   have   little
impact   on   the   debt   situation.   Instead   we   find
that   bilateral   grants   primarily   reduce   central
government   deficits.   This   result   is   consistent
with   the   categorization   of   local   currency   loans
as   grants   in   the   OECD   data.   More   important,
however,   there   appears   to   be   little   economic
policy   leverage   obtained   by   this   form   of
bilateral   aid.

SUMMARY AND CONCLUSION

This chapter has analyzed the impact of foreign assistance on central government budgeting. The goal has been to assess the impact of foreign aid on expenditure and revenues, and to examine how resulting budget deficits are financed. A crucial part of the analysis involves determining the efficacy of strings attached to foreign economic assistance. We find that the strings attached to multilateral aid are crucial for understanding its budgetary impact. In particular, project aid by the multilateral development banks causes relatively large expenditure responses in recipient countries apparently due to the matching funds requirements of these loans. Similarly, highly constrained IMF aid is shown to profoundly impact public sector expenditure and foreign debt. Conversely, IMF aid with few constraints, as well as bilateral aid, show virtually no effects on public expenditure and debt patterns. The conclusion is that the form of aid conditionality is crucial in determining how aid is filtered through the public sector. This determination is necessary before the impact of aid on debt or growth can be ascertained.

The latter part of the chapter used the public sector model of aid and its strings to examine the impact of foreign aid on public sector foreign debt. We find that MDB project lending offsets alternative sources of borrowing, and therefore does not generally represent additional sources of capital for LDCs. Despite this finding, MDB lending does have important implications for public sector debt levels of recipient governments because the recipients appear willing to increase public sector deficits considerably in order to meet the matching expenditure requirements. The severity of this finding is ameliorated because the resulting deficits are internal, not external. Nonetheless, to the extent that internal deficits cause other economic problems, recipient governments are paying for access to concessional foreign resources with considerable distortion of their internal economies. Consistent with previous research, this illustrates the fact that access to foreign exchange lending has been a significant problem for LDCs.

Highly conditional IMF aid is found to successfully reduce public sector debt by reducing central government expenditures. The preference of recipients for expenditure reduction rather than tax increases is also shown by our results concerning debt service expenditures. Debt service is financed exclusively through expenditure reductions, and not by revenue increases. Again the pattern of these results is consistent with finding that LDCs are constrained in the amount of credit they can obtain. Only bilateral aid and access to first credit tranche IMF resources appears to expand LDC access to credit.

Two policy implications emerge from the results of our examination of aid and public sector budgets. The first is that donors have not successfully convinced LDCs to increase public sector revenue in response to development assistance. Whether this is desirable or not depends crucially on the macroeconomic impacts of the public sector budget, and on the particular manner in which revenue increases are obtained. The second policy question concerns a reassessment of the form of foreign assistance. The three major types of donors, MDBs, IMF, and bilateral

assistance agencies, have vastly different
impacts on public sector budgets. It has been
suggested that a movement toward unconstrained
aid would be one means of solving the debt
crisis. This policy recommendation would
certainly appear to reduce the policy leverage
currently enjoyed by aid donors. What is
needed is a stronger assessment of how the aid
community can refine its existing policy
leverage to obtain some short-term debt relief
while continuing to foster long-term growth
potential.

NOTES

1. This assumes the objective of aid donors is
to stimulate growth. Clearly, aid can be used
to achieve multiple objectives. The basic
statement in the text holds, however, in that
there is a trade-off facing recipients
concerning access to concessional aid and
adopting certain policy changes.

2. One possible reason for the establishment
of multilateral aid agencies may have been to
obtain greater leverage over recipients.
Further, the formation of the DAC was
motivated, in part, by the belief that greater
cooperation among the donor countries could
increase the leverage available to the donors
(Thorp 1965). These efforts show that policy
leverage of bilateral programs is perceived to
be relatively weak.

3. The definition of a developing country used
here is one with a per capita GDP of less than
$3,900. This includes the poorest 90 countries
in the world. See Appendix I for a list of the
countries used in the empirical analysis.

4.   This means that the interest rates are relatively near market rates. For example, the hard window of the World Bank is the IBRD. In 1984, its lending terms were at an interest rate of 9.89 percent, with interest to accrue starting three to five years after disbursement, and a loan term of 15 to 20 years.   In contrast, the soft window of the World Bank is IDA, which charges a service charge of .75 percent, with interest accruing starting 10 years after disbursement, and a repayment period of 50 years.

5.   Reflows in 1980 were $3 billion, compared to only $800 million a decade earlier.

6.   Also called structural adjustment loans. These type of loans would still have conditionality, or strings, attached that are oriented toward macroeconomic policies rather than the sector specific recommendations that usually accompany traditional project lending (see Michalopoulos, 1987, for a description). Program loans through 1980, the time period used for the empirical analysis, were very small for the MDBs.

7.   Altering policy in response to aid is costly to the local authorities, in that if the opportunity to receive aid were not available, these policy changes would not occur.   The basic idea is that local authorities may be willing to alter policies in return for access to concessional resources.

8.   Strictly, the IMF does not consider itself as providing development assistance.   The classification of IMF aid as ODA is not important for this article, however, because

what is of interest is whether IMF
conditionality has impacted LDC budgetary
behavior. It should also be noted that the IMF
does not provide loans per se, but repurchase
agreements. These agreements allow countries
to purchase convertible currency (such as
dollars or pounds) for local currency. After a
specified period of time, the recipient is
required to repurchase its local currency with
the convertible currency it originally
received. For convenience, we will refer to
repurchase agreements as loans.

9. The bilateral donors are the DAC. Aid from
the CMEA Eastern Bloc countries and from the
OPEC countries is excluded. CMEA aid is quite
small for the countries in our sample (see
Appendix I for a list of recipients), and the
Middle Eastern countries have been excluded
(see footnote 17) so OPEC aid is also quite
small.

10. See Mason and Asher (1973) for a
discussion of the merits of project-oriented
aid as opposed to un-tied aid. In part, the
relative merits of the form of aid depends on
the success of aid strings at altering policy
behavior.

11. Our model, unfortunately, is not able to
distinguish among alternative categories within
the central government budget. For example,
aid for population control may end up in the
infrastructure budget. The data are not
sufficiently refined to test for detailed
categories of expenditures. To the extent that
nondefense to defense reallocations occur,
additional reallocations would be expected
within the nondefense budget. Thus the
estimate on nondefense to defense reallocations

may be considered a lower bound on the tendency to reallocate funds generally.

12.   It should be noted, however, that in general income effects are rather small, so the more likely scenario is the first - that is, recipients may be forced into the extra expenditures because of the implicit policy reforms required. If this is the case, then our model presents the first methodology that is able to measure this difficult to observe phenomena.

13.   One important source of strings is that bilateral aid must frequently be spent in the donor country. Also see footnote 2.

14.   Delineation between the structure and demographic variables is unimportant. Both sets of variables are included to control for differences in the political control of various coalitions, and for different demands on the public sector. Hamilton (1983) has also suggested that the effectiveness of public output may vary with these variables, resulting in different preferred spending levels.

15.   A very small portion of MDB lending during the sample period (1975-1980) is for balance of payments support or for sectoral development. These loans are not project-oriented, and may not be of the form closed-end matching. These loans have been dropped from the data.

16.   Potential simultaneous equation bias comes because country budgetary behavior or characteristics may determine loan commitments. See Cline and Sargen (1976) or Behrman and Sah (1984) for a model of loan commitments.

17.   See van de Laar (1980).   Thus the
coefficient in the expenditure equation of a
$1.00 commitment one year ago will reflect the
proportion of the loan disbursed, times the
impact of that disbursement on expenditure.   If
this impact is added over each of the lagged
periods, the total disbursed will be $.90
(IDA).   Adding the six coefficients will give
the impact on expenditure of that $.90.   If the
final $.10 has the same impact as the first
$.90, then the total impact of the loan
commitment will be the sum of the coefficients
divided by .9.   Assuming the expenditure impact
is equal each year indicates that differences
in the individual year estimated coefficients
should only be due to the rate of disbursement.

18.   The grant component of a loan is
calculated by determining the discount from
market terms.   The OECD (various) uses a fixed
10 percent interest as the market rate of
interest.   If a loan contains more than a 25
percent grant element, and if it is for social
development (not defense), it is considered to
be ODA.

19.   Initially, the model was estimated for 46
countries, the addition being six countries
from the Middle Eastern region.   Pooling tests,
however, indicate that these six countries are
significantly different than the pooled sample
of the rest of the world.   While the parameter
estimates of the aid variables change little,
these six countries were nonetheless dropped
from the data set.

REFERENCES

Baltagi, B. H. "Pooling: An Experimental Study of Alternative Testing and Estimation Procedures in a Two-Way Error Component Model," Journal of Econometrics 17, 1981, pp. 21-49.

Behrman, J. R., and Sah, R. K. "What Role Does Equity Play in the International Distribution of Development Aid?" In Syrquin, M., L. Taylor and L. Westphal (eds.), Economic Structure and Performance. Orlando: Academic Press, 1984.

Cashel-Cordo, P., and Craig, S. G. "The Public Sector Impact of International Resource Trans-fers," Journal of Development Economics: 1987, forthcoming.

Craig, S. G., and Inman, R. P. "Federal Aid and Public Education: An Empirical Look at the New Fiscal Federalism," Review of Economics and Statistics 64, 1982, pp. 541-552.

Craig, S. G. and Inman, R. P. "Education, Wel-fare, and the 'New' Federalism: State Budget-ing in a Federalist Public Economy." In H. Rosen (ed.), Studies in State and Local Public Finance. Chicago: University of Chicago Press, 1986, pp. 187-222.

Edwards, S. "LDC Foreign Borrowing and Default Risk: An Empirical Investigation, 1976-80," American Economic Review 74, 1984, pp. 726-734.

Gramlich, E. "Intergovernmental Grants: A Review of the Empirical Literature." In W. Oates (ed.), The Political Economy of Fiscal Federalism. Lexington, MA: Lexington Books, 1977, pp. 219-240.

Hajivassiliou, V. A. "The External Debt Repayments Problems of LDC's: An Econometric Model Based on Panel Data," Journal of Econometrics 36, 1987, pp. 205-230.

Hamilton, B. W. "The Flypaper Effect and Other Anomalies," Journal of Public Economics 22, 1983, pp. 347-361.

Heller, P. S. "A Model of Public Fiscal Behavior in Developing Countries: Aid, Investment, and Taxation," American Economic Review 65, 1975, pp. 429-445.

International Monetary Fund (IMF). "How Members Use Fund Resources to Meet Balance of Payment Needs," IMF Survey, Supplement to the Fund, September, 1979, pp. 7-11.

International Monetary Fund (IMF). "How Members Use Fund Resources to Meet Balance of Payment Needs," IMF Survey, 14, 1985, pp. 6-10.

International Monetary Fund. International Financial Statistics, Washington, annual.

Inman, R. P. "The Fiscal Performance of Local Governments: An Interpretative Review." In P. Mieszkowski and M. Straszheim (eds.), Current Issues in Urban Economics. Baltimore: Johns Hopkins University Press, 1979, pp. 270-321.

Jennings, A. "The Recurrent Cost Problem in the Least Developed Countries," The Journal of Development Studies, 1983, pp. 504-521.

Leipziger, D. M. "Lending Versus Giving: The Economics of Foreign Assistance," World Development 11, 1983, pp. 329-335.

Mason, E. S. and Asher, R. E. The World Bank Since Bretton Woods. Washington, D.C.: The Brookings Institute, 1973.

Mosley, P. "Aid, Savings, and Growth Revisited," Oxford Bulletin of Economic Statistics 6, 1980, pp. 628-641.

National Advisory Council on International and Monetary Affairs (NAC). International Finance Annual Report to the President. Washington, D.C.: U.S. Government Printing Office, annual.

Organization of Economic Cooperation and Development (OECD). Geographical Distribution of Financial Flows to Developing Countries. Paris: Organization for Economic Development, 1977, 1980, 1981.

Shepsle, K. "Institutional Arrangements and Equilibrium in Multidimensional Voting Models," American Journal of Political Science 23, 1979, pp. 27-59.

Singh, R. D. "State Intervention, Foreign Economic Aid, Savings, and Growth in LDC's: Some Recent Evidence," Kyklos 38, 1985, pp. 216-232.

Thorp, W. L. Development Assistance Efforts and Policies. Paris, OECD, 1965.

van de Laar, A. The World Bank and the Poor. Boston: Martinus Nijhoff Publishing, 1980.

World Bank. IDA in Retrospect. New York: Oxford University Press,

World Bank. <u>World Tables</u>. Baltimore: Johns
Hopkins University Press, Vols. I, II, 1976,
1980, 1983.

TABLE 6-1.

INTERNATIONAL AID STRUCTURE BY DONOR

A.   Multilateral Development Banks (MDBs)[a]

   I.   Bypass Loans (BYPASS):   50% of the total of hard flows[b]
                                       10% of the total of soft flows[c]

   II. Direct Loans (DIRECT):   50% of the total of hard flows
                                       90% of the total of soft flows

B.   International Monetary Fund (IMF) Repurchase Agreements (loans)

   I.   Low Conditionality (LIMF):   Ordinary Credit Tranche
                                       policies

   II. High Conditionality (HIMF):   Extended Facility or
                                       Supplemental Financing Facility

   III. Commodity Facilities (COMIMF): Commodity Facilities (oil, and
               buffer stock), and Compensatory Financing Facility

C.   Bilateral Aid from DAC Countries[d]

   I.   Bilateral loans (BLOAN)

   II. Bilateral grants (BGRANT)

---

a.   The development banks which are included are: the African
Development Fund (AfDF), the Asian Development Bank (ADB), the Inter-
American Development Bank (IDB), and the World Bank (including the
International Bank for Reconstruction and Development (IBRD), the
International Development Association (IDA), but excluding the
International Finance Corporation.

b. Hard MDB loans are made at interest rates which are relatively close
to market rates. These include loans from the IBRD, the Ordinary
Capital (OC) window of the IDB, and the OC window of the ADB.

c.   Soft MDB loans are made at interest rates which are highly
concessional.   These include loans from IDA, the Fund for Special
Operations window of the IDB, the Special Funds window of the ADB, and
the AfDF.

d. The members of the DAC are the developed countries, including the
OECD, Japan, Australia, and New Zealand.

TABLE 6-2.

IMPACT ON FOREIGN AID SPENDING AND REVENUE

	PUBEX	DEX	DEBT	TAX	REV
BYPASS[a]	1.59	-0.46	0.12	-2.98	-2.48
	(2.41)	(0.43)	(1.73)	(2.25)	(2.48)
Lag1	0.04	-0.02	0.39	-0.33	-0.20
	(0.38)	(0.07)	(0.28)	(0.36)	(0.39)
Lag2	-0.19	-0.08	0.57*	-0.82*	-0.55
	(0.43)	(0.08)	(0.30)	(0.40)	(0.44)
Lag3	-0.38	-0.10	-0.02	-0.70	-0.54
	(0.57)	(0.10)	(0.41)	(0.53)	(0.59)
Lag4	0.81	-0.10	-0.21	-0.02	0.04
	(0.58)	(0.11)	(0.42)	(0.54)	(0.59)
Lag5	0.73	-0.04	0.26	-0.61	-0.71
	(0.58)	(0.11)	(0.42)	(0.54)	(0.59)
Lag6	0.58	-0.12	-0.87*	-0.50	-0.52
	(0.51)	(0.09)	(0.37)	(0.48)	(0.53)
DIRECT[a]	2.37	-0.09	0.01	0.37	0.06
	(1.12)	(0.19)	(0.80)	(1.01)	(1.15)
Lag1	0.31	0.01	0.21	-0.28	-0.28
	(0.26)	(0.05)	(0.19)	(0.24)	(0.27)
Lag2	0.70*	-0.003	0.28	0.11	0.11
	(0.27)	(0.05)	(0.19)	(0.25)	(0.28)
Lag3	0.47	-0.05	0.21	0.08	0.01
	(0.31)	(0.06)	(0.22)	(0.29)	(0.32)
Lag4	0.41	-0.09	-0.01	0.26	0.16
	(0.31)	(0.06)	(0.22)	(0.29)	(0.32)
Lag5	0.49*	0.01	-0.18	0.20	0.11
	(0.29)	(0.05)	(0.21)	(0.27)	(0.29)
Lag6	-0.01	0.03	-0.50*	0.001	-0.05
	(0.33)	(0.06)	(0.24)	(0.31)	(0.34)
LIMF	0.70	-0.23	0.92	-0.16	-1.58
	(1.25)	(0.23)	(0.90)	(1.16)	(1.28)
HIMF	-1.68*	0.06	-1.44*	-0.05	0.49
	(1.01)	(0.18)	(0.72)	(0.94)	(1.04)

COMIMF	-0.77*	-0.23*	0.08	-1.49*	-1.88*
	(0.32)	(0.06)	(0.23)	(0.29)	(0.32)
BLOAN	-1.38*	-0.12	0.59	-0.47	-0.30
	(0.78)	(0.14)	(0.56)	(0.72)	(0.80)
BGRANT	-0.22	0.03	0.23	-0.39	-0.31
	(0.77)	(0.14)	(0.55)	(0.71)	(0.79)
DSV	-1.03*	-0.02	-0.03	-0.10	-0.11
	(0.15)	(0.03)	(0.11)	(0.14)	(0.16)
INC	0.09*	0.01*	0.02*	0.07*	0.08*
	(0.01)	(0.002)	(0.01)	(0.01)	(0.01)

* Indicates coefficients are signigicant at the 10% level.

Standard errors are in parentheses.

[a] These results are the sum of the coefficients of the six lags. The * i these cases represents significance at the 10% level using a Student's t test on the group of coefficients. See text, and footnote 15.

NOTE: See Appendix II for the remainder of the coefficient estimates.

TABLE 6-3.

IMPACT OF FOREIGN AID ON DEBT AND BUDGET DEFICITS

Aid	Budget SURP (DEF) [a]	Expected Debt	Actual Debt [b]	Change in Other Debt [c]	Internal SURP (DEF) [d]
BY-PASS	$(3.61)	$ .90[e]	$ .12	$- .78	$(3.49)
DIRECT	(2.22)	.90[e]	.01	- .89	(2.21)
LIMF	(2.05)	1.00	.92	- .08	(1.13)
HIMF	2.11	1.00	-1.44	-2.44	.67
COMIMF	(0.88)	1.00	.08	- .92	(0.80)
BLOAN	1.20	1.00	.59	- .41	1.79
BGRANT	(0.12)	.00	.23	.23	1.11

a   Calculated from budget constraint (equation 6.3) using estimates from Table 6-2. (see text).

b   See Table 6-2 for standard errors.

c   Calculated by subtracting expected debt from actual debt.

d   Equals budget surplus (deficit) plus actual debt.

e   About 90% of MDB commitments are disbursed in a six-year period (see footnote 15).

APPENDIX I: DATA DESCRIPTION

The data consists of observations for 40 non-European LDC countries over the 12-year period of 1969-1980. The model is tested for 1975-1980, the additional six years are for the lagged MDB commitment data (see text). A two-tier selection process is used in country selection. First, the country has to be ranked in the lower 90 countries on a GNP per capita basis, as done by the World Bank in its 1982 World Development Report. Middle Eastern countries are excluded for poolibility reasons (see text). Secondly, countries are selected on a data availability basis. The resulting 40 countries represent a broad cross-section across regions and income levels.

Government budget data are derived from the World Bank's World Tables. Excepting debt service, all of these variables are denominated in local currency. Debt service is in U.S. dollars. The par/market annual average exchange rate, from the World Tables, is used to convert from local currency to U.S. dollars. The multilateral commitment data are obtained from NAC International Finance Annual Reports, for the years 1972 to 1980. Prior to 1972, these data are obtained from the respective MDB reports. The bilateral aid data are obtained from the OECD's Geographical Distribution of Financial Flow to Less Developed Countries. The IMF data are derived from the IMF's International Finanical Statistics Yearbook, (various volumes). With the exception of the IMF data, all aid data are denominated in U.S. dollars. The IMF data, originally in SDRs are converted to U.S. dollars using the IMF's annual average exchange rate. Structural/taste data are also from the World Tables. Some of these variables are denominated in U.S.

dollars, and the rest are measured in
appropriate units (see below). All variables
either obtained in U.S. dollars or converted to
U.S. dollars are deflated to 1975 dollars by
use of the World Tables' implicit GDP deflator
for the United States. The LSDV regressions
are normalized against the Republic of the
Philippines and the year 1980.

COUNTRY LIST:

Latin America and Caribbean: Argentina,
Barbados, Bolivia, Brazil, Chile, Costa Rica
Dominican Republic, Ecuador, El Salvador,
Guatemala, Honduras, Mexico, Nicaragua,
Paraguay, Peru, Uruguay.

Sub-Sahalien Africa: Burkina Faso, Ghana,
Kenya, Liberia, Malawi, Mali, Mauritius, Niger,
Rwanda, Sierra Leone, Sudan, Tanzania, Uganda.

Asia: Burma, Fiji, India, Indonesia, Korea,
Malaysia, Nepal, Pakistan, Papua New Guinea,
Philippines, Thailand.

APPENDIX II

REMAINING VARIABLES OF THE BUDGETARY MODEL

	PUBEX	DEX	DEBT	TAX	REV
AG	-1.70	1.74*	-1.55	1.63	0.65
	(3.14)	(0.57)	(2.24)	(2.91)	(3.21)
MAN	-3.65	3.87*	-6.32*	1.99	0.41
	(4.88)	(0.88)	(3.49)	(4.53)	(4.99)
YNG	-6.47	1.40	6.40	5.62	5.13
	(7.48)	(1.36)	(5.35)	(6.94)	(7.66)
OLD	11.53	7.41*	-1.14	40.95*	47.80*
	(14.11)	(2.56)	(10.10)	(13.10)	(14.46)
URB	3.16	0.91	0.10	-0.001	0.92
	(2.27)	(0.41)	(1.62)	(2.10)	(2.32)
POPDEN	0.16	0.11	1.12*	-1.03*	-0.89
	(0.54)	(0.10)	(0.39)	(0.50)	(0.55)
LIFEX	-1.01	1.38*	-1.03	2.52	1.85
	(4.56)	(0.83)	(3.26)	(4.23)	(4.67)
INFM	-1.61	0.02	-2.09*	0.67	0.45
	(1.09)	(0.20)	(0.78)	(1.01)	(1.11)
PRIM	-0.05	0.04	-0.29	-0.004	-0.01
	(0.39)	(0.07)	(0.28)	(0.36)	(0.40)
SECD	-0.17	0.08	-1.04	2.02*	2.01*
	(0.90)	(0.16)	(0.64)	(0.84)	(0.92)
LAB	3.10	4.12*	0.62	12.31*	16.95*
	(7.39)	(1.34)	(5.29)	(6.86)	(7.57)
FEMLAB	11.70*	-0.09	-3.40	16.72*	15.96*
	(5.66)	(1.03)	(4.05)	(5.26)	(5.80)
POP	-0.23	-0.16*	-0.47	0.001	-0.19
	(0.46)	(0.08)	(0.33)	(0.42)	(0.47)
DEFL	0.95*	0.23*	-0.24*	1.06*	-1.35*
(0.19)	(0.19)	(0.03)	(0.14)	(0.18)	(0.20)
CONSTANT	64.16	-508.80*	644.95	-1434.44*	-1481.46*
	(724.92)	(131.37)	(518.66)	(672.87)	(742.53)
R²	0.98	0.95	0.52	0.98	0.98

NOTE: Standard errors are in parentheses.
* Indicates significance at the 10% level.

See Table 6-2 for the other coefficient estimates. Dummy variables are also included for each year, and for each country, with the constant terms representing Phillipines in 1980.

Structure/Taste		MEAN	STANDARD DEVIATION
MAN	percentage of the labor force in industry	16.150	7.602
AG	percentage of the labor force in agriculture	56.087	22.787
URB	percentage of the population residing in urban areas	35.283	21.298
INC	per capita G.D.P.	694.839	575.191
YNG	percentage of the population under 14 years of age	42.422	5.311
OLD	percentage of the population over 65 years of age	3.627	1.736
POPDEN	density of population per square kilometer	85.672	129.482
LIFEX	life expectancy, average number in years remaining for a newborn	56.085	9.314
INFM	infant mortality, annual numbers of deaths of infants less than one year old per thousand live births	95.250	48.612
PRIM	enrollment of all ages in primary schools as a percentage of the population of primary school age	83.365	27.210
SECD	enrollment of all ages in secondary schools as a percentage of the population of secondary school age	30.174	20.572
LAB	participation rate of the labor force as a percentage of the population of all ages	36.454	7.072
FEMLAB	female labor force participation as a percentage of the female population of all ages	21.694	12.389
POP	population in millions	34.478	95.754
DEFL	implicit G.D.P. deflator (1975=1)	3.230	13.315

VARIABLE	DEFINITION	MEAN	STANDARD DEVIATION
Aid ($ per capita)			
BYPASS	multilateral development bank commitments to non-central government agencies		
t-1		2.658	5.444
t-2		2.651	5.410
t-3		2.328	4.796
t-4		2.302	4.754
t-5		2.143	4.791
t-6		2.138	4.552
DIRECT	multilateral development bank commitments to the recipient central government		
t-1		6.826	8.949
t-2		6.147	7.874
t-3		5.663	7.638
t-4		4.938	6.827
t-5		4.466	6.680
t-6		3.572	5.659
HIMF	highly conditional I.M.F. disbursements	0.526	2.736
LIMF	low conditional I.M.F. disbursements	0.805	2.230
COMIMF	I.M.F. commodity disbursements	4.687	7.538
BLOAN	DAC bilateral ODA loan disbursements	1.941	2.860
BGRANT	DAC bilateral ODA grant and local currency disbursements	6.149	10.705
Central Government Budgets ($ per capita)			
PUBEX	nondefense expenditures	106.374	116.939
DEX	defense expenditures	13.037	14.671
DEBT	end of year change in public and public guaranteed external debt	11.935	18.180
TAX	own tax revenues	107.434	113.440
REV	own revenue (including TAX)	120.507	127.928
DSV	debt service on public and public guaranteed external debt	18.795	23.324

COMMENTARY BY WENDELL GORDON

Professors Cashel-Cordo and Craig have assembled a major amount of data and imaginatively organized them in an effort to answer a variety of questions.

An important thrust of the article seems to involve the implications of fungibility and conditionality in analyzing the effect of official development assistance on the public finance arrangements in the assistance-receiving countries.

According to a dictionary, fungibility involves "the quality or state of being fungible" and fungible means "of such a kind or nature that one specimen or part may be used in place of another specimen or equal part in the satisfaction of an obligation." It also means "interchangeable." In their discussion of fungibility the authors remark: "The source of fungibility can be ascertained by examining the impact of foreign aid funds in different sectors of the central government budget." And later on the same page they say: "The budgetary model we present measures fungibility through an examination of different sectors of the central government budget."

The data actually presented in the report permit comparing military and nonmilitary spending and effect on debt. But the authors do not seem to have had available to them the data that would permit "an examination (in any detail) of different sectors of the central

285

government budget." Some interesting possibilities are thereby missed in terms of
identifying diversion of funds to projects of
particular interest to insiders in the aid
receiving countries - a not unimportant
consideration. There well may be "playing of
games" going on. The aid-recipient country
representatives may ask for foreign aid to
support projects which they have reason to
believe are viewed sympathetically by potential
donors. Then the receipt of such aid will
permit them to divert their own funds to more
congenial projects.

It would seem that it might have been
useful to have been able to say that "foreign
aid intended to assist with corn production on
the central plateau" had been largely negated
by a governmental reduction in internal funds
being provided to the agricultural development
bank that might have been providing internal
funds for that purpose. The authors do not
seem to be in position to identify diversion at
this level, for example, as among expenditures
on agriculture, or education, or high living by
the country's diplomatic corps.

The meaning and role of conditionality in
all this is important and obscure. Conditionality involves the extent to which the
aid providers impose conditions on the behavior
of the aid recipients as a condition for
providing the aid. One would seem not to have
said very much by merely classifying in terms
of high or low conditionality. What were the
conditions? Whose interests are they really
serving? How much meaningful exchange occurred
between donors and recipients in identifying
the conditions? Was there arm twisting or
reasonably pleasant understanding and agreement? To indicate the range of uncertainty it
should suffice to notice that the conditional-

ity imposed by MDBs generally involved pressure on the recipients to put more of their own money into the project in question or into other development projects. On the other hand IMF conditionality generally has involved effort to force (considerable arm twisting frequently being involved) the recipients to cut government expenditures and move toward balanced budgets. (This latter type of conditionality has frequently been criticized as contributing to depression or stagnation in poor countries).

Also the recipient countries may be quite favorably disposed to conditions that either involve their putting matching funds into the project or involve their being able to shift funds (the previously mentioned fungibility) to other projects. The authors seem to make no effort to set up cirteria as to whether the results of fungibility are helpful to economic development, helpful to the pocketbooks of local movers and shakers, or a little of both. It should be confessed that adequate information on these matters might not be obtained if the authors had written a separate book on each of their 40 countries. One cannot do everything in one short chapter.

At all events conditionality and fungibility remain buzz words that the reader can love or hate according to one's feelings. They do not provide a clearcut criteria as to desirability. Just saying "conditionality" merely opens Pandora's box in terms of both the nature of the conditions and their desirability for dealing with problems that have not been precisely identified.

The authors conclude that the forms of official development aid, which encourage additional expenditures by the recipient, actually result in additional spending by the recipient! The conditions of the conditionality are implemented. And this means larger domestic deficits, since this process seems to discourage international borrowing from alternative sources and taxes are not increased to make up the difference.

On the other hand, highly conditional IMF aid fosters reduction in domestic expenditures and balanced budgets. The statistical model indicates that such programs not only have this effect but they also work to reduce dramatically borrowing from other foreign sources. The authors are obviously aware, but do not emphasize, that these results of highly conditional IMF aid seem to be generating fiscal contraction in the aid receiving country and consequent recession and lack of growth.

Also, the authors plead for effort to assess "how the aid community can refine its existing policy leverage to obtain some short-term debt relief while continuing to foster long-term growth potential." But the question remains as to how to accomplish this. In fact, in view of the unsatisfactory results both when assistance is conditioned on matching expenditures from domestic funds and when it is conditioned on reduction in domestic spending and deficits, one might be inclined to suspect that the exercise of "policy leverage" by the "aid community" may be part of the problem rather than being part of the solution.

Beyond this it may be that really constructive work in the fiscal field needs to be in connection with the structure of government spending as among the major areas of activity: education, social security, health, public services, the military, housing, business regulation, and so on. And there is not going to be any substitute for more conscientious and effective implementation of programs by public servants with integrity. By its nature, the model presented by Professors Cashel-Cordo and Craig does not deal with structural problems at this level. The implications of fungibility or substitutability as among different government programs are not discussed.

The authors obviously have done a painstaking, thoughtful, and professionally competent job of assembling and processing data in an effort to get at how the foreign aid process works in relation to the role of fiscal policy as an intermediary in that process.

7 IMPORTATION AND LOCAL GENERATION OF TECHNOLOGY BY THE THIRD WORLD: AN INSTITUTIONALIST PERSPECTIVE

Dilmus D. James

INTRODUCTION

Following the second World War, the economic development of less developed countries (LDCs)[1] came into its own as a distinct subdiscipline of economics. For most of that period the technological dimension of development was dominated by the issue of transferring technology from wealthy, industrial nations to the third world. Early optimism was transformed into a more sober attitude as it became apparent that establishing sustained socioeconomic development in developing countries was far less facilely achieved than economic recovery in war-torn Europe. The size and rate of increases in LDCs' payments for technology imports became cause for concern. Having grown from around U.S. $300 million in 1965, and topping U.S. $1 billion in 1975, such outlays were predicted to reach U.S. $4 to 6 billion by 1985 (Janiszewski, 1981).

Yet, in retrospect, the accomplishments of the third world as a whole are rather impressive. As Morowetz observed, "The growth performance of developing countries as a group grew at an annual average rate of 3.4 percent a

year during 1950-1975.... This was faster than
either the developing countries ... or the
developed nations ... had grown in any comparable period before 1950 and exceeded both
official goals and private expectations" (1977,
p. 12). Since 1965, LDCs' economies and those
of low-income countries within that group
expanded more rapidly than industrial market
economies (Table 1). Even in per capita terms,
the South does not compare unfavorably to the
industrial market economies.

TABLE 7-1.

	1980 GNP per capita (dollars)	Average Annual Growth - GNP					
		1965-1973	1973-1980	1981	1982	1983	1984[1]	1985[2]
Developing countries	2,064	6.6	5.4	3.5	2.0	2.0	5.4	4.3
Per capita basis		4.1	3.2	1.0	-0.7	0.0	3.3	2.4
Low income countries	550	5.6	4.7	5.0	5.3	7.8	9.4	7.8
Per capita basis		3.0	2.7	3.0	3.2	6.1	7.4	6.1
Industrial Market Economies		4.7	2.8	1.9	-0.6	2.3	4.6	2.8
Per capita basis	7,540	3.7	2.1	1.1	-1.3	1.6	3.9	2.4

1.   Estimated
2.   Projected
_____
     Source: World Development Report, 1986.

Source: <u>World Development Report</u>, 1986.

Naturally, such aggregate data mask
crucial questions of income distribution. In

this regard it is noteworthy that Latin
America, which contains many countries with
extremely skewed incomes (high Gini coefficients), every country experienced an improvement in its Physical Quality of Life Index
between 1960 and 1980.[2]

Turning more specifically to technology,
most economists have been caught off guard.
Many countries of the South, especially those
in the upper and middle industrial tiers, are
exporting products and services which indicate
fairly elevated levels of technological
competence.[3] Information on third world
technology exports has only recently become
available; thus economists and other social
scientists are still digesting it and mulling
over its significance. It was also found,
primarily through plant-level studies of
manufacturing firms, that while not universal,
many enterprises in LDCs routinely improve
their technologies.[4] Ordinarily, individual
innovations, taken in isolation, have a minor
impact, but the cumulative effect through time
is a significant source of productivity and
product quality gains. Technology exports and
local innovation provide convincing evidence
that domestic technological capabilities are
present and accumulating in many LDCs. This,
plus a political impetus encouraging technological self-reliance, has caused the
spotlight to shift to internal technological
mastery and how it can be enhanced.

This chapter will examine the acquisition
of technology, whether through imports or local
generation. The growing awareness of the
complexities of technology transfer will be
highlighted in the following section. The
mounting dissatisfaction on the part of LDCs
with the transfer mechanisms, and LDCs'
attempts to regulate technology imports are

discussed in the section entitled "Objections
and Regulations." Several characteristics of
promoting indigenous technological capabilities
are explored in the section "Internal Technological Capabilities." In the next section,
I will allege that mainstream economics does
not do justice to some important aspects of
third world technology experiences and that
orthodoxy should receive poor marks by failing
to assign technology a central role in the
development process. In broad contours, the
Veblen-Ayres institutionalist (or evolutionary)
thesis of technological change is presented.[5]
Ways that an institutional perspective might
contribute to a better understanding of
technology transfer and building internal
technological capabilities are then considered,
followed by a discussion of future problems and
opportunities. A short summary concludes the
chapter.

The reader deserves advance notice of two
limitations. First, due to the concentration
and specialization of my previous work, an
inordinate reliance is placed on examples from
Latin America. I intend and trust, however,
that the generalities that emerge have some
applicability to third world nations in Africa
and Asia. Second, due to limitations of space,
selectivity has necessarily influenced the
content of the chapter; indeed no section of
the chapter has escaped. On several occasions
the reader is referred to more comprehensive
surveys of in-depth treatments of relevant
topics.

MOUNTING COMPLEXITY[6]

As the investigation of third world
technology imports proceeded, what first

appeared a simple matter of the South employing
technology bought, borrowed, begged, or stolen
gave way to a more complicated array of (1)
forms and levels of technology, (2) participants in the transfer process, (3) institutional conditions within which technology
transfer is accomplished, and (4) arrangements
for achieving a connection between suppliers
and recipients.   The following may at least
provide some feel for the escalating number of
differentiations.   Part of the picture was
progressive discovery of existing variations;
the rest resulted from continual innovations in
the transfer process.
     Erdilek and Rapoport (1985:252) convey one
facet of the complexity well:

> The principle channels of ITT
> (international technology transfer)
> are licensing; direct foreign
> investment; sale of turnkey plants;
> joint venture,   cooperative
> research arrangements, and co-
> production agreements; export of
> high-technology products and capital
> goods; reverse engineering; exchange
> of scientific and technical person-
> nel; science and technology conferen-
> ces; trade shows, and exhibits;
> education and training of foreigners;
> commercial visits;   open litera-
> ture (journals, magazines, technical
> books, and articles); industrial
> espionage; end-user or third country
> diversions; and government assistance
> programs.

     Private firms might transfer technology
within institutional arrangements involving
wholly owned foreign subsidiaries, joint

ventures, foreign minority holdings, "fade-out"
options, franchising, management contracts,
turnkey ventures, or international subcontract-
ing (Buckley, 1983).

Technologies can be proprietal or in the
public domain; they can represent levels
ranging from traditional through intermediate,
conventional and newly emerging; and they may
be relatively disembodied and easily inserted
into prevailing modes of production, free-
standing turnkey types, or anywhere between
these extremes.

Initially, in its most straightforward
guise, technology transfer was represented by
entity X in the developing country acquiring
technology from entity Y, usually located in a
developed country. If private firms are
involved, the calculus of profit expectations
governs the transaction. If X is a parastatal
enterprise or nongovernmental organization, net
social benefits should be the paramount
consideration. If Y is an aid agency, economic
and/or political quid pro quo or altruism serve
as motives. As experience with transferring
technology accumulated, however, all sorts of
characters began to join this rudimentary cast.
For example, private firms differ by size,
industry, and amount of experience in international affairs. Moreover, there are frequently
different vistas, motivations, and designs of
key actors within firms. The same is likely
true of parastatal units, aid agencies, and
nongovernmental organizations that implement
the international movement of technology to the
South. This is just the beginning. Experts
performing preinvestment analyses, financial
institutions providing the funding, engineering
consultants hired for establishing a new
facility, or workers' representatives apprehen-
sive about the consequence of new technology

are examples of others that may be involved
with technology transfer. Regulatory agencies
and ministries concerned with employment,
balance of payments, and industrial or agricultural policy frequently impact on technology
imports.

How ample is the "technological menu" from
which developing countries can choose meaning-
fully? Early models of third world economies
pictured an extreme bifurcation between modern
(mainly industrial) and backward (mainly
agricultural) sectors (Lewis, 1954). This
dualistic conception was extended to technology
in a seminal article by Richard Eckaus (1955).
While production in backward activities tends
to be small-scale with generous opportunities
for substitution between labor and capital,
such is not the case in the modern sector.
Nathan Rosenberg (1986, pp. 4-5) who goes on to
critique the theory, characterizes technological dualism as follows:

> Thus, modern industrial societies
> have developed technologies whose
> main features broadly accord with the
> special characteristics of their
> historical growth paths. Their
> technologies reflect an adapta-
> tion to conditions of labour
> scarcity and capital abundunce, the
> exploitation of scale economies that
> provide low per unit costs when the
> volume of output is sufficiently
> large, and they have well-educated
> labour forces that are able to
> generate new scientific knowledge,
> as well as exploit it. --- oppor-
> tunities for substituting labour in
> general for capital in general are
> very limited, but emphasis is also

frequently placed upon the inability
to substitute unskilled labour or
capital.

While no serious observer questions the
existence of real constraints on varieties of
technologies that developing countries can
effectively employ (scale effects, product
quality considerations, cost of search or
adaptation, risk differentials, etc.), the
feasible menu is undoubtedly more plentiful
than previously believed. Rosenberg (1986)
reminds us by citing Ranis (1957, 1973) and
Granick (1957) that the Japanese and Russians
found ways of substituting labor for capital
effectively in industrial production. Jorge
Katz and his associates uncovered instances of
capital-stretching innovations by Latin
American manufacturing firms.[7] Technologies
with more varied technical specifications have
become more prevalent as Japan, Eastern Europe,
and newly industrializing countries (NICs)
became exporters of capital equipment and other
forms of technology. Developing countries
import significant amounts of secondhand
equipment which further broadens the choice of
vintages, fator intensities, scales of output,
and skill requirements (James, 1974, 1982).
    Reviews of elasticities of factor sub-
stitution support the conviction that LDCs are
seldom relegated to a narrowly defined capital-
labor conbination.[8] Collections of product
case studies justify the notion that there is
much from which to choose (Bhalla, 1985).
    To all of this must be added the conscious
effort poured into producing and disseminating
technologies aimed at populating the intermediate void between traditional and modern
technologies. This takes us into the controversial realm of intermediate (or "ap-

propriate") technology, and the lesser known, more recently explored possibilities of "technology blending." These issues are more conveniently discussed later. We only note here that such technologies further expand the stock of technologies from which to select.

It appears that during the past several decades, due to accumulated practical experience, our conceptualization of technology transfer has become increasingly Byzantine. This is far from hair-splitting or indulging in taxonomical exercises for their own sake. Practitioners as well as observers recognize that changes in the permutations, minor though they may seem, can have a palpable effect on the chances for a successful transfer. John Enos (1985), using a game theory approach, and Peter Buckley (1983), employing a typology-matrix of corporate forms matched against manner of transfer, are convincing on this score.

The welter of individuals, enterprises, and agencies reflecting various viewpoints and bundles of priorities will influence importantly who gets what technology when and for how much, as well as for how effectively it is eventually employed. Nevertheless, much of what orthodox economics has to offer remains handicapped by the underlying residual of analysis resting on behavior of profit-oriented firms that are homogenous within their given market structures.

OBJECTIONS AND REGULATION

To illustrate the South's ambivalent attitude toward technology exports, Paul Streeten tells the story of two ladies returning from a cruise. When their welcoming

spouses inquired about their gastronomical
experiences, one traveller replied, "The food
was like poison!" "And the portions were so
small!" complained the other.[9] Similarly,
while recognizing overall benefits from
technology, developing countries have found
considerable fault with prevailing transfer
mechanisms.

Objections that became more vociferous
during the 1960s and early 1970s were fed by at
least three sources. First, there was a
growing recognition that foreign investment,
and technology transfer associated with it, was
taking new forms. The sheer size of many
multinational firms represented such a mammoth
quantitative leap over previous movements of
international capital that it could only be
regarded as a change in kind. And, of course,
there were momentous qualitative alterations in
the range of products, geographic scope of
sourcing and marketing, managerial practices,
and business organizations. Perhaps it was
inevitable that the multinational enterprise
would bear the brunt of the discontent over
commercially oriented technology transfer - it
was awesome, it had all the advantages attendant to global operations, and it was alien.

Not incidentally, this was the heyday of
the dependency school of thought. Always more
influential in Latin America, the
dependentistas soon had a following among
African and, to a lesser extent, Asian students
of development (or underdevelopment). The
complete argument need not detain us here.[10]
Suffice it to say that one of the concrete
contributions of the dependency school was to
call attention to the rise of the multinational
corporation and to demonstrate convincingly
that this new institution had transformed the
international economic landscape forever. In

addition, dependency thought, to put it mildly, cast suspicion on any resources, technology included, obtained from first world sources. The third ingredient that stimulated discontent was empirical studies that uncovered unsatis- factory elements in the transfer process.[11]

Complaints were legion, but some of the most worrisome can be enumerated here.   As already discussed, most new technology is developed in wealthy, industrial economies where economic conditions biases (research and development) toward turning out relatively capital-intensive, large-scale production methods.   Multinational enterprises received the brunt of such criticism as they were accused of being particularly blase about selecting technologies with a closer fit to LDCs' factor endowments and market sizes, and even more cavalier with respect to engaging in research, development, and adaptation of technologies.   A substantial amount of am- bivalence creeps in also.   Suppliers, usually assumed to be multinational enterprises, were often accused of not marketing their most modern technologies, which presumably would be most inappropriate in the sense described below.

Second, it was believed that there were significant monopoly elements in the technology markets.   Contracts involving the international movement of technology to the third world, very frequently packaged with direct foreign investment and expatriate management, routinely contained clauses advantageous to the sellers. Common examples were export restrictions or prohibitions; tying agreements for purchases of material inputs or technical assistance; stipulations that technical improvements be ceded to the seller ("grant back" provisions); and parent enterprise control over quality,

price,   and   quantity   of   output.   Empirical
studies revealed considerable overcharging of
third world affiliate firms by their parent
counterparts.   This   practice   of   "transfer
pricing" came under keen scrutiny and was
considered detrimental to the host country's
balance of payments, tax revenues, and local
investment.[12]
     The   theory   of   duopoly   or   bilateral
monopoly was revived and applied to bargaining
conducted between LDCs' buyers and supplying
multinationals.   Alternatively, multinationals
were looked upon as discriminating monopolists
who   compartmentalized   the   purchasers   of
technology by nation or firm and took advantage
of different elasticities of demand in their
pricing policies.   In either case the chips
were thought to be stacked decisively on the
side   of   those   possessing   the   technology.
Naturally buyers faced the problem inherent in
the   "fundamental   paradox   of   knowledge"-
sellers necessarily know more about the
technology than those seeking to acquire it
(Arrow, 1952).   Purveyors of technology were
thought likely to be more knowledgeable about
the   global   market   for   technology   and   more
experienced at international bargaining than
their developing country counterparts.
     Selling firms may encounter a private risk
in   selling   technology   since   there   is   some
chance   that   the   new   users   will   allow   the
knowledge to "filter out" to third parties,
thereby weakening the monopolists' position.
This leads either to a higher selling price or
to a transfer of an absolute minimum of know-
how to operate the technology.   But, it is
claimed   that   past   R&D   expenditures   were
predicted on sales in major markets, not in
marginal markets in LDCs, thus ex post, the
marginal social cost to transferring technology

to LDCs is zero.[13] Put differently, any positive price paid by LDCs for the technology constitutes monopoly rent.

Patents came to be regarded as another institutional advantage of developed-country suppliers.[14] The third world has consistently called for various reforms in the international patent system.

Finally, imported technology was viewed as a conspicuous link in a self-perpetuating cycle that exacerbated socioeconomic injustices in some developing countries. Known as the "Brazilian-model" (Furtado, 1973), the sequence involves a skewed economic distribution which generates a demand for a wide range of modern products through spending by upper-income strata of the society. These products tend to require recent-vintage, capital-intensive, large-scale technologies. Importation and use of these technologies tend to worsen employment and favor the owners of capital and those fortunate to have well-paying industrial jobs, thus completing the cycle. It takes little imagination to embellish the model with unconscious or overt political actions by those benefitting from the system to perpetuate it.

One major response to this catalogue of dissatisfaction was the instigation (or, in India's case, the tightening) of regulations on technology imports. Argentina, Brazil, Mexico and the Andean Pact countries in Latin America; Nigeria in Africa, and Indonesia, South Korea, Malaysia, and the Phillipines in Asia have such regulations, most of which were imposed in the early 1970s. India, having established controls in 1947, eventually developed an extremely protectionist stance on technology transfer.

Various institutional arrangements were created as screening mechanisms, the primary

motivation being to reduce the damage stemming
from unfair or undesirable practices in the
international commerce of technology. Owing to
the importance of direct foreign investment as
a vehicle for technology transfer, it was
common to coordinate legislation and enforcement measures in both areas. Typical provisions in the restrictions were: a ceiling on
rates of royalty for technology licenses, a
limit on the duration of a technology transfer
contract, prohibitions of tying contracts for
purchases of inputs, requiring that technical
host country improvements on licensed technology can be used by the innovating firm,
disallowing export prohibitions, and so forth.
    Many of these regulations have been in
place for over 15 years, and some have had
significant embellishments (e.g., Mexico in
1976 and 1982). Originally conceived as
"defensive" and vaguely analogous to anti-trust
legislation in developed nations, there has
been a recent tendency to regard these screening mechanisms as part of a policy to protect,
and thereby encourage technological activities.
We will return to these matters in a later
section when speculating on future technology
acquisition by the South.

INTERNAL TECHNOLOGICAL CAPABILITIES

    A second response to perceived disad-
vantages in the transfer process is a heightened vigor by LDCs in becoming more self-
sufficient in technology. Below is discussed
what is understood about fostering local
technology at the enterprise level, at the
sectoral level (capital goods), and through
national science and technology councils.

Enterprises-level Learning

We know enough about local generation of technical knowledge by manufacturing enterprises in developing countries to venture a suggestive sequence of learning activities:[15]

1. The ability to identify an opportunity, the reaping of which, or a problem, the amelioration of which, involves a technological dimension.

2. The capacity to scan the existing technological shelf, screen, and select the appropriate technologies and, if proprietary considerations are involved, bargain effectively for the acquisition of the new knowledge.

3. The competence for operating the technology and adapting it to local conditions (as may be mandated by factor prices, ranges of skills available, consumer tastes, local inputs, climate, and a host of other possibilities).

4. The talent for modifying technologies in response to a changing economic environment (as may be motivated by changes in tariff structures, tax laws, availability of inputs, industrial structure, etc.)

5. The capability of producing and acting upon enterprise-generated designs leading to major equipment modifications of new (or substantially modified) products.

6. The talent for conducting long-run research and development in an organized, systematic fashion.

Several qualifications and embellishments are warranted. First, the sequence is not inviolate - step four may precede step two, for example. Second, there are interdependencies- illustratively, an excellent job of screening and selecting may preclude extensive adapta- tions to local conditions. Third, most observers agree that important learning effects can accrue to the enterprise if its technical staff fully participates in the setting up of a new plant or expanding an existing facility. This, of course, could come at any point in the sequence. Fourth, the jump from step four to step five is particularly crucial, yet espe- cially difficult to accomplish. In effect, steps one through four represent know-how - a familiarity with how the technology can be utilized. Going from these to steps five and six which represent "know-why," implying some insight into the basic principles of the technology - requires a discrete, order of magnitude jump in enterprise-level learning (Lall, 1980). Fifth, it is rare for an enterprise to sustain success through routine, relatively inexpensive, learning-by-doing. At some point, continued accumulation of tech- nological mastery is likely to rest on con- scious commitment of resources, with consequent assumption of risks, in training of key personnel, hiring to fill gaps, or similar investments (Bell, 1984).

What is puzzling is that there appears to be no correlation between level and success of innovative activity and such factors as industry, type of firm ownership (proprietor- ship or corporation), size of enterprise, or proportion of foreign participation.

Capital Goods Sector

That capital goods production played a crucial role in the industrial development of

Western Europe and the United States is clearly recognized by economic historians (Rosenberg, 1963). Indeed the capital goods sector has been referred to as "a _sine qua non_ for industrial progress" (UNIDO, 1985, p. 5) and "at the heart of the process of technology generation and diffusion" (Fransman, 1985, p.17). What makes the capital goods sector so special with respect to enhancing local technological capacities?[16]

First, a tremendous variety of worker skills and demands on managerial abilities are associated with the wide range of products that characterize the industry. Furthermore, since many of these skills and abilities are in demand throughout the larger industrial sector, labor and management circulate technical learning more broadly throughout the economy when they change jobs. Improvements in capital goods spread productivity increases and concomitant technical change to manufacturing generally. Moreover, production of capital goods ordinarily requires a sophisticated level of design capability that must be sporadically or continuously upgraded as material and technical inputs change and user specifications are altered. Important capital goods producers frequently rely on subcontractors and other local sourcing arrangements, and it is often in the best interest of the larger firm to assist the supplier enterprises in becoming more technologically competent. Finally, there is a significant amount of knowledge and stimuli for learning and technical innovation flowing back to the producer from product users in the forms of expressions of dissatisfaction, constructive suggestions, and stipulations of the need for entirely new designs.[17]

Such epicenters or nexuses for learning are not unique. Evidently the manufacture of

clocks during the Middle Ages served the same
purpose in Europe (Bourstein, 1985). The
contemporary computer industry, if one includes
the fashioning of software and abilities to
apply computer innovations, displays many or
all of the characteristics ascribed to capital
goods production. This may explain and justify
special treatment being accorded to the
computer industry by several third world
nations.[18]

National Science and Technology Councils

At the macro-level, many developing
countries looked to national science and
technology councils to coordinate and encourage
national science, research and development, and
technological activities. Establishment of
councils were especially popular during the
late 1960s and early 1970s with Latin America
leading the way: Chile (1967), Venezuela
(1967), Argentina (1968), Colombia (1968), Peru
(1968), Mexico (1970). Latin America was not
alone, however. India established a Department
of Science and Technology (1971), the Republic
of Korea a Council for Science and Technology
(1972), and Malaysia a National Institute for
Scientific and Industrial Research (1974).
Some nations (e.g., Brazil, the Phillipines,
and Thailand), having set up national organs
for science and technology much earlier, took
measures to strengthen existing institutional
infrastructure during the 1965-1975 period.[19]
These national institutions often became
heavily involved in planning for national
science and technology promotion.
How effective have these agencies been?
Many observers are rather critical. Francisco
R. Sagasti was involved in a five-year study on

Science and Technology Policy Instruments (STPI) which over a five-year period covered Argentina, Brazil, Colombia, Egypt, India, Mexico, Peru, Republic of Korea, Venezuela, and Yugoslavia. In general, Sagasti (1979) finds serious shortcomings in science and technology policy instruments.[20] The heterogeneity and diversity of instruments meant that contradictory policy orientations coexisted; many promotional provisions were not effective because the majority of firms in target industries were unaware of them; and redundancy abounded in some areas while harmful gaps remained in others. While these observations apply to the entire spectrum of STPI, national councils, given their central position, must bear the brunt of the blame for deficiencies.

Amadeo (1979) believes the national councils of Latin America are mainly motivated by theoretical considerations with little to do with indigenous productive and technological forces. The model is more applicable and useful in center countries than in the periphery. The councils tend to push "big science" rather than more direct means of enhancing local technological mastery. Finally, Amadeo claims that there is a general lack of social support:

> Without any structural need for locally generated S & T in our countries, given the features of the dependent model in force, and with the potentially interested social actors (national bourgeoisie) limited in their possibilities for political expression, who would fight for an indigenous science and technology (p. 163).

For even more emphatic declarations regarding the lack of social and political underpinnings for a science and technology policy in Mexico see Miguel S. Wionczek (1981) who was instrumental in developing an _Indicative Plan for Science and Technology_ which appeared in 1976 (CONACYT, 1976) while serving as Deputy Director of Mexico's National Council of Science and Technology. Wionczek was bitterly disappointed when this superb planning document fell on evil times, a victim of a financial crisis, an administrative change, and a policy of neglect.

The jury is still out on national councils on science and technology. Some of their promotional and educational efforts take a great deal of time before results become manifest, but if there is a dearth of social and political enthusiasm, what better way to begin eliciting and bolstering support than hammering away at spreading awareness about the potential of technological progress? As to the general ignorance about programs designed to encourage local technological undertakings, this is not a problem confined to LDCs. Approximately one-fourth of the manufacturing firms in the United Kingdom were in the dark about governmental financial and consultancy support for the introduction of microelectronics innovations (James, 1984).

Furthermore, the "outputs" of such councils are difficult to measure; the interactions between science and applied technology are not well understood, especially in a developing country context; and political or financial instability have led many scientific and technical professionals to emigrate to developed countries.[21]

INSTITUTIONAL APPROACH TO TECHNOLOGICAL DEVELOPMENT

In the main, economics has been sadly inadequate through the failure to assign technological change a central role in development, and at best, it has a spotty record in treating effectively new perspectives and adjustments that have unfolded. A review of several textbooks on economic development is revealing.[22] Early on, much attention was focused on choice of production techniques under circumstances likely to prevail in developing countries, e.g., abundant labor/scarce capital, distorted factor prices, and small market sizes. This analysis, showcasing isoquants, factor price lines, and expansion paths, still tends to be featured in a chapter or section devoted to technology in economic development texts.

Either explicitly or tacitly, the receiving entity, be it private firm or governmental agency, is seen as making an arms-length purchase based on an assessment of cost and prospective returns. The important exception is an affiliate of a foreign firm acquiring technology from its parent. If the deal is not arms' length, there is considerable question, as we have observed, over whether gains by the affiliate or the parent predominate. A complicated literature on shadow pricing has emerged that provides a methodology for adjusting technology choice for differences between private and social costs and benefits arising from price market frictions and externalities. Often it is assumed, once again either stated or understood, that the technological "menu" or stock of technologies on the "shelf" are known to the prospective user, and that once the

technology is acquired, there is perfect
knowledge about the relevant production
functions.[23] Very little attention is devoted
to producing technologies de novo either in
mature industrial countries or in third world
nations.

Currently used texts are of interest, of
course, because presumably they contain the
distillation of received doctrine on the
subject. Stated slightly differently, a great
deal of selectivity takes place and what
survives should signify what economists think
is most important and useful. In this context
it is enlightening to note that of the five
economic development textbooks perused, three
do not include "technology transfer" or
"transfer of technology" in their indices.

Yet the analysis deserves softening
through several observations. First, by and
large, the texts do perform well on some
matters reviewed in the previous section, e.g.,
in recognizing that multinational firms have
altered many features of the economic
landscape, technology transfer included.
Second, some notable changes in priorities,
e.g., more weight accorded to achieving
internal technological mastery within the
South, are of quite recent origin. Given the
lags involved, perhaps text authors and
compilers can be excused. Third, if we move
outside textbooks, orthodox economics has shed
much light on such issues as the economics of
producing technology ex ante.[24]

Fourth, to their credit, some
noninstitutionalist economists have felt
constrained by traditional economic renditions
of technology and technological advance and
have attempted to deal with real world
complexities of the transfer process, the
fiction of omniscience about production

functions, and the incomplete analysis inherent
in demand-induced technological progress.[25]
The fourth observation affords a useful point
for departure. If economists, more or less
rooted in the mainstream, grow dissatisfied
with existing economic explanations of
technology transfer and technological change,
it at least suggests that an alternative
perspective might be useful. With this in
mind, I will attempt to outline the
evolutionary or institutional thesis of
technological change.[26] The rendition will
lean almost exclusively on the Veblen-Ayres
axis of institutionalism with some recent
embellishments.

Institutional economics is concerned with
solving or ameliorating problems that have an
economic dimension. However, the institutionalist approach to eliminating or lessening an
economic shortcoming goes far beyond relying on
pure economics as conventionally defined. The
methodology employed is "holistic" or
multidisciplinary, and unapologetically so.
Using history, cultural anthropology,
sociology, social psychology, logic, political
science, engineering, or mathematics is fair
game, not necessarily because institutionalists
are more intellectually inquisitive, but
because they are firmly convinced that problem-
solving works better that way. Most real world
difficulties worthy of attention do have
interdependent, multidimensional properties.
When each discipline acts in isolation, the
often crucial interdependencies are not given
sufficient weight. At the barest minimum,
institutionalists believe, the most egregious
blunders due to disciplinary blinders are
avoidable.

In addition, institutional economists,
while not discounting entirely the insights

provided by examining equilibria models, find
situations of disequilibria much more
interesting and revealing. Human culture is in
constant flux as alterations in beliefs,
material environments, and human capabilities
transform the human condition and,
concomitantly, the nature of society's
discomforts and aspirations. Institutionalism
is an evolutionary science. After attempting
to fathom the fundamentals of the dynamics
involved, by considering "the achieved
technological potential and the full range of
culturally relative behavior and interests at
play" (Lower, 1984, p. 1172), the trick is to
intervene judiciously in order to steer the
course of events toward a better outcome.

The word "intervene" in the previous
sentence hints that institutional economists
advocate the exercise of some reasoned,
deliberate guidance for the economy. Indeed,
most do believe that some form of indicative
planning is desirable. The term "better
outcome" is also loaded with implications.
Institutionalism, by its problem-solving
nature, is valuational. Heavy reliance is
placed on Deweyian instrumentalism which seeks
to make some reasonable, weighted evaluation
among often conflicting social values, and use
such an assessment as the basis for action.[27]
Thus, after appropriate study of the origins
and contemporary ramifications of a
socioeconomic problem, and perhaps bolstered by
knowledge of similar experiences elsewhere in
time or location, the typical institutionalist
will feel comfortable in recommending a change
that might lead to an improved situation.
There are no certainties; emphasis is on trial
and error, experimentation, pushing successes,
and expeditiously abandoning failures. By and
large, the usefulness of the institutional

approach does not rest on its reputation as a predictive science other than in the very broad sense of prognosticating the general direction and pace of technological change.

We have identified at least four characteristics that distinguish institutional from mainstream economics. Economic orthodoxy is more likely to view interdisciplinary approaches as either adventurous or deviant excursions rather than the norm; it is preoccupied with equilibrium models; it eschews value judgments; and it devotes an enormous amount of energy and effort to formulating rigorously constructed highly abstract models that only remotely relate to, or influence, the identification and solution of pressing problems.

Against this backdrop, we can introduce the role of technology explicitly through what is known as the "Veblen-Ayres dichotomy."[28] Starting with the notion that human culture provides the core concept on which to base a study of the human condition,[29] Thorstein Veblen made a distinction between two aspects of human behavior; institutional or ceremonial behavior and tool-using behavior. This dichotomy that ran throughout Veblen's work was retained by Clarence Ayres who clarified many of Veblen's earlier ideas and formulated these ideas into a coherent theory.

Institutional or ceremonial behavior rests on cultural institutions, values, folk-beliefs, and mores. Such behavior is culture-specific. The idea of eating a chicken egg will evoke revulsion in some societies and be seen as perfectly normal in others; markings on a rock that represent an ancestor to an Australian aborigine will be meaningless to others; and so on.

At a very early age, members of society are taught "right" from "wrong," thus engendering a powerful emotional authoritarianism associated with existing behavioral norms. This emotional commitment is further heightened by myth, ceremony, symbols, and ritual (e.g., singing the school song before an athletic contest or donning cap and gown for convocation). Thus, social institutions, be they religious, financial, educational, familial, etc., being imbued with the prevailing cultural values, tend to be change resistant or supportive of the status quo.

Technology can be defined as tool-using if one makes clear that "tools" include artifacts (hammers, computers, or copper smelters), conceptual instruments (mathematical formulae, managerial techniques, or the latest valence table), and associated skills. Technological advance comes about through devising a new tool by combining two or more existing ones.[30] Technology operates across cultures in the sense that a tool is capable of performing the same, or very similar, productive task regardless of the culture.

Technological change disturbs comtemporary institutional arrangements since virtually any new technology will require alterations in the ceremonial aspects of life if it is to be used effectively. This can range from a mantled chimney replacing a hole in the roof leading to a major change in social status and class consciousness during the Middle Ages,[31] to the enormous institutional upheavals resulting from the printing press.

Technology tends to be dynamic for at least three reasons. First, as technological progress unfolds, the number of permutations-additional raw material for new productive combinations - expand. Second, if technological advance becomes sufficiently robust, institutional resistance is likely to attenuate - the institutional environment becomes more permissive.[32] Finally, there is a certain amount of "automaticity" or supply-push involved. If the requisite tools for an invention or discovery come into juxtaposition within a culture, and prevailing institutions are not utterly intractable, the tools are very likely to be combined appropriately and quickly. In support of this position, Ayres often cited evidence of simultaneous inventions and discoveries, of serendipitous discoveries, and of instances of premature attempts at invention before the required complement of tools existed.[33] It also explains why many institutionalists, including Ayres, have been fascinated by frontier situations - it is on geographic frontiers where institutional inhibitions are weakest, and where very often cultures, and their tools, first come into contact.[34]

This, as I interpret it, was the state of the Veblen-Ayres dichotomy as of the early 1960s. Since that time, institutional analysis has been applied to industrial organization, economic history, labor relations, public finance, economic development and other fields - analyses that are readily available in such publications as the <u>Journal of Economic Issues</u> and <u>American Journal of Economics and Sociology</u>. Institutional economists populate such professional organizations as the Association for Evolutionary Economics, Association for Institutional Thought, and Association for Social Economics.

Recently there has been an effort to further clarify concepts and correct past and avoid future misconceptions. It is one thing to say that ceremonial <u>behavior</u> is based on social institutions and tool-<u>using</u> is technology. It is quite another, however, to pose a dichotomy between the social institutions and the technology (hardware) themselves. From here, there is only a short descent on a slippery slope to picturing social institutions as "backward" and technology as "progressive." Sliding still further, one might decide, therefore, that social institutions are "bad" and technology is "good."

This is fatal on at least two counts. First virtually any purposive human act will involve both ceremonial and technological behavior. Whether it is planning a meal, planning a banquet, or planning a nation's agricultural policy, the actions take place in a cultural setting where behavior is influenced by prevailing folk-beliefs and available technical artifacts and know-how for using them. This is why Ayres, when accused once of being "against institutions," replied that it was like being "against air."

Second, and equally important: although true that technology, in the broadest sense, explains why material aspects of the human condition is superior to any previous time, it does not follow that every specific application of technology is desirable. Anne Mayhew has reminded us recently (1981) that it is the starkest form of ceremonial behavior to accept any new technological application in an unquestioning, ritual-like manner - the use of a novel technology or an untried application of existing technology should be subject to careful instrumental valuations just as should any important cultural mutation.

If some specific technological applications can be too dynamic for our own good, the other side of the coin is that some useful applications may go unexplored or unexploited. Several institutionalists have been investigating the possibility that in some cases, power exercised through social institutions can be so potent that technology is captured, controlled, and steered in socially undesirable, or at least in suboptimal ways. Such "institutional encapsulization" of technological capabilities appears most likely when institutional pluralism erodes and one institution emerges with cultural dominance or hegemony.[35]   One hopes these and other insights will continue to be explored by institutional economists and that fruitful policy derivatives will emerge.

     If the above constitutes a reasonably accurate skeleton of how ceremonial and tool-using behavior condition the pace and trajectory of technological change within a culture, the next question is "so what?" or "who cares?" The payoff must be in how valuable institutionalist analysis is in dealing with real-world problems. In short, institutionalist economics must commit itself to an evaluation along instrumentalist lines. For the broad sweep of institutional analyses in all its manifestations and assorted subdisciplines, I leave the reader to the outlets for institutionalist works cited above. Attention will now be directed to what an institutional perspective may contribute to improving third world acquisition of technology.

POSSIBLE CONTRIBUTIONS OF AN INSTITUTIONALIST PERSPECTIVE

Central Role of Technology

     The fundamental reason we are not grubbing in the ground for a root to eat or chasing

buffalo off cliffs for meat and other basic
needs is past technological advance. Savings
may have something to do with it, as may
capital accumulation, and in some societies
buying and selling activities most certainly
impinge on social welfare, but basically and
ultimately, technological progress is at the
heart of socioeconomic development and the
motor power for economic progress.

To say that this idea fits comfortably
into the institutional perspective understates
the case - it is axiomatic. A student of
economics can read neoclassical economics until
he/she drops and will never be led to such an
insight. "North-east" shifts in production
possibilities frontiers, "south-west" movements
of production functions, or the analysis of
mysteriously materialized new vintages of
capital equipment, and similar analytical
apparatuses, while worthwhile if used cautious-
ly, fail individually or collectively to give
technology a central place in economic development.[36] This remains true despite an emerging
interest in the economics of research and
development that was spurred in part by
research conducted in the 1960s which uncovered
a "residual," i.e., growth left unexplained by
the accumulation of unaltered factors of
production. Recognition that technology is
fundamental to economic development should give
institutionalists a "leg up" on other contemporary eocnomic perspectives.

Holism, Ideology, and Power

In addition, the holistic approach may
help explain behavior that would seem
irrational in a purely economic analysis. Why
does local sourcing account for around 40

percent of material inputs in Taiwan's manufactured exports to the United States under United States tariff provisions 806.3 and 807, while Mexican inputs amount to only 2 percent of such exports? Why do firms seemingly underutilize consultancies when empirical evidence (Johnston, 1963) suggests a very high rate of return on expenditures for these services?[37] Or how can one explain why a very successful innovation sits as an isolated micro-enclave, tried once and forgotten, in Colombia, and is built into a five-year development plan and the subject of further scientific experimentation in Thailand?[38]

The author has no doubt that conventional economic analysis can offer perhaps a substantial part ot these questions, but a priori it would seem that extra-economic forces are operative. The identification and understanding of these forces are essential to maximizing improvements through achieving an institutional configuration that will result in more effective use of technical capabilities.

The interdisciplinary nature of institutional economics should also stand it in good stead in analyzing the exercise of power, through political, financial, religious, military, or other institutional vehicles. This is especially true when combined with another advantage of institutionalism. James Street and the author (1982) have claimed that institutional economics is less encumbered by "ideological baggage" than either structuralist or dependency approaches. The same case can be made regarding institutional economics vis a vis neoclassical economics applied to problems of economic development. For example, International Monetary Fund (IMF) stabilization policy pronouncements have gone far beyond technical economic prescriptions - it is not difficult to read between the lines and determine who is being "sinful" versus who is behaving "righteously."[39]

Economic prescriptions and the consequences emanating from their implementation get even more serious when supreme institutional power and ideologically laden economics go hand in hand. The recent applicaton of neoconservative or monetarist measures in the Southern Cone countries of Latin America provide a case in point. It is ironic in the extreme that a brand of economics that takes pride in maximizing freedom of individual choice could not be introduced or sustained in these countries without an oppressive, totalitarian political system. But more instructive to our point is the character of the neoclassical post mortem.

Most Latin Americans and Latin Americanists not in the neoclassical camp, and perhaps many who are, would agree with Albert Hirschman who, speaking of the period from 1973, remarked: "Few will deny that the deindustrialization experience in Chile and Argentina was a most unhappy chapter in Latin American economic history. As often happens with such aberrations, its perversity is almost incomprehensible in retrospect" (1987, p. 16). To their credit, neoclassical economists are attempting to divine what went wrong; however, anything but laudable is the steadfast refusal to examine critically the paradigm of Newtonian economics per se or whether it may not be universally applicable in all cultural, social, and historical settings.[40]

Mainstream efforts have concentrated on: if only wage rates had been indexed properly; if only the adjustable peg had allowed the peso to depreciate more rapidly, etc. The possibility of that the whole framework was

rickety or wrong for the occasion does not seem
to be raised.   It reminds one of David
Hamilton's comment·on ritual or ceremonial
behavior: "Adhere rigidly to some prescribed
ritual and belief and the desired outcome will
be achieved.   If it is not achieved, it is not
because of the inefficiency of the ritual
belief, but because of failure to adhere to all
of the prescribed canons for proper
manipulation" (1986, p. 527).

By no means are institutionalists entirely
free from ceremonial patterns of thought.
Occasionally an institutionalist has to chide
the flock: "Unfortunately, too many
institutionalists have preferred to play the
role of perpetual outsider - - abandoning any
idea as soon as it enters the intellectual
mainstream of economics" (DeGregori, 1987, p.
477).   Yet I am suggesting that an economic
analysis with strong pragmatic roots will be
less encumbered in this respect than other
analytical approaches.   We are contemplating a
matter of degree, not a pristine cleavage
between ceremonial and nonceremonial patterns
of thought.

Being relatively ideologically unbiased
does not mean the same thing as being
apolitical.   If it is true that global research
and development is unduly skewed toward
preventing and curing diseases common in
temperate zones to the relative neglect of
tropical ailments, political pressures may well
be part of the mix of policies needed to right
the imbalance.   If the configuration of
photovoltaic-powered street lights in an Indian
village are suspiciously concentrated around
the village headman's and friends' houses
(Bhatia, forthcoming), any move to a more
equitable sharing of the benefits of technology
will necessarily involve political action.

Formulating national strategies for balancing technology transfer with expanding domestic technological mastery is utterly dependent on the political arena.

As these examples imply, a major deficiency of world development is the unequal distribution of the benefits of technology. Reasons include inadequate purchasing power by a large chunk of the world's population, uneven access to education, and heavy-handed usurpation by those in power. To the extent that income distribution is involved, orthodox economics, because of a taboo on making interpersonal utility comparisons, is notoriously impotent. At times their only way out is to "cheat" - sometimes with apologetic caveats when introducing "community indifference curves" - usually with no qualifications when aggregating consumer surplus under a demand curve (Whalen, 1987). It goes without saying that virtually any policy worth its salt will hurt some groups and benefit others. Perhaps it is advantageous, from the standpoint of getting problems solved, to employ an economic analysis that incorporates distributional considerations in its analysis and as one functional component of policy prescriptions. The alternatives are not recognizing distribution of income (or wealth) as a legitimate economic problem or spelling out in positive economic terms what the distributional consequences will be and letting the political arena decide. The latter option forfeits insights garnered from a holistic vantage.

Success of NICs: Korea

Finally, institutional perspective can help understand the astonishing success of newly industrializing countries. Precise policy packages have differed intertemporally within countries, as well as among countries, but with the exception of Hong Kong, all saw economic expansion accompanied by persistent government policy interventions. We focus here on South Korea because her rationale for intervening and the style and methods for doing so appear to have employed instrumental approaches for acquiring technological prowess. I rely exclusively on a remarkable article by Howard Pack and Larry Westphal (1986). In the synopsis that follows, I take considerable liberty with the sequence of presentation but not, I trust, with the substance of their analysis and conclusions.

Korea has made very wise and extensive use of market forces, especially with respect to established industries, and when intervening, policymakers went to some pains to get the prices right. But intervene she did with tariffs, import licensing, local-content requirements, and credit rationing. In addition, the government helped develop effective marketing agents (<u>chaebols</u>), established public enterprises, and participated in investment decisions regarding "capacity creation and expansion, market creation and overseas marketing, human capital accumulation, technology acquisition, infrastructure provision, and so on" (p. 100).

These measures were anything but random interventions - they were strategic intercessions designed to choose infant industries reasonably close to the margin of international comparative advantage and make

them competitive, both at home and abroad, in
relatively short order. Strategy focused on
flexibility and selectivity. Usually the total
number of infant industries encompassed within
the strategy was small, and the composition
evolved through time. It is difficult to
choose industries for special treatment ex
ante, and indeed failures occurred, but on
balance the strategists have been quite
successful. This has been due in part to a
concerted effort to gather information on all
aspects of infant industries (and presumably
prospective ones). This is a process with
continuous monitoring as prices, market
conditions, and industries' technological
sophistication evolved together. In this way,
the center of gravity of tactics could be
shifted, and in some cases reversed, in
response to an evolving stream of signals. In
effect, government became an integrated
decision-maker which was necessary to overcome
externalities associated with a fledging
industry with future promise.

All of this led Pack and Westphal to see
technological matters very close to the heart
of industrialization strategies. Despite
Korea's vaunted export-led growth the authors
believe "that trade considerations are
secondary to technological ones in searching
for an understanding of industrializiation that
is relevant to policy making" (p. 91).

Korea's experience cannot be understood
fully in neoclassical terms. There is, of
course, the obvious heresy of industry-specific
biases of policy interventions. Also, for
reasons explained in some detail by the
authors, neoclassical theory underestimates by
a wide margin the beneficial externalities
garnered through accumulating technological
capacity. The need of "an explicit recognition

that sociopolitical factors are the primary determinants of the efficacy of different forms of government intervention" (p. 103) may well disadvantage mainstream analysis, as well as neoclassical economists' tendency to "assume a world of platonic ideals" (p. 118).

Pack and Westphal are careful to caution against attempting to apply this strategy indiscriminately to the third world, although they believe insights gained from their analysis can be useful in tailoring a country-specific approach. I agree on both counts. The reason that their study is singled out here is that (1) Korea appears to have adopted a policy that is perfectly compatible with an instrumental approach to problem-solving with emphasis on flexible experimentation and stress on integrating imported technology with domestic learning, and (2) with slight changes in terminology, the paper could have been read comfortably, accompanied by much nodding of heads at the annual meeting of the Association for Evolutionary Economics. As far as I know, the two economists do not consider themselves institutionalists, but the insights and perspective of their analysis are so congruent with an institutional approach, that I rest my case on the assertion contained in the first sentence of this subsection.[41]

FUTURE PROBLEMS AND OPPORTUNITIES

It is here, more than in any other section, where the tight pinch of space limitations is felt. I hope to elaborate elsewhere on additional themes that could have been equally appropriate here (James, in preparation). With this limitation in mind, we consider below (1) possible trade reversals and

LDCs' technological strategies, (2) the case
for rethinking regulations on technology
imports, and (3) an advocacy for technology
pluralism.

Trade Reversal and Technological Responses

Juan Rada (1984) reminds us of India's
loss of comparative advantage in textile
production due to innovations in the British
textile industry and new technologies for
producing nitrogen which sank the Chilean
saltpeter exports. Are there incipient
contemporary examples of dynamic comparative
advantage shifting away from developing
countries? Certainly there is mounting
trepidation that the application of microelectronic innovations will erode LDCs' competitive
edge in manufacturing activities based on low-
wage, skilled labor. No one can be certain --
it is simply too early to tell. At this stage
we can only take a look at some "straws in the
wind."

Some of the evidence adduced is the
enumeration of abandoned overseas operations by
affiliates of developed countries' parent
firms. For example, Werner Olle (1986) cites
West German plant closures in entertainment
electronics in Mexico (AEG, 1982), camera
lenses in Taiwan (Bosch, no date), TV and hi-fi
equipment in Taiwan (Grundig, 1983), electronic
mounting material in Brazil (Busch-Jaeger,
1984), power plants in South Korea (Deutsche
Babcock, 1982), and electronic components in
Mauritius (Siemens, 1981). Of itself, such
fragmenting information is of little use since
it says nothing about the net flow of
production and, as Olle recognizes, many

factors unrelated to technology could have motivated the withdrawal.

Other studies attempt to project the pace of automation. Susan Sanderson (1987), citing work by her and associates, have estimated that for electrical and electronic products in Mexico's assembly plants (maquiladoras) 80 percent automation will come about in component fabrication (5 years), board assembly (7 years), subsystem assembly (10-15 years), and system assembly (15 years). Presumably if Mexico fails to keep pace, she will lose comparative advantage; if she does, the assembly plants will become considerably less labor-intensive.

Jones and Womack (1985) review what they call the third and fourth transformation of the automobile: Japan's organization of automobile production and the application of electronic and new materials innovations respectively. They conclude:

> For the developing countries, the third and fourth transformations mean that the product cycle is not coming their way. In fact, the future for anyone plotting a low wage, high labor content strategy to gain world export markets is bleak (p. 405).

One of the most thorough investigations of technology-induced transformation of international competitiveness is a study by Hoffman and Rush (1984) on the global garment industry. After surveying microelectronic innovations in clothing production, they found considerable automation at the preassembly stage and finishing stage. In the assembly stage, which occupies 80 percent of the work force, incremental innovations are taking place, but

the basic pattern of one person, one sewing
machine remains.

Still, the garment industry's pace of
adoption of innovations and, partly as a
consequence, capital-goods suppliers
development of new innovations, have both been
slow. Reasons include: (1) the industry is
dominated by small, capital-starved firms with
tradition-bound management; (2) the industry
spends only a nominal amount on research and
development; (3) capital-goods suppliers form a
staid oligopoly that has been reluctant to
innovate; and (4) formidable technological
barriers face those attempting to produce a
cloth-manipulating robot.

Significantly, however, all of these
inhibiting factors appear to be weakening. The
industry structure is gradually becoming more
concentrated as the average firm size grows;
management is confronting competitive
conditions which motivates learning about the
new technology; "new blood" in the form of
electronics firms entering the capital-goods
sector has forced older supplier to become more
innovative; and finally, both the European
Community and Japan have well-funded research
and development programs geared (in part)
toward developing an efficient cloth-handling
robot.

The authors estimate that by the mid-1990s
the cumulative effect of incremental
innovations will begin to shift comparative
advantage in favor of developed countries, at
least for some products. About the same time,
they speculate, flexible manufacturing systems
will become available in assembly operations,
complemented by computer-based innovations in
other stages of garment production. Unit costs
will decline as bugs are worked out and
economics of scale are realized, and these

integrated automation systems will be capable of causing a fundamental reversal of comparative advantage in the next 15 to 20 years.

We concentrate here on microelectronic innovations since other emerging technologies are just edging into the application phase. Gerd Junne (1984), however, sees the likelihood of manufactured substitutes for third world agricultural and food exports resulting from modern biotechnology. Also, it appears that applied conventional biotechnology techniques are already taking their toll in depressing LDCs sugar exports (Ruivenkamp, 1986).

Certainly the possibility of trade reversal has to be taken seriously, and a technological dimension must loom large in any responses contemplated by developing countries. The usual prescription is that LDCs adopt newly emerging technologies on a selective basis and in accordance with market conditions, other national priorities, and level of the nation's overall development. This is well and good, but it leaves 99 percent of the work undone. One formidable challenge that must engage development planners and economists is the fleshing out of these essentially vacuous dictums in detail sufficient for industry-, country-, and regional-specific operational guidelines that are translated into suitable policies for achieving an adequate level and composition of technology acquisition, as well as a proper balance and integration between technology obtained from abroad, and hardware, knowledge, and skills generated internally.

Rethinking Defensive Restrictions on Technology
Imports

If the institutionalist emphasis on
acquiring, constructively utilizing, and
improving technology is sound, there is an
urgent need for countries of the South to
review policies governing technology imports.
As we observed earlier, many upper-tier
developing countries regulated technology
transfer as a response to imperfections in the
market for technology which disadvantaged the
buyer. A thorough review of these measures is
in order due to (1) changing perceptions about
how the technology market has worked all along,
(2) changing conditions in commercial
technology transactions, and (3) questions as
to whether the old "defensive" regulations are
compatible with policies for encouraging
internal technological capabilities.

Without attempting to be definitive,
several examples of changing perceptions can be
adduced. For example, contrary to earlier and
still lingering views, there is convincing
evidence that suppliers of existing technology
often incur positive direct costs, and in some
cases these reach significant levels. After
investigating 26 technology transfer projects
involving U.S. multinational firms as
providers, David Teece concluded: "The
resources required to transfer technology
internationally are considerable. Accordingly,
it is quite inappropriate to regard existing
technology as something that can be made
available to all at zero social cost" (1977, p.
259). Bell and Scott-Kemmis surveyed 93
technology transfer agreements between British
providing and Indian receiving firms. They
found that "few of the supplier firms incurred
trivial or zero costs - for most firms they

were clearly of considerable significance"
(1985, 1978). They go on to cite an example of
one British firm that incurred a cost of around
300,000 British pounds covering the expense
costs of sending a team of engineers to India
to pinpoint needs, determine the content of the
technology package to be transferred and
initiate negotiations.

As to another perception, there is no
conclusive evidence that multinational
enterprises employ a more capital-intensive
technology than their nationally owned
counterparts. Lall (1978) reviewed the
empirical investigations, and results vary by
methodology and country studied.
Significantly, the only studies attempting to
compare matched pairs of national and foreign
firms failed to find consistent patterns of
factor intensities. When meaningful
differences in intensities are found, they
appear to be associated with a heavier concentration of multinationals in more modern
industries rather than any greater proclivity
for capital intensity per se (ILO, 1984).

During the initiation of defensive
regulation of technology imports, domestic
affiliates of foreign firms and national
enterprises were viewed as the prime
"exploitees" by international purveyors of
technology. It is therefore somewhat
astonishing that technology regulations are not
a universal hit with LDCs entrepreneurial and
managerial corps. Some technology-receiving
enterprises are frustrated by regulatory
delays, feel that in somes cases they lose out
on technology purchases because of prohibitions
on meeting the stipulated price, and some
prefer a longer term contractual relationship
than regulations allow. Some firms get around
the regulations by "informal" agreements with

the foreign supplier (Chudnovsky, 1981; Bell
and Scott-Kemmis, 1985b).

Have conditions changed since defensive
regulations were instigated around a decade and
a half ago?   Perhaps so.   I know of no conclusive evidence, but certainly there are
strong implications that royalty payments for
technology have been declining (Chudnovsky,
1981).   Naturally, this may be because of
defensive measures, but they may also be partly
owing to a proliferation of sources for
technologies and enhanced bargaining skills on
the part of technology purchases.   The extent
to which a decline can be attributed to the
last two causes diminishes the value of the
older type of technology transfer laws.

There is also evidence from India that the
technology transfer process has changed
markedly since studies were made during the
1970s.   Bell and Scott-Kemmis (1985b), who
looked at technology agreements between British
suppliers and Indian buyers, found, among other
things, that usually the Indian firm made the
first overture to enter into negotiations; in
about three-fourths of the cases, the firms had
no prior relationship; nearly half the British
firms had no transnational investment, and many
others could not be considered "major
multinationals"; and for most supplying firms,
India had numerous alternative suppliers, and
in "a considerable number of cases" Indian
firms had performed a systematic search.   All
of these findings do considerable damage to the
stereotyped view, perhaps justified earlier, of
a multinational monopolist anxious to extract
economic rents from foreign firms, often their
affiliates.   I know of no similar studies for
other developing countries, but it is not
implausible to suppose that some evolutionary
alterations have taken place in the global

technology market.   If so, this is an added reason for critically reviewing existing science and technology policy instruments, especially restrictions on technology imports.

Science and technology policy instruments need to be reviewed for a third reason involving the following question: since the production of new technologies calls for risky commitments of resources over an extended period of time, will not reducing external competition in domestic technology markets encourage domestic production?   This proposition had been suggested casually by many observers, but it was stated most fully and persuasively by Sanjaya Lall (1980).

We are not lacking in real-world experiments.   Perhaps most intriguing is that India, which has had an extremely strict policy on technology imports, has a remarkable record for two crude indicators of internal technological capabilities, namely (1) capital goods production and (2) technology exports. Mexico, on the other hand, has had the most liberal imports of technology (as a proportion of GDP) of any major NIC, and has a dismal record in both capital goods output and exports of goods and services with high technology content.   Are cause and effect operating here? Brazil, like Mexico, has been very free with technology imports, but has protected her important capital goods "learning nexus," while Mexico has done little (until very recently) to promote capital goods.   Brazil's extremely strict stance on reserving microcomputer production and markets for domestic firms is also an interesting experiment.[42]

I have written at greater length on the matter of infant industry protection for technological activities with respect to Mexico (James, forthcoming).   My position is that it

is unwise for Mexico to screen technology
imports more stringently across the board.
Some effective protection of capital goods as
part of a promotional package for that sector,
would, in my opinion, greatly speed and deepen
Mexico's progress toward building internal
technological capability. In addition, Indian
experience suggests that a stringent stance on
technology imports, while leaning to rapid
domestic accumulation of know-how, is less
successful in fostering mastery at the know-why
level of technological mastery (Lall, 1985, and
forthcoming). But these remain tentative
conclusions. Students of technical change in
the South still need to milk the existing and
future policy permutations for clues helpful in
reconstructing science and technology policy
instruments. The primary aim is to achieve a
productive balance, composition, and
integration of technology imports with internal
learning. You find very few individuals
experienced in this process who advocate
completely unfettered trade, a la neoclassical
dictums, or autarkic delinking, sometimes
recommended by dependency writers. However,
the expanse between these extremes is vast, the
number of policy instruments are many, and
viable strategies are likely to show country-
specific differences.

Technological Pluralism

Thus far, either overtly or tacitly,
technology for the modern industrial sector has
been emphasized. This bias is reflected in the
literature. Most studies of accumulating
internal technological capabilities deal with
manufacturing activities,[43] and a similar
concentration of investigative effort has been

applied to newly industrializing countries, not
second- and third-tier developing nations.
Presumably, judging from economic and socioeconomic data, some long-term trickle-down of
benefits to the very poor has taken place, thus
technology-propelled expansion of output has
had some beneficial impact. But are there no
technological avenues for more directly and
palpably affecting the welfare of the world's
lower-income strata?

One possibility is the development and
dissemination of "intermediate technology."[44]
These technologies will ordinarily exhibit
many, if not all of the following characteristics compared to conventional production
methods: (1) involve low investment cost per
work-place, (2) employ a relatively labor-
intensive technique, (3) require low to
moderate skill levels and entrepreneurial
abilities, (4) be ecologically sound, (5) use a
high proportion of locally available inputs,
and (6) operate efficiently on a small-scale
basis. Detractors notwithstanding, there is
substantial evidence that many individual
applications of intermediate technology succeed
in raising productivity and output in traditional economic activities, and not infrequently, relieve the drudgery and discomfort visited
on traditional-sector workforces.

An additional approach, "technology
blending," also seeks to upgrade traditional
technologies and, in addition, attempts to
bring the advantages of frontier technology to
the very poor. Due to its novelty and potential, it will receive more detailed attention
here. Technology blending has come to be known
as the constructive integration of emerging
technologies with small-scale, low-income
sectors.[45] More concretely, it is the fruitful
merger of modern biotechnology, photovoltaic

power, microelectronics, satellite communications, and new materials technology with small
holder agriculture and agribusiness, the
informal urban sector, small manufacturing
enterprises, and traditional systems for
delivering services (e.g., health and education). Larger scale operations that clearly
meet basic needs criteria and sometimes
included as "traditional" activities. As the
word blending implies, the frontier technology
does not completely replace traditional
technology (the very contraposition of blending), but leaves some sizeable, recognizable
elements of traditional production technique
and organizational configurations intact.

Examples include an electronic load
controller for mini-hydroelectric power
generation in Colombia, Sri Lanka, and
Thailand; cloning of palm oil trees in Malaysia
and Costa Rica; village education via
satellite-based communication in India;
microbial leaching for metal extraction in
Andean Pact countries; photovoltaic-powered
street lighting for Indian villages, remote
sensing for resource development in West
Africa, laser-guided land leveling in Egypt,
and single-cell protein production in Mexico.[46]

Although intermediate technology and
technology blending are both pathways for
upgrading traditional technologies, they are
clearly distinct. Very often blending will
entail far higher capital costs than those
envisioned by intermediate technology
proponents; most developing countries will have
to import emerging technologies for blending
for many years to come; and sometimes blending
makes substantial demands on skills and
abilities of those using the technology.

What hope do intermediate technology and
technology blending hold? Focusing on the

former, the growth in number of organizations, manpower, and expenditure devoted to developing and promoting such technologies has been impressive (Jaquier and Blanc, 1983).   The generation of intermediate technology has been dynamic, but the technology itself has been less so.   There is scant evidence that the introduction and employment of intermediate technology leads to progressive, imaginative recombinations, adaptations, and novel uses that lead to self-sustained technological advance.

Several reasons suggest themselves. Although the rate of growth in research, development, and dissemination of intermediate technologies has been high, it still represents a tiny fraction of the world's total expenditures on such activities. Perhaps the endeavor remains short of some aggregate threshold of activity beyond which more innovative behavior would be stimulated. Government policies often knowingly or incidentally discourage the adoption of more labor-intensive production methods.[47] The ease of replication of simpler technologies ordinarily rules out commerical investment in developing and promoting intermediate technologies.   There may be technical limitations to many simpler technologies.[48]

We could extend this list considerably, but one further question is certain to occur to an institutionalist.   Is it possible that intermediate technologies fit so cozily with the surrounding cultural millieu that ceremonial patterns of thought and behavior go virtually undisturbed?   If so, we are confronted with a different type of threshold problem and a somewhat different sense in which technology can be encapsulated.

I am convinced that a host of intermediate
technologies, the stock of which continues to
be augmented by research, are useful, productive, innovations. Furthermore, given
prevailing conditions among the world's abject
poor, only very infrequently will using modern
technology be a feasible option. For improving
productivity, in many circumstances, it is
intermediate technology or nothing. It is
quite plausible then that world welfare will be
served by devoting resources to developing a
small tractor with a reduced turning radius
that saves small-holder's growing space; and
inexpensive roofing material for low-cost
housing; an efficient, low-cost winnowing
machine; an effective soap made from locally
available substances; and so on. Assuming they
are effective, their adoption by a multitude of
individuals in a profusion of third world
village and urban slums, quite feasibly can
result in a net gain in global social welfare
even if no further village-level or slum-level
innovations take place. There is nothing
inherently wrong in squeezing out gains from
what would amount to a million tiny technological enclaves (or encapsulizations). But if
there is anything on which all economists
(conventional or otherwise) agree upon, it is
that really imposing gains come from dynamic,
cumulative, and routine technological advance.

If this analysis is on the mark, the first
order of business is to attend to such questions as: To what extent, if any, do technical
considerations circumscribe dynamic technological trajectories for intermediate technology?
Do intermediate technologies, taken individually, agitate prevailing social institutions so
imperceptibly that cultural constraints on
further technical change remain as confining as
ever? If the answer to the last question is

yes, is a "cluster effect" possible wherein the introduction of a package of intermediate technologies would eventually lead to a more favorable cultural environment for technical change?   Are there some classifications (by using sector of application, level of technical sophistication, etc.) of intermediate technology that are currently or potentially more dynamic than others?   It is obvious that social scientists have much work to be done.   Equally clear, one should think, a "holistic" approach in addressing these questions is the most productive way to go.

Technology blending proffers a different array of problems and opportunities.   Research is still in its early stages, but indications are that technology blends can elevate levels of productivity and incomes in traditional sectors.   From case study material, it appears that technology blends are especially fruitful in augmenting resources and improving social services without compromising levels of employment.   Two hypotheses can be advanced. First, since technology blending by definition involves high technology, the resulting marriage with prevailing production methods may encounter fewer technical "dead ends" compared to intermediate technology.   Indeed, some blends have led to considerable scientific effort and indigenous technical learning within LDCs.[49]   Furthermore, the insertion of a more radical technology - compared to the intermediate variety - may achieve the necessary "shake up" of social institutions, thus rendering the institutional surroundings more conducive to further technical progress. However, since (again, by definition) important aspects of traditional modes of production are preserved, the level of social disruption and attendant psychological discomfort may be more bearable than cataclysmic perturbations occasioned by the complete displacement of traditional technology by modern production. In short, we are suggesting that both technical and institutional inhibitions to progressive innovational activity may be less confining in the case of technology blending vis a vis intermediate technology.

These are only partially tested hypotheses. We need de novo blending experiments with early data gathering that permit more complete socioeconomic appraisals. Especially needed are trials of blending projects in which technology is centrally provided and maintained (government entity, aid agency, nonprofit organization, cooperative, etc.) and made available as a quasi-public good to a wide constituency of users in small-scale, low-income occupations.

Technological pluralism is not coterminous with satisfying basic needs, but it is an essential element of a basic needs approach. If intermediate technology and technology blending continue to be geared toward relieving the plight of the abjectly poor, and join conventional and emerging technologies as part of the technological amalgam in the South, far more can be accomplished if we can learn how to discover, nourish, and encourage propulsive innovational trajectories.

SUMMARY

After the second World War, developing countries became preoccupied with obtaining technology from abroad. As the transfer process proceeded, the full range of technologies, transfer mechanisms, and participants began to be appreciated. At the same time, imperfections in the market for technology, believed to be deleterious to third world interests, were identified. Many LDCs responded with defensive regulations designed to eliminate or ameliorate undesirable effects of technology imports. Recently the South has shown a growing concern with building their own technological capabilities.

Orthodox economics has failed to handle some aspects of technology acquisition satisfactorily. Partly this is because technological change is seen as arising incidentally to market activity, and partly because analysis tends to focus narrowly on purely economic manifestations. Institutional economics, which places technological change at the epicenter of socioeconomic development, employs a multidisciplinary approach. This situates it well for examining how vested interests, and power relationships that arise from them, affect technological progress and access to existing technologies. The pragmatic, experimental, valuational process espoused by institutionalists should also prove useful in analyzing third world technology strategies and experiences.

Of the many issues deserving attention by social scientists interested in improving technology requisition and mastery by the South, three were singled out. It was argued that defensive regulations of technology imports should be revamped because (1) some older perceptions were not so accurate, (2) the transfer process has seen important changes, and (3) the older restrictions may not be compatible with the higher priority given to accumulating internal technological capacities. Second, the danger of trade reversals due to shifting configurations of comparative advantage is real, yet no concrete guidelines on

intelligent responses by nations of the South
have been forthcoming. This issue must be
addressed. Finally, a plea was made for a
technology strategy of technological pluralism
wherein technologies of different levels of
sophistication would be nurtured. Intermediate
technology and technology blending can be
targeted to raising income levels and produc-
tivities in traditional sectors and serve as a
major component of a basic needs approach.
However, we need to know much more about the
extent to which these levels of technology can
lead to dynamic trajectories of technological
advance and how any such potential can be
realized.

NOTES

1. For the sake of variety "LDCs,"
"developing countries," "third world," and
"South" will be used synonymously.

2. See Dixon (1985). The PQLI is based on
the average life expectancy at age one,
infant mortality, and literacy rates.

3. See Dahlman and Sercovich (1984) and the
special edition of World Development on
technology exports edited by Lall (1984).
Lall has a useful overview in this issue.

4. See case studies in Katz (1987) and a sum-
mation of cases of productivity gains in Bell
and associates (1984).

5. In some contexts the terms "institutional
economics" and "evolutionary economics" can be
used interchangeably. Indeed the Association
for Evolutionary Economics is the most impor-

tant professional body of institutionalists. Since other variants of evolutionary concepts have emerged, which have different emphases from mainstream institutional thought (Nelson and Winter, 1982; Clark and Juma, 1987), I will use "institutional" and "institutionalist" to avoid confusion.

6.   This section has benefitted greatly from the following surveys of technology transfer: Contractor and Sagafi-Nejad (1981), Stewart (1981), and Buckley (1983).

7.   On capacity-stretching by steel plants see Maxwell (1987) on the Acindar plant in Argentina, Dahlman and Fonseca (1987) on the USIMINAS plant in Brazil, and Perez y Peniche (1987) on Altos Hornos in Mexico. See Pearson (1987) on the Latin American cement industries. All of these are based on earlier research done under the auspices of the Research Program on Scientific and Technological Development in Latin America. For an overall appraisal of capacity-stretching, see Sercovich (1978) and Maxwell and Teubel (1980).

8.   See Acharyn (1974), Morawetz (1974), Stewart (1974), and White (1978).

9.   Presentation, University of Tennessee-Knoxville, April, 1987. Streeten is Director, World Development Center, Boston University.

10.   For reviews and critiques of dependency thought, see Bath and James (1974) and Palma (1981).

11.   For example, see Subrahmanian (1972) and Vaitsos (1974, 1975).

12.   See Vaitsos (1974).

13.   See Vaitsos (1970) and Stewart (1977).
This view is not confined to those sympathetic
to the dependency perspective - see Johnson
(1970).

14.   See Vaitsos (1972) and Lall (1976).

15.   From James (forthcoming). The sequence
benefitted from similar lists by Lall (1979)
and Fransman (1984).

16.   On capital goods production in the South,
see Chudnovsky and associates (1983), UNIDO
(1985) and Fransman (1986).

17.   For some types of capital goods that are
extremely "'design'intensive," user feedback is
essential to product development. See Rosenberg (1982) on aircraft development.

18.   Country studies can be found in Rushing
and Brown (1986).

19.   See Guide to World Science, 2nd ed.,
various volumes, various dates (F.H. Books
Ltd.: Guernsey, British Isles).

20.   For a more comprehensive evaluation of
STIP, see Sagasti (1978).

21.   I have relied heavily here on Teitel
(1984).

22.   The texts perused are Herrick and
Kindleberger (1983), Meier (1984), Todaro
(1985), Gillis and associates (1987), and
Hugendorn (1987).

23. For an interesting variation, see Stoneman and David (1986) who do assume limited knowledge about a new technology, but go on to assume perfect foresight on prices once the technology is obtained and that capital goods suppliers have perfect knowledge of the demand environment.

24. For illustrative works on the economics of generating scientific and technical knowledge, see Nelson (1959), Arrow (1962a, 1962b), Mansfield (1968), and Freeman (1982).

25. See my (1987) analysis of dissent from the neoclassical position on the economics of technological progress which purports to find similarities between institutionalist and non-institutionalist misgivings. When commenting on an earlier draft presented at the 1986 Association for Evolutionary Economics, David Hamilton remarked that if the noninstitutionalists discovered with whom they were converging, they would run like hell. I yearn for a less negative response.

26. There is a large, outstanding and growing literature on this topic.

27. For a contemporary review of the role of instrumental valuation in institutional economics, see Hickerson (1987).

28. Since the theme permeates Veblen's writings, it is difficult to point any uninitiated reader to any one of his works. See Mayhew (1987) and relevant references. To a lesser extent, the same applies to Ayres, but most agree that his single most revealing exposition is Ayres (1944). For years there has been a lack of a reasonably condensed body

of literature that conveys what institutional economics is all about. "Where do you send a colleague or graduate student who stumbles over an orthodox anomaly or by chance or design is intrigued by a reading of Thorstein Veblen, Clarence Ayres or William Kapp, and wishes access to a general presentation of the institutionalist approach?" (Tool, 1987, p. 952). A two-volume series of "paradigm papers" were designed to fill the void. As I pen this note, the first set, "Evolutionary Economics I: Foundations of Economic Thought," is contained in the September 1987 issue of the <u>Journal of Economic Issues</u>, the second set, "Evolutionary Economics II: Institutional T h e o r y   a n d Policy," will follow soon in the same journal.

29.   On culture as a core concept, see Mayhew (1987b).

30.   See Ayres (1938, p. 13, 1944, p. 112, 1952,   p.   56),   Gilfillan   (1935,   p.   6), Kaempffert   (1930,   p.   17),   Mumford   (1938,   p. 52),   Ogburn   (1922,   p.   881),   Russman   (1931,   p. 9),   Usher   (1929,   p.   11),   and White   (1949,   p. 169), and others too numerous to mention.

31.   "Mantled chimneys, built into the walls, were a feature in every part of the castle. As distinct   from   a   hole   in   the   roof,   these chimneys were a technological advance   of   the 11th century that by warming individual rooms, brought lords and ladies out of the common hall where all had once eaten together and gathered for warmth, and separated owners from retainers.   No other invention brought more progress in comfort and refinement, although at the cost of a widening social gulf" (Tuchman, 1978, p. 11).

32.   For any single society or civilization,.
this is not undirectional.   Once improving
welfare is attributed to hallowed institutions
rather than technical competence, a technological breakthrough can be halted and cemented.
Arnold Toynbee's nine-volume <u>A Study in History</u>
is strewn with civilizations fallen victim to
this "feedback" mechanism.

33.   As in other matters, Ayres' "oral tradition" stemming from class lectures and seminar
discussions is richer than his writings.   See,
however, Ayres (1944, pp. 112-119) and James
(1958), a thesis done under Ayres' supervision.

34.   For an interesting offshoot of this
literature, see Street (1976).

35.   On "ceremonial encapsulation" see Bush
(1979), Junker (1982), and Waller (1987).
Waller, who develops the point on institutional
hegemony, has further citations.

36.   A good part of the problem is the habit of
treating technological change as an exogenous
variable.   Eight of ten works in the neoclassical mold on technology transfer reviewed by
Pugel (1981) make this assumption.

37.   The author recently completed analyzing
survey data for 46 metal-engineering
enterprises in Mexico.   The firms had been
divided into a top, middle, and lower
(roughly one-third each) groups according to
their technological capabilities.   The lower
group (14 enterprises) had one consultancy in
1980 and one in 1986.   A priori this seems
suboptimal.   Data to appear in James
(forthcoming).

38.   For a somewhat lengthier account, see
Bhalla and James (1986).   For a description of
the innovation and its use in three countries,
see Whitby (1984).

39.   On ideology and the IMF, see Horowitz
(1985-1986); on ideological tendencies of
the Reagan administration with respect to Latin
America, see Hirschman (1987).

40.   Corbo and de Melo (1987) is a good example
of this literature, and many more citations are
found   in   their   bibliography.   It   should   be
clear from the context, but is perhaps prudent
to say explicitly, these economists and their
colleagues are doing excellent economics within
the   neoclassical   framework.   It   is   the
framework   that   is   questionable   in   this
application   -   a   fine   example   of   Veblen's
assertion that economics is the most advanced
social science - but in the wrong direction.

41.   Pack's   and   Westphal's   reputations   are
sufficiently   established   to   survive   such
accusations - see note 25.

42.   Adler (1986), Erber (1985), Evans (1986),
Frischtak (1986), and Schwartzman (1985) are
useful on Brazil's computer policies.

43.   It is my understanding that Martin Bell
and associates at the Science Policy Research
Unit, University of Sussex, are well into a
study on enhancing local technology mastery
with respect to petroleum technology transferred to China.   Also Alyson Warhurst, of
SPRU, and Chilean colleagues are looking into
internal technological capacity building in
mining activities.   Fransman (1986b) provides a
few hints as to how building internal tech-

nological capabilities in agriculture might differ from the industrial sector.

44.   The term "appropriate technology" is studiously avoided here, although in practice it is often associated with technologies having the same characteristics as I list in the text for intermediate technology.   But many use the term to mean any technology that is appropriate to achieving national development goals.   There are two definitional flaws here. First, it is so vacuous it fails to tell us much, if anything.   Who is going to advocate "inappropriate technology?"   Second, and perhaps more subtle, it excludes national goals from the instrumental valuational process. Furthermore, we can expect an evoluation of national priorities as conditions change - one of these conditions will be the state of technological capabilities itself.

45.   For a pioneer attempt to explore technology blending, see Von Weizsacker and associates (1983), but it is evident that many of the contributors did not catch on to the concept of technology blending.   Many cases dealt with intermediate technology or application of emerging technologies in LDCs without an integration to traditional sectors or basic needs.   For collections of case studies, see Bhalla and associates (1984) and Bhalla and James (forthcoming).   The latter source includes analytical and conceptual material, which was largely ignored in the earlier volume of cases.

46.   The first four are cases in Bhalla and associates (1984); the latter four are included in Bhalla and James (forthcoming).

47.   Technology, Institutions, and Government
Policy (James and Watanabe, 1985) is useful in
this   regard.   Especially   so   are   the   two
contributions by Frances Stewart and David J.C.
Forsyth contained herein.

48.   As a reductio ad absurdum, Bhalla and I
have used the bullock drawn cart as an example.
Disregarding   costs,   there   is   only   so   much
biotechnology   applied   to   the   bullock   and
microelectronic-driven   stabilization   devices
can do to improve the technology.   At some
point, a discrete change to an alternative,
more   efficient   mode   of   transportation   is
warranted.   We   suspect   other   more   subtle
technical limitations exist, but we haven't a
clue as to how prevalent or constricting they
may be.

49.   Thailand   is   showing   considerable
initiative and producing and improving mini-
hydroelectronic technology (Bhalla and James,
1986);   Andean   Pact   countries   have   (by
necessity) developed indigenous capability in
metal   extraction   using   microbial-leaching
techniques   (Warhurst,   1984);   and   Mexico   is
making   strides   in   assimilating   and   adapting
food-producing   biotechnologies   (Bifani,
forthcoming).

REFERENCES

Acharya, S.N.   "Fiscal/Financial Intervention,
Factor   Prices,   and   Factor   Proportions: A
Review of the Issues.   World Bank Staff Working
Paper No. 183, Washington, D.C.:   World Bank,
1974.

Adler, Emanuel. "Ideological 'Guerillas' and the Quest for Technological Autonomy: Brazil's Domestic Computer Industry," _International Organization_ 40: Summer, 1986, pp. 673-705.

Amadeo, Eduardo. "National Science and Technology Councils in Latin America: Achievements and Failures of the First Ten Years." In D. Babatunde Thomas and Miguel S. Wionczek (eds.), _Integration of Science and Technology with Development: Caribbean and Latin American Problems in the Context of the United Nations Conference on Science and Technology for Development_. New York: Pergamon Press, 1979, pp. 149-166.

Arrow, Kenneth J. "Economic Welfare and the Allocation of Resources for Invention." In National Bureau of Economic Research, _The Rate and Direction of Inventive Activity: Economic and Social Factors_. Princeton: Princeton University Press, 1962, pp. 609-626.

Ayres, Clarence E. _The Industrial Economy, Its Technological Basis and Institutional Destiny_. Boston: Houghton Mifflin, 1952.

Ayres, Clarence E. _The Theory of Economic Progress_. Chapel Hill: University of North Carolina Press, 1944.

Ayres, Clarence E. _The Problem of Economic Order_. New York: Farrar and Rinehart, Inc., 1938.

Bath, C. Richard, and James, Dilmus D. "Dependency Analysis of Latin America: Some Criticisms, Some Suggestions," _Latin American Studies Association_ 11 (3), 1974, pp. 3-54.

Bell, Martin.   "Learning and the Accumulation
of Industrial   Capacity   in   Developing
Countries."   In Fransman, Martin, and King,
Kenneth, (eds.), Technological Capability in
the Third World.   London: Macmillan, 1984, pp.
187-209.

Bell, Martin, Ross-Larson, Bruce, and Westphal,
Larry E.   "Assessing the Performance of Infant
Industries," Journal of Development Economics,
16 (1/2), 9 Sept/Oct, 1984, pp. 101-128.

Bell, Martin, Scott-Kemmis, Don.   "Technology
Import Policy: Have the Problems Changed?"
Economic and Political Weekly 20 (45), 46 and
47:   November, 1985b, 1975-1990.

Bhalla, Ajit S. (ed).   Technology and Employment   in   Industry,   3rd   edition.   Geneva:
International Labour Office, 1985.

Bhalla, Ajit S., and James, Dilmus D., (eds.)
New Technologies and Development: Experiments
in "Technology Blending." Boulder, CO: Lynne
Rienner Publishers, forthcoming.

Bhalla, Ajit S., James, Dilmus D., and Stevens,
Yvette, (eds.) Blending of New and Traditional
Technologies: Case Studies.   Dublin: Tycooly
International Publishers, 1984.

Bhatia, R.   "Photovoltaics for Street-Lighting
in India."   In A.S. Bhalla and D.D. James
(eds.), New Technologies and Development:
Experiments in "Technology Blending." Boulder,
CO.: Lynne Rienner Publishers, forthcoming.

Bifani, Pablo.   "New Biotechnologies for Food
Production in Developing Countries with Special
Reference to Cuba and Mexico."   In A.S. Bhalla

and D. James (eds.), New Technologies and Development: Experiments in "Technology Blending." Boulder, CO.: Lynne Rienner Publishers, forthcoming.

Bourstein, Daniel J. The Discoverers: A History of Man's Search to Know His World and Himself. New York: Vintage Books, 1985.

Buckley, Peter J. "New Forms of International Industrial Cooperation: A Survey of the Literature with Special Reference to North-South Technology," Aussenwirtshaft Heft 2: June 1981, pp. 195-222.

Bush, Paul D. "The Ceremonial Encapsulation of Capital Formation in the American Economy." Paper, Western Social Science Association, Lake Tahoe, Nevada, 1979.

Chudnovsky, Daniel. "Regulating Technology Imports in Some Developing Countries," Trade and Development: Winter 1981, pp. 133-149.

Chudnovsky, Daniel, Nagao, Masafumi, and Jacobsson, Steffan. Capital Goods Production in the Third World: An Economic Study of Technology Acquisition. New York: St. Martin's Press, 1983.

Clark, Norman, and Juma, C. Long Run Economics: An Evolutionary Approach to Economic Growth. London: Frances Pinter, 1987.

Consejo Nacional de Ciencia y Technologia. National Indicative Plan for Science and Technology. Mexico, D.F.: CONACYT, 1976.

Contractor, Farok J. and Sagafi-nejad, Tagi. "International Technology Transfer: Major Issues and Policy Responses," Journal of International Business Studies 12:2: Fall, 1981, pp. 113-135.

Corbo, Vittorio, and de Melo, Jaime. "Lessons from the Southern Cone Policy Reforms," The World Bank Research Observer 2 (2): July, 1987, pp. 111-142.

Dahlman, Carl J. and Sercovich, Francisco C. "Exports of Technology from Semi-Industrial Economies and Local Technological Development," Journal of Development Economics 16 (1/2): September/October, 1984, pp. 63-99.

Dahlman, Carl J. and Fonseca, Fernando Valadares. "From Technological Dependence to Technological Development: The Case of the USIMINAS Steel plant in Brazil." In J.M. Katz (ed.), Technology Generation in Latin American Manufacturing Industries. New York: St. Martin's Press, 1987, pp. 154-182.

DeGregori, Thomas R. "Finite Resources or Finite Imaginations? A Reply to Gowdy," Journal of Economic Issues 21 (1): March, 1987, pp. 477-481.

Dixon, William J. "Progress in the Provision of Basic Human Needs: Latin America, 1960-1980," Journal of Developing Areas 21 (2): January, 1987, pp. 129-140.

Eckaus, Richard S. "The Factor Proportions Problem in Underdeveloped Areas," American Economic Review 45 (4): September, 1955, pp. 539-565.

Erber, Fabio Stefano. "The Development of the 'Electronics Complex' and Government Policies in Brazil," World Development 13 (3): March, 1985, pp. 293-310.

Erdilek, Asim, and Rapoport, Alan. "Conceptual and Measurement Problems in International Technology Transfer: A Critical Analysis," In A. Cockun Samli (ed.), Technology Transfer: Geographic, Economic, Cultural and Technical Dimensions. Westport, CT: Quorum Books, 1985, pp. 249-261.

Evans, Peter B.   "State, Capital and the Transformation of Dependence: The Brazilian Computer Case," World Development 14 (7): July, 1986, pp. 791-808.

Forsyth, David J.C. "Government Policy, Market Structure, and Choice of Technology in Egypt." In J. James and S. Watanabe (eds.), Technology, Institutions, and Government Policies. London: Macmillan press, 1985, pp. 137-182.

Fransman, Martin. (ed.) Machinery and Economic Development. London: Macmillan Press, 1986.

Fransman, Martin. A New Approach to the Study of Technological Capability in Less Developed Countries. World Employment Programme Research Working Papers No. 166. Geneva: International Labour Office, 1986b.

Fransman, Martin.   "Conceptualizing Technical Change in the Third World in the 1980s: An Interpretative Survey," Journal of Development Studies 21 (4): July 1985, pp. 573-651.

Fransman, Martin. "Technological Capability in the Third World: An Overview and Introduction

to Some of the Issues Raised in this Book." In
M. Fransman and K. King (eds.), Technological
Capability in the Third World, London:
Macmillan Press, 1984.

Fransman, Martin, and King, Kenneth. (eds.)
Technological Capability in the Third World.
London: Macmillan Press, 1984.

Frischtak, Claudio. "Brazil [High Technology
Policies]." In Francis W. Rushing and Carole
Ganz Brown (eds.), National Policies for
Developing High Technology Industries:
International Comparisons. Boulder, CO.:
Westview Press, 1986.

Furtado, Celso. "The Brazilian Model," Social
and Economic Studies 22: March, 1973, pp. 121-
131.

Gilfillan, S. Colum. The Sociology of Invention. Chicago: Follett Publishing Co., 1935.

Granick, David. "Economic Development and
Productivity Analysis: The Case of Soviet
Metalworking," Quarterly Journal of Economics,
71 (2): May, 1957, pp. 205-233.

Hamilton, David. "Technology and Institutions
are Neither," Journal of Economic Issues 20
(2): June 1986, pp. 525-532.

Hickerson, Steven R. "Instrumental Valuation:
the Normative Compass of Institutional Economics," Journal of Economic Issues 21 (3):
September 1987, pp. 1117-1143.

Hirschman, Albert O. "The Political Economy of
Latin American Development: Seven Exercises in

Retrospecting," Latin American Research Review 22 (3): 1987, pp. 7-36.

Hoffman, Kurt, and Rush, Howard. Microelectro-nics and Technological Transformation of the Clothing Industry, World Employment Programme Research Working Paper No. 163.   Geneva: International Labour Office, 1984.

Horowitz, Irving Louis.   "The 'Rashomon' Effect: Ideological Proclivities and Political Dilemmas of the IMF," Journal of Inter-American Studies and World Affairs 27 (4): Winter, 1985-1986, pp. 37-55.

International Labour Office. Technology Choice and Employment Generation by Multinational Enterprises in Developing Countries, Geneva: ILO, 1984.

James, Dilmus D.   "Acquiring and Utilizing Internal Technological Capacities in the Third World," Presidential Address, Association for Evolutionary Economics, Chicago, December 1987.

James, Dilmus D.   "The Impact of Technology Imports on Internal Technological Capacity: A Case Study of Mexico,"   World Employment Programme Research Working Paper.   Geneva: International Labour Office, forthcoming.

James, Dilmus D.   "The Economic Feasibility of Employing Used Industrial Machinery in Develop-ing Countries." In Mangalam Srinivasan (ed.), Technology Assessment and Economic Development. New York: Praeger Publishers, 182, pp. 228-247.

James, Dilmus D. Used Machinery and Economic Development. East Lansing: Division of Research, Michigan State University, 1974.

James, Dilmus D. "The Instrumental and Induced Theories of Technological Development: A Critical Study." Unpublished, M.A. Thesis, The University of Texas at Austin, 1958.

James, Jeffrey and Watanabe, Susumu. (eds.) Technology, Institutions and Government Policies. London: Macmillan Press, 1985.

Janiszewski, Hubert A. "Technology-Importing National Perspectives." In Tagi Sagafi-nejad, Maxon, Richard W., and Perlmutter, Howard V. (eds.), International Technology Transfer: Issues, Perspectives, and Policy Implications. New York: Pergamon Press, 1981, pp. 306-320.

Jequier, Nicolas, and Blanc, Gerard. The World of Appropriate Technology: A Quantitative Analysis. Paris: Organization for Economic Cooperation and Development, 1983.

Johnson, Harry G. "The Efficiency and Welfare Implications of the International Corporation." In Charles P. Kindleberger (ed.), International Corporations. Cambridge, MA: MIT Press, 1970, pp. 35-56.

Johnston, John. "The Productivity of Management Consultants," Journal of the Royal Statistical Society, Series A, 126.

Jones, Daniel T., and Womack, James P. "Developing Countries and the Future of the Automobile Industry," World Development 13 (3): March, 1985, pp. 393-407.

Junker, Louis.   "The Ceremonial-Instrumental Dichotomy in Institutional Analysis: The Nature, Scope and Radical Implications of the Conflicting Systems," <u>American Journal of Economics and Sociology</u> 41 (2): April, 1982, pp. 141-150.

Junne, Gerd.   "New Technologies: A Threat to Developing Countries' Exports," paper, Seminario Revolucion Technologica y Empleo, Mexico City, November, 1984, (mimeo).

Kaempffert, Waldemar.   <u>Invention and Society</u>. Chicago: American Library Association, 1930.

Katz, Jorge M. (ed.) <u>Technology Generation in Latin American Manufacturing Industries</u>.   New York: St. Martin's Press, 1987.

Lall, Sanjaya. <u>Learning to Industrialize: The Acquisition of Technological Capacity in India</u>. London: Macmillan Press, forthcoming.

Lall, Sanjaya.   "Multinationals and Technology Development in Host Countries."   In his <u>Multinationals, Technology and Exports: Selected Papers</u>.   New York: St. Martin's Press, 1985a, pp. 114-130.

Lall, Sanjaya.   "Trade in Technology by a Slowly Industrializing Country: India."   In Nathan Rosenberg and Claudio Frischtak (eds.), <u>International Technology Transfer: Concepts, Measures, and Comparisons</u>. New York: Praeger, 1985b, pp. 45-76.

Lall, Sanjaya.   "Exports of Technology by Newly-Industrialized Countries: An Overview,"

World Development 12 (5/6): May/June, 1984, pp. 471-480.

Lall, Sanjaya. "Developing Countries as Exporters of Technology," Research Policy 9 (1): January, 1980, pp. 24-51.

Lall, Sanjaya. "Developing Countries as Exporters of Technology: A Preliminary Analysis." In Herbert Giersch (ed.), International Economic Development and Resource Transfer. Kiel: Institut fur Weltwirtshaft an der Universitat Kiel, 1979, pp. 589-616.

Lall, Sanjaya. "Transnationals, Domestic Enterprises, and Industrial Structure in Host LDCs: A Survey," Oxford Economic Papers 30 (2): July, 1978, pp. 217-221.

Lall, Sanjaya. "The Patent System and the Transfer of Technology to Less-Developed Countries," Journal of World Trade Law 10 (1): January, 1976, p. 1-16.

Lall, Sanjaya. (ed.) Special Issue on "Technology Exports by Newly Industrializing Countries," World Development 12 (5/6), May/June 1984.

Lewis, W. Arthur. "Economic Development with Unlimited Supplies of Labour," Manchester School of Economics and Social Studies 22 (2): May 1954, pp. 139-191.

Lower, Milton D. "The Concept of Technology Within the Institutionalist Perspective," Journal of Economic Issues 21 (3): September 1987, pp. 1147-1176.

Maxwell, Philip. "Adequate Technological Strategy in an Imperfect Economic Context: A Case-Study of the Evolution of the Acindar Steel Plant in Rosario, Argentina." In J.M. Katz (ed.), Technology Generation in Latin American Manufacturing Industries. New York: St. Martin's Press, 1987, pp. 119-153.

Maxwell, Philip, and Teubal, Morris. "Capacity Stretching Technical Change: Some Empirical and Theoretical Aspects," Working Paper No. 36. Buenos Aires: IDB/ECLA/UNDP Research Programme on Scientific and Technological Development in Latin America, 1980.

Mayhew, Anne. "The Beginnings of Institutionalism," Journal of Economic Issues 21 (3): September 1987a, pp. 971-998.

Mayhew, Anne. "Culture: Core Concept Under Attack," Journal of Economic Issues 21 (2): June 1987b, pp. 587-603.

Mayhew, Anne "Ayresian Technology, Technical Reasoning, and Doomsday," Journal of Economic Issues 15 (2): June 1981, pp. 513-520.

Morawetz, David. Twenty-five Years of Economic Development, 1950-1975. Washington, D.C.: World Bank, 1977.

Morawetz, David. "Employment Implications of Industrialization in Developing Countries - A Survey," Economic Journal (84): September 1974, pp. 491-542.

Mumford, Lewis. Technics and Civilization. New York: Harcourt Brace and Co., 1938.

Nelson, Richard R. and Winter, Sidney G.   An
Evolutionary Theory of Economic Change.
Cambridge, MA: Belknap Press of Harvard
University Press, 1982.

Ogburn, William F.   Social Change, New York:
B.W. Heubsch, Inc., 1922.

Olle, Werner.   "New Technologies and the
International Division of Labour: Retransfer
of Foreign Production from Developing
Countries?" Vierteljahresberichte (103): Marz
1986, pp. 3-10.

Pack, Howard and Westphal, Larry.   "Industrial
Strategy and Technological Change: Theory
versus Reality," Journal of Development Studies
22 (1): June 1986, pp. 87-128.

Palma, Gabriel. "Dependency: A Formal Theory
of Underdevelopment or a Methodolgy for the
Analysis of Concrete Situations of Underdevelopment?" In Paul Streeten and Richard
Jolly (eds.), Recent Issues in World Development: A Collection of Survey Articles. Oxford:
Pergamon Press, 1981, pp. 383-426.

Pearson, Ruth.   "Transfer of Technology and
Domestic Innovation in the Cement Industry."
In J.M. Katz (ed.), Technology Generation in
Latin American Manufacturing Industries. New
York: St. Martin's Press, 1987, pp. 352-427.

Perez, Luis Alberto, and Perez y Peniche, Jose
de Jesus. "A Summary of the Principal Findings
of the Case Study on the Technological Behavior
of the Mexican Steel Firm, Altos Hornos de
Mexico."   In J.M. Katz (ed.), Technology
Generation in Latin American Manufacturing

Industries. New York: St. Martin's Press, 1987, pp. 183-191.

Pugel, Thomas A. "Technology Transfer and the Neoclassical Theory of International Trade." In Robert G. Hawkins and A.J. Prasad (eds.), Technology Transfer and Economic Development. Greenwich, CT.: JAI Press Inc., 1981, pp. 11-37.

Rada, Juan. "A Third World Perspective." In Gunter Friedrichs and Adam Schaff (eds.), Microelectronics and Society, For Better or For Worse. Oxford: Pergamon Press, 1984, pp. 213-242.

Ranis, Gustav. "Industrial Sector Labor Organization," Economic Development and Cultural Change 21 (3) April, 1973.

Ranis, Gustav. "Factor Proportions in Japanese Economic Development," American Economic Review 47 (5): September, 1957, pp. 594-607.

Rosenberg, Nathan. "On Technology Blending," World Employment Programme Research Working Paper No. 159. Geneva: International Labour Office, 1986.

Rosenberg, Nathan. "Learning by Using." In N. Rosenberg, Inside the Black Box: Technology and Economics. Cambridge: Cambridge University Press, 1982, pp. 120-140.

Rosenberg, Nathan. "Capital Goods, Technology and Economic Growth," Oxford Economic Papers 15 (3): October 1963, pp. 217-227. Reprinted in Nathan Rosenberg, Perspectives on Technology. Cambridge: Cambridge University Press, 1963, pp. 141-150.

Rossman, Joseph. The Psychology of the Inventor. Washington D.C.: The Inventor's Publishing Co., 1931.

Ruivenkamp, Guido. "The Impact of Biotechnology on International Development: Competition Between Sugar and New Sweeteners," Vierteljahresberichte (103) Marz, 1986, pp. 89-101.

Rushing, Francis, and Brown, Carole Ganz. (eds.) National Policies for Developing High Technology Industries: International Comparisons. Boulder, CO.: Westview Press, 1986.

Sagasti, Francisco R. National Science and Technological Policies for Development: A Comparative Analysis." In Jairam Ramesh and Charles Weiss (eds.), Mobilizing Technology for World Development. New York: Praeger Special Studies, 1979, pp. 162-171.

Sagasti, Francisco R. Science and Technology for Development: Main Comparative Report on the STPI Project. Ottawa, Canada: International Development Research Center, 1978.

Sanderson, Susan Walsh. "Automated Manufacturing and Offshore Assembly in Mexico." In Cathryn L. Thorup (ed.), The United States and Mexico: Face to Face with New Technology. Washington, D.C.: Overseas Development Council, 1987, pp. 127-148.

Schwartzman, Simon. High Technology vs. Self-Reliance: Brazil Enters the Computer Age. Cambridge, MA.: Center for International

Studies, Massachusetts Institute of Technology, 1985.

Sercovich, Francisco C.   "Ingenieria de Diseno y Cambio Tecnico Endogeno,"   Working Paper No. 19.   (IDB/ECLA/UNCP Research Programme on Scientific and Technological Development in Latin America; Buenos Aires: 1978.

Stewart,   Frances.   "Macro Policies for Appropriate Technology: An Introductory Classification." In J. James and S. Watanabe (eds.), Technology, Institutions and Government Policies.   London: Macmillan Press, 1985.

Stewart,   Frances.   "International Technology Transfer: Issues and Policy Options." In Paul R. Streeten and Richard Jolly (eds.), Recent Issues in World Development: A Collection of Survey Articles.   Oxford: Pergamon Press, 1981, pp. 67-110.

Stewart, Frances. Technology and Underdevelop- ment. London: Macmillan Press, 1977.

Stewart, Frances.   "Technology and Employment in LDCs." In Edgar O. Edwards (ed.), Employment in Developing Nations.   New York: Columbia University Press, 1974, pp. 83-132.

Street, James H.   "The Technological Frontier in Latin America: Creativity and Produc- tivity," Journal of Economic Issues 10 (3): September, 1976, pp. 538-558.

Street,   James   H.   and   James,   Dilmus   D. "Institutionalism,   Structuralism,   and Dependency in Latin America," Journal of Economic Issues 16 (3): September, 1982, pp. 673-689.

Subrahmanian, K.K.   Imports of Capital and
Technology: Study of Foreign Collaboration in
Indian   Industry.   New   Delhi: Peoples
Publishing House, 1972.

Teece,   David   A.   "Technology   Transfer   by
Multinational   Firms: The   Resource   Cost   of
Transferring Technological Know-How," Economic
Journal 87 (346): June, 1977, pp. 242-261.

Teitel, Simon.   "Technology Creation in Semi-
Industrial Economies," Journal of Development
Economies 16 (1/2): September/October, 1984,
pp. 39-61.

Tool, Marc R.   "Introduction," Special edition
on "Evolutionary Economics I: Foundations of
Institutionalist Thought," Journal of Economic
Issues 21 (3): September, 1987, pp. 951-967.

Tuchman, Barbara W.   A Distant Mirror: The
Calamitous 14th Century. New York: Balentine
Books, 1978.

United Nations Industrial Development Organiza-
tion.   Capital Goods Industry in Developing
Countries: A Second World-Wide Study.
Sectoral Studies Series No. 15, Volume 1.
Vienna, UNIDO, 1985.

Usher, Abbot Payson.   A History of Mechanical
Inventions. New York: The Viking Press, 1929.

Vaitsos, Constantine V.   "Foreign Investments
and Productive Knowledge." In Guy F. Erb and
Valeriana Kallab (eds.), Beyond Dependency:
The Developing World Speaks Out.   Washington,
D.C.:   Overseas Development Council, 1975, pp.
75-94.

Vaitsos, Constantine V. "Empirical Evidence on Monopoly Rents." Chapter 4 in his <u>Intercountry Income Distribution and Transactional Enterprises</u>. Oxford: Clarendon Press, 1974, pp. 52-65.

Vaitsos, Constantine V. "Patents Revisited: Their Function in Developing Countries," <u>Journal of Developing Studies</u> 9 (1): October, 1972, pp. 71-97.

Vaitsos, Constantine V. "Bargaining and the Distribution of Returns in the Purchase of Technology of Developing Countries," <u>Bulletin of the Institute of Development Studies</u> 3 (1): 1970, pp. 16-23.

von Weizsacker, Ernst U., Swaminathan, M.S., and Lemma, Aklilu. (eds.) <u>New Frontiers in Technology Application: Integration of Emerging and Traditional Technologies</u>. Dublin: Tycooly International Publishers, Ltd., 1983.

Waller, William T. "Ceremonial Encapsulation and Corporate Cultural Hegemony," <u>Journal of Economic Issues</u> 21 (1): March, 1987, pp. 321-328.

Warhurst, Alyson. "The Application of Biotechnology to Metal Extraction: The Case of the Andean Countries." In A.S. Bhalla and D.D. James (eds.), <u>New Technologies and Development: Experiments in "Technology Blending</u>." Boulder, CO: Lynne Rienner Publishers, 1984, pp. 135-153.

Whalen, Charles J. "A Reason to Look Beyond Neoclassical Economics: Some Major Shortcomings of Orthodox Theory," <u>Journal of</u>

Economic Issues 21 (1): March, 1987, pp. 259-280.

Whitby, Gary. "Electronic Load-Controlled Mini-Hydroelectric Projects: Experiences from Colombia, Sri Lanka, and Thailand." In A.S. Bhalla and D.D. James (eds.), New Technologies and Development: Experiments in "Technology Blending." Boulder, CO: Lynne Rienner Publishers, 1984, pp. 122-138.

White, Lawrence J. "The Evidence on Appropriate Factor Proportions for Manufacturing in Less Developed Countries: A Survey," Economic Development and Cultural Change 27 (1): October, 1978, pp. 27-60.

White, Leslie A. The Science of Culture. New York: Farrar, Straus and Co., 1949.

Wionczek, Miguel S. "On the Viability of a Policy for Science and Technology in Mexico," Latin American Research Review 16 (1): 1981, pp. 57-78.

COMMENTARY BY RANDAL JOY THOMPSON

In his thought-provoking article, Dilmus James sketches an institutionalist perspective on the importation and local generation of technology by LDCs, derived from the centrality of technological progress to development. James applies a holistic, multidisciplinary approach to the transfer of technology, arguing that, rather than study production functions, the effect of technology on capital accumulation, or other neoclassical scenarios, one must look at the complexity of socioeconomic systems that impinge on the transfer process. One must look at the underlying dynamics, consider the technological potential and "the full range of culturally relative behavior and interest at play," and then intervene in order to "steer the course of events toward a better outcome." As James states, intervention is a key aspect of the institutionalist perspective, for instrumental valuation, which "seeks to make some reasonable, weighted evaluation among often conflicting social values," is the basis not only of action but also of knowledge. James counsels, however, that the best we can do is attempt to improve a situation, not with any certainty, but rather by trial and error and experimentation.

James reviews the post-World War II period of development, showing how the tansfer of technology grew more complex as we came to identify critical variables in the process and how some countries responded by restricting the

import of technology and by trying to build up
their own capabilities at the enterprise and
sectoral levels and through national science
and technology councils. James argues that
orthodox economics has failed to understand
fully the transfer process. The maximization
of profit, net social benefit, political
dictums, or altruism cannot explain specific
transfers. Nor can these account for the
nurturing of internal technological mastery.
The menu of technologies appropriate for LDCs
is also larger than that predicted by neoclassical models. As James says, "The welter of
individuals, enterprises, and agencies reflecting various viewpoints and bundles of priorities will influence importantly who gets what
technology when and for how much, as well as
for how effectively it is eventually employed."

James then calls on development planners
to provide operational principles for selecting
technologies which will "achieve an adequate
level and composition of technology acquisition
as well as a proper balance and integration
between technology obtained from abroad and
hardware, knowlege, and skills generated
internally." James asserts that such principles, needed for the industry, country, and
regional level, are required to take advantage
of technology as the driving force of development rather than as an exogenous variable and
also to have ready scenarios in case of trade
reversals.

James also advises LDCs to rethink
defensive restrictions on technology imports,
given the fact that the market for the international transfer of technology imports has not
been successful in fostering indigenous
technological mastery.

James advises that LDCs should focus on
other than industrial technologies which have a

more direct impact on lower income populations.
He recommends "intermediate technology" and
"technology blending." Intermediate technology
integrates emerging technologies with small-
scale, low-income sectors and leaves "recognizable elements of traditional production
techniques and organizational configuration
intact." Technology blending marries high
technology with prevailing production methods.
James calls for more research into these two.
He clearly prefers technology blending since it
may provide the necessary shakeup of institutions required, according to institutionalists,
for technological progress, while "moderating
social disruption and attendant psychological
discomfort." He is concerned that intermediate
technology may have overly confining technical
and institutional inhibitions.

As a practitioner who designs and
evaluates development projects, I am always
interested in approaches that may provide
guidelines for solving complex development
challenges. Thus, I read James's essay from a
practical perspective (and according to his
assertion that institutionalist analysis itself
must be evaluated along instrumentalist lines),
asking how effectively his approach accounts
for the transfer of technology in the context
of a donor project. Although, as James points
out, the donor channel is only one of a myriad,
it may provide interesting insights since
donors take a pluralistic approach to
technology. Donors focus on nonindustrial and
soft technologies such as planning methods and
management techniques, in addition to
industrial technologies.

As a project design officer for a donor
organization, I am a technology broker to a
large extent. Through the project development
process, I look for new technologies to

introduce into LDCs, to eliminate "development
constraints," and spark a creative "take-it-
and-run" process. The project cycle is set up
to introduce new technologies into LDCs via
hardware, software, technical advisors who
impart the know-how required, organizational
development and adequate budgetary commitments
to support the new technology, and policy
changes to assure that it is worth people's
while. When my colleagues and I design a
project, we attempt to determine whether a
technology will benefit the LDC, and then
assess its feasibility by conducting an
economic, technical, environmental, social,
institutional, and administrative analysis. In
undertaking these analyses, we do practice what
James preaches. That is, we identify and
attempt to understand extra-economic forces in
order to guage whether the technology has a
chance of being adopted and supported without
causing undue disruptions while having a "pro-
development" impact. As James states, "The
identification and understanding of extra-
economic forces are essential to maximizing
improvements through achieving an institutional
configuration that will result in more effective use of technological capabilities." Of
course, it is ultimately a political process of
negotiation which determines whether the
project will be attempted. Then, during
project implementation and evaluation, we work
through our predictions and rough blueprints in
the reality of the situation and make changes
in our design, our assumptions, our objectives,
our beneficiaries, our schedule, or even the
technology. Reflection and flexibility,
progressive approximations, or "muddling
through" are, we have found, the key to
successful transfer.

This multidisciplinary, flexible method
has evolved from a long series of mistakes
since the early days of development assistance.
We used to think that a road was a road was a
road, for example. Only after we had built a
number of them and they deteriorated because
they were built of materials that could not
survive the tropics, or they were not used or
used for other than foreseen purposes, or not
maintained, or did not lead to desired
behavioral changes in the target beneficiaries,
did development practitioners recognize that a
technology is a lot more than the apparent
hardware. As tool-using behavior, not an
object, the supposedly lone hardware carried
with it a presumed cultural context, a whole
array of ideas, an institutional framework and
a complex of skills to reinforce, use, and
maintain it, and a presumed interactive
relationship with the people who were to employ
it. The holistic approach to project selection
and appraisal as well as the broader view of
technology thus evolved out of the necessity of
producing something that was useful. And it
was the political context that forced
accountability.
    The imagery of the project cycle is
clearly the institutionalist imagery of the
steersman, moving, as James asserts, with
"flexible experimentation and stress on
integrating imported technology with domestic
learning...pushing successes and expeditiously
abandoning failures." Certainly as a purposive, directed approach, intervention is, as
James states, a necessary component. At the
level of the government, policies are made and
modified to better assure the success of the
project approach at the specific-case level and
to assure that the individual benefits are also
shared at the social level.

On the level of human action, thus, it does appear that technological progress is the "motor power for economic progress." For it is with technology that we directly work. Although our project logical frameworks, which set out the input-output logic of the project and the hierarchy of objectives, generally include macro-level indicators which will hopefully change as a result of the project and its technology, these indicators are usually out of our control and very difficult to link directly to project activities.

In the project process, one gauges one's way both on the basis of information at hand in the specific situation, as well as on the basis of the experiences of similar projects elsewhere. "Theories" are built up about what works where, but even these theories are being constantly modified based on new occurrences. There are no absolute imperatives which, like neoclassical theory, inform one what to do—only a body of shared and collected experiences in an information system or by word-of-mouth or in development lore. Of course, development professionals, like everyone concerned about cost and simplicity attempt to "replicate" projects. But these attempts often end up in failure.

Neoclassical economists claim to explain, in economic terms, what James asserts is unexplainable. And in the project business, there is a vast analytic literature, based on the premises of neoclassical economics, which directs project selection and appraisal from shadow prices and other macro indicators. However, the literature fails to account for actual choices, as James points out. This leads one to ask whether it is the theory that is in error, or the lack of information which makes the decision maker appear less than rational, or his institutional/ceremonial behavior which, in the spirit of the Veblen-Ayres dichotomy, makes him choose according to existing behavioral norms rather than choose a technology which may disturb them.

One is reminded, in the debate which James outlines, of the schism between prescriptive and descriptive or behavioral decision-making and that between administrative man as optimizer versus satisfier. Institutionalist analysis certainly seems to describe the actual process of technology selection, transfer, and dissemination. But can this analysis also prescribe what technological choices we should make, the way that neoclassical constructs at least purport to do? This question is critical in the context of James's article because he calls on us to develop operational guidelines to assist LDCs develop effective technology policies and an appropriate mix between imported technology and internal technological mastery. He specifically calls on development planners and economists to flesh out what he calls the vacuous dictums for LDCs to "adopt newly emerging technologies on a selective basis and in accordance with market conditions, other national priorities, and level of the nation's overall development." What should the nature of these guidelines be, and are such guidelines even possible under the institutionalist perspective?

After all that James argues, it would certainly be disastrous to have policy guidelines which, like typical policies, inform decisions out of context and imply absolute choice prescriptions. This may lead, as it did in some Latin American countries, to totalitarian political systems trying to make reality achieve abstract ideals, or to closed door reactive policies such as those against

multinationals in the 1970s. And it would
certainly be wasteful to have policy guidelines
which are overly theoretical and hence, like
the national science and technology councils of
Latin America, negligent of "indigenous
productive and technological forces." Nor do
we evidently want too many institutions and
individuals involved in the policy-making
process because this may lead to the
heterogenity and diversity of instruments
which, as Sagasti found, "meant that
contradictory policy orientations coexisted;
many promotional provisions were not effective
because the majority of firms in target
industries were unaware of them; and redundancy
abounded in some areas while harmful gaps
remained in others." Nor do we want policies
which are restricted only to industry. As
James states, we need guidelines for
technological pluralism, since many nonindustrial technologies are critical to
balanced development.

In his discussion of Korea's success
story, James presents a criterion which was
beneficially applied, that of choosing infant
industries "reasonably close to the margin of
international comparative advantage" and making
them competitive, "both at home and abroad in
relatively short order." Yet he then qualifies
this statement by asserting that "it is
difficult to choose industries for special
treatment ex ante." In his discussion of
intermediate technology versus technology
blending, James presents as possible criteria
for technological selection "that technology
which would shakeup social institutions thus
rendering the institutional surroundings more
conducive to further technical progress," and
"that technology which would lead to considerable scientific effort and indigenous

technical learning," and "that technology which
will encourage propulsive innovational trajectories."   In his discussion of achieving
technological   mastery,   he   also   emphasizes
developing the capital goods sector.

From all of these examples, which are
certainly only a sprinkling of possibilities,
it seems as if the fleshing out of operational
guidelines would be extremely difficult.   We
have   here   economic   criteria,   criteria   about
types   of   technology,   technical   progress,   and
social change, criteria about the generality of
guidelines, about who is involved in making and
promoting the guidelines.   Some of the criteria
suggested would be difficult for many of us to
employ.   Working for a donor organization, I
politically would not be able to select between
technologies based on the criterion of which
one   has   the   best   possibility   of   unbalancing
social   institutions   to   cause   technical
progress, a criterion which James posits for
choosing between intermediate technology and
technology blending.   Other criteria may change
from   one   situation   to   another.   Or   the
situation may change faster than one can apply
the criteria.   Those technologies that lead to
"trajectories of technological advance" in one
situation may not do so in another.   Moreover,
there are "fads" in technology like anything
else.   After careful analysis which concludes
that   intermediate   technology   or   technology
blending are more appropriate, an LDC may
choose to buy computers instead, in order to be
a part of the "in crowd" in technology.   In
addition, there are certain technologies which
have become a basic component of "the good
society"   which   cannot   always   be   completely
justified by rigorous analysis, but which every
country wants.   Finally, when one employs a
broader conception of technology as "ideas," as

Thomas   DeGregori   does,   one   realizes   that
technology flows are occurring so rapidly that
it would be difficult for guidelines to keep
up.

What we can conclude from James's discussion is that the operational guidelines must be
flexible   enough   so   that   they   do   not   become
absolutes, yet not open-ended and hence wishy-
washy.   From all that James has said, and from
the   broader   philosophy   of   the
institutionalists, it seems that the guidelines
should   focus   more   on   the   process   of
technological mastery rather than on specific
assetions as to which technology to select and
apply where.

Guidelines that focus on the process of
technological mastery would be prescriptive in
the sense that they would prescribe the best
process to follow to achieve technological
progress and descriptive in the sense of
containing the wisdom gathered from experiences
of technology transfer, mastery, and progress.
The descriptive component could offer insight
into such things as how to promote enterprise
level learning through the steps that James
outlines in his essay.   The prescriptive
process element would contain guidelines as to
how to engage in a process which maintains
flexibility, how to keep policies from becoming
rigid, how to obtain access to data on technological experiences, how to keep creativity
and the spirit of change alive and well.   For
in a world in which the best we can do is to
intervene in a trial-and-error fashion, only
approximating ideal solutions, the most
effective way for improving our approximations
is not to try to force solutions that work well
in theoretical constructs, but to assure that
the process of choice and action allows for
flexibility, quick response, the availability

and use of relevant data, and a critical element of creativity. That is, by following the process we can be better assured that what we are engaging in will lead us in the right direction, hence the evolutionary imagery of institutionalist thought. This creative process works better, certainly, if information on relevant experiences is available and if the choice itself is based on the information, economic theory, and creativity. Development is a discovery process, and this process should be encouraged through process-oriented guidelines.

Recommending that by "operational guidelines" James should mean "process guidelines," I am going further to suggest that the most effective level at which to practice the prescribed process is at the specific "project level." Since the project cycle is really how technology transfer and technology mastery gets operationalized, it should be here that we assure that project design, implementation, and evaluation provides some structure but also nurtures creativity. By keeping this process a process and not a rigid construct which merely delivers goods is the best way to assure that creativity is used creatively. Such creativity can never be expressed at the policy or government guideline level, although as James points out, government policies are certainly required at critical stages of growth. In order to keep these government policies dynamic, however, the project process serves as a review of and dialectic to these policies. In a flexible, creative project process, these policies are put under critical scrutiny. Of course, the success of this process rests ultimately upon an open political system which fosters free exchange between the project level and the

policy level and in which the vested interests
served by policies are not protected from
review.

By following such a process, the three
areas that James cites for further investigation - technological responses for possible
trade reversals, modifications of restrictions
on technology imports, and intermediate
technology and technology blending - would
naturally get treated. In addition, a wider
view of technology would also get taken into
consideration. This is the one slight disap-
pointment I have with James's chapter. He
discusses industrial technology primarily and
then rightly calls for technological pluralism.
His choices here are narrower than need be.
"Soft" technologies such as planning
methodologies, research approaches, management
techniques, and general methodological outlook
should also be included and reviewed in this
process. After working for several years in
development, I see some of the major challenges
in these areas. Even when a specific
technology transfer is not successful, the
interactive process between industrialized
nation and LDC can result in the transfer of
new approaches and the linkage of the LDC to
new systems of knowledge generation and
technology.

While I certainly agree with James that
countries should review and revamp their
restrictive import of technology policies, I do
not see that the transfer of technology process
has changed since the 1970s. I researched
foreign private investment in India during the
late 1970s and am thus very familiar with
India's then stringent stance against
multinationals. But the stance was not antitechnology so much as a concern over
disadvantageous terms of the transfer. LDCs

have most probably, as James points out, improved their bargaining skills. Certainly, as James states, "technology regulations are not a universal hit with LDCs' entrprenerial and managerial corps." They never were, even in India of the 1970s. Individuals all along the decision tree were making gains, even during the most virulent attacks on transnationals. That was never the point, of course, but rather disparity between individual and social payoffs and India's commitment to an import substitution policy. In the pharmaceutical industry, which I studied, local drug companies without international linkages were pressuring the government to protect them. And arguments abounded as to whether indigenous firms, which did not have research and development capabilities, could ever effectively develop an adequate pharmaceutical industry there. Even then, individual Indian entrepreneurs were taking the first step toward contacting foreign firms, which were not necessarily multinationals for know-how and technology agreements. James's argument that restrictive policies do not lead to technological mastery is probably the key to modification of import restrictions, not the fact that the technology transfer process has changed.

I found James's discussion of intermediate technology and technological mastery fascinating, and more comparative research should certainly be done in this area. But I would hate to make a selection of a technology on the basis of its impact on institutions. Certainly LDCs are seriously looking at both types of technologies to solve critical problems at the grassroots level, but the determinants of choice are more likely to center around effectiveness in addressing the

problem, cost, maintenance, and applicability
to particular milieus, rather than impact on
propelling progress.

    After working in development for a number
of years, I see the technology transfer and
mastery process, as James states, as
essentially a human, not only an economic
process. While I see the necessity for and
usefulness of economic analysis, I also clearly
see, when push comes to shove, the need for a
much broader perspective. Perhaps, in this
sense, then, James is correct when he says that
institutionalists have "a 'leg up' on other
contemporary economic perspectives."

SUBJECT INDEX